DAVE MORTON
TAPES, BREAKS & HEARTACHES

My Sixteen Years in British Speedway

To Lindsey
Best Wishes
Dave
Mike

First published in December 2015 by
Retro Speedway
Tel: 01708 734 502
www.retro-speedway.com

Copyright Retro Speedway & Dave Morton

Designed by Jan Watts
Cover design: Paul Hewitt at Battlefield (www.battlefield-design.co.uk)
Printed by Henry Ling Ltd
Distributed by Retro Speedway
103 Douglas Road, Hornchurch, Essex, RM11 1AW, England
Distribution email: subs@retro-speedway.com

ISBN 97809927427-1-3

In memory of George and Jamie Morton

Acknowledgements

THERE are a number of people I need to thank for helping to get my story into print. Firstly, Mark Potts and Kevin Tew, two avid Crewe Kings fans, who followed my speedway career from day one.

Sharen and Dave Beresford for getting pictures and information sorted, and Bernadette for encouraging me to do it when Mark first approached me about writing the book nearly five years ago.

Encouragement also came from the Ellesmere Port trio of Mervyn Porter, Chris Bond and Judith Ward, Hackney fans Paul Tadman and Chris Fenn, not forgetting my old Hawks team-mate Barry Thomas or Colin Tucker. All the others who helped with stories and confirmation of dates. And a special mention for PC, for writing the foreword.

Finally, thanks to Tony and Susie McDonald at Retro Speedway for taking on the publishing role, ensuring the book finally came out and advertising it.

Dave Morton

PUBLISHERS Retro Speedway would also like to add our thanks to Mark Potts for supplying the original manuscript, designers Jan Watts and Paul Hewitt, and our good friends at *Speedway Star* Richard Clark and Andrew Skeels.

A number of the photographs came from Dave's personal collection and although we've done our best to credit all photographers where they are known, we apologise if anyone's name has been omitted in error.

Credit for photographs and other images must go to: the late Alf Weedon and Wright Wood, Mike Patrick and Trevor Meeks (whose volume of work now form part of the vast and unrivalled John Somerville Collection at www.skidmarks1928.com), plus John Milburn, Bill and Wayne Meyer (Australia), Gail Crowther, Alan Legg, Jeff Baker, Ian Gill and Marilyn Suckling.

Finally, thanks to Ken Carpenter, who covered the latter part of Mort's career with Sheffield, Newcastle and Long Eaton.

Contents

My school pal Peter Collins in his Belle Vue days, relaxing
by the greyhound traps between races at Sheffield in 1984,
and (inset) looking happy in 2015.

Foreword

By Peter Collins MBE

IWAS delighted when asked to write the foreword to Dave's book. We go back a long way, having grown up together, as did our fathers, Bill and George. They were also from the same village of Partington in what used to be a small backwater farming community before it became a large overspill area for Manchester.

I was born in 1954 and brought up on Homestead Farm on Manchester Road, which was only about a quarter of a mile from the Morton residence. George rented an outbuilding/garage at our next-door-but-one neighbour's, Miss Annie Hardstaffe, which was around 200 yards from our farm. He used this to repair cars for the locals and also worked on his own cars and motorbikes for sons, Dave and Chris. This is where I met the two Morton boys and from an early age we became good friends.

I do remember, when very young, my father and Uncle Tom (who worked at my dad's farm) talking about the time when George was a young man, and how good he was on his motorbike. He used to speed past when they were working in the fields, lying flat on the tank, squeezing every ounce out of the engine. These were the lanes that would claim the life of Belle Vue legend Ken

PC and his father Bill both played a huge part in my early love of motorcycles and racing.

Sharples, who was killed in a car crash. Looking back, it was obvious where Dave and Chris got their ability on a motorbike and the desire to go fast.

My father was also into motorbikes; he and many other local lads were always riding around the farm fields. We had a number of different tracks, including the farmyard, which was covered in packed cinders – ideal for sliding and broadsiding. Dave and Chris were regulars at the farm, as well as a number of others who also went on to be professional speedway riders.

Saturday night was always eagerly anticipated during the speedway season, when we ventured to Hyde Road to watch our beloved Belle Vue Aces. We often went with our parents but would usually meet up on the back straight/pit bend (known as the 'Pop Side'). During this time, in the mid-to-late 60s, the riders wore old army gas goggles, and on a wet night these were discarded on the track when they became filled with shale. Dave turned out to be the master of collecting these.

Once the race had finished and the riders had cruised past us on the back straight heading back to the pits, we would climb the safety fence and attempt to retrieve the discarded 'trophies'. However, Dave was usually too quick, and had the pick of the best ones. He had the most fantastic collection at home, with the name of each rider written on the rim. His pride and joy were those which had belonged to his favourite Ace, Cyril Maidment.

There were, of course, dangers attached to this pursuit – the first by way of track curator Stan Ford sweeping the track on his tractor and grader. Then, as often as not, as soon as we had climbed back over the fence, the security men would give chase. Again, Dave was too quick and he would always escape under the stands and around the back of the stadium. I did manage to get a few pairs myself but Dave was the master in the art of 'goggle collecting'.

As for Dave's riding, after taking up speedway following his grass-tracking exploits, he definitely had his fair share of success, although his dream to be the very best was cruelly hampered by a string of serious injuries. In his early days he rode for Crewe Kings, with the massive Earle Street bowl the quickest track in the world. There, Dave would set a number of track records, and on one particular night, went so quick, he earned a place in *The Guinness Book of Records* as the fastest man in speedway.

At one time in the mid-70s while riding for Hackney, he was top of the British League averages with over 11 points per match, ahead of Ole Olsen, Ivan Mauger and myself. How many of today's stars could achieve a figure like that?

On our travels, racing all over the world, I always shared a room with Dave, and I remember some really funny moments – but will save them for my own book!

Although I don't see as much of Dave as I would like to, I still regard him as one of my best mates. We grew up together, went to school together and had the good fortune of racing together on the international stage. Long overdue, his story has now been written, and he thoroughly deserves his spot in the speedway limelight.

Peter Collins
October, 2015

Introduction

by Dave Morton

PICTURE the scene: a three-way run-off for the 1963 speedway World Championship, with Belle Vue trio Cyril Maidment, Peter Craven and Soren Sjosten all desperate to win the coveted crown.

The tapes go up and Maidment hits the first corner, a tyre-width ahead of Craven, with Sjosten a few yards back following a poor gate.

Lap two sees a tremendous tussle develop, with the lead changing hand several times. Swedish sensation Sjosten battles to the front, until a slip as he enters the back straight bend on the penultimate lap allows British ace Craven to lead right up to the final corner. When all seems lost for the other two Aces, Craven drifts slightly wide on the very last turn, to allow the emerging English star Maidment to dive inside and take the chequered flag.

Now before you all start scratching your heads and reaching for the speedway record books, the race *did* take place . . . but the venue wasn't Wembley Stadium.

It happened in a field at Bill Collins' farm, where I 'was' Cyril Maidment, Peter Collins rode as the original PC, Peter Craven, and our Chris as Soren Sjosten.

On push bikes!

We raced as though our lives depended on it. Because we all shared the same crazy dreams – not to emulate George Best, or any other famous footballer, cricketer or rugby league star of the day, but to become professional speedway riders and one day win the World Championship.

So can you imagine how we all felt just 12 years later, when three Partington lads lined up together for England Lions during the speedway Test series in Sweden – but more about that 'crazy dream

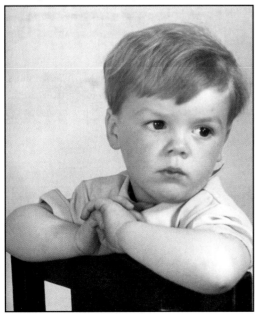

Dreaming of the World Championship . . .

With my younger brother Chris.

coming true' a bit later.

School in those days was basically an interruption in the day which prevented us spending more time honing our racing skills in the fields. All three of us attended Partington primary school, which was quite an uneventful period in my life apart from the time I broke my arm during an after-school activity. The accident occurred while doing the high-jump – I landed awkwardly on an uneven foam mat. Bad luck and broken bones would be a regular occurrence in the next 30 years.

I laugh now at some of the daft things we did as kids. I remember when Mum first pestered me to take Chris with me to ride the bikes at PC's dad's farm. We'd get as far as our garden gate and then I'd leg it, leaving him standing there helpless because he couldn't run fast enough to catch me. He'd have to turn around and go back indoors and when I arrived home much later, after an enjoyable few hours dreaming of becoming World Champion, I'd get a bollocking from our parents.

I remember Chris' first ride on a chopped-up scooter in the yard behind the garages where Dad worked. He could only have been about 10 or 11-years-old but as soon as he opened the throttle he crashed straight into a garage door.

Once he was old enough to join PC and me, Chris would take his riding seriously – he's like Mum in the sense that he has always applied himself fully to whatever challenge he faces and does it right, whereas I've always been more, 'if it happens, it happens, we'll sort it out later' and a bit more cavalier, just like Dad.

Sometimes, if I was tormenting Chris while we were at the farm, because he was a bit sensitive he'd walk off down the end of the lane, sit down and sulk, until PC went to console him and persuade him to rejoin us.

With an age gap of almost three years between us (I was born on September 24, 1953 and he came along on July 22, 1956), I naturally adopted the role of 'big brother' and exploited it for all its worth. Nanna – Hilda Morton, our dad's mum – worked for Priestner, one of the big haulage companies in Carrington, Manchester who delivered good quality brand names toys all over the country. She also looked after the boss's children, so, as a perk at Christmas, Gerald Priestner would let her have a couple of toys off the wagon that she'd then take home to wrap up for me and Chris. Being the eldest, and before Nanna added the gift-wrapping, I'd go with her to the depot where she worked and

Two of the Partington pushbike mafia.

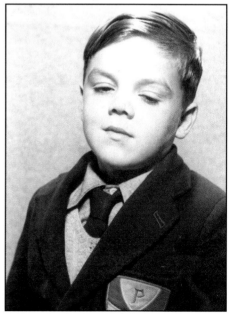

Partington Primary's woodwork expert.

The 1963 Belle Vue Aces, including the trio at the front who contested the run-off for the unofficial World Championship. The full line-up is: Gordon McGregor, Bill Powell, Jim Yacoby, Dick Fisher. Front: Soren Sjosten, Peter Craven, Cyril Maidment. Peter was tragically killed racing at Edinburgh later in the '63 season.

have first pick of the two toys, which of course meant I always got the best one.

One year I chose a big battleship that was about four foot long and fired torpedoes and all sorts, while Chris was left with a little cannon that only fired tame plastic bullets. Once we'd finished opening our presents and set up the battleground in our bedroom, of course my battleship destroyed his feeble cannon within seconds! We used to wrestle on the bed – another childhood activity where he came off second best in our sibling scraps.

We had bunk beds and if I woke up first in the morning, from the top bunk I'd pull the mattress back a few inches and dribble spit on his head while he slept below! A horrible, tight thing to do, I know, but it seemed dead funny at the time. We were all t***s at that age!

Chris was never really into football but our uncle Adrian used to take me to Old Trafford every home game to see Manchester United play. We used to stand on the Stretford End, where I'd marvel at the skills of all-time greats such as Bestie, Denis Law and Bobby Charlton and the team that famously won the European Cup in 1968.

However, as Chris and I were brought up as catholics, I had to leave most of my old schoolmates behind when moving up to high school. Now it was daunting enough making the step-up to 'big school' but it seemed even more stressful for me when boarding the bus on my first day for the journey to the Blessed Thomas Holford School in Altrincham. But within a few weeks, I had settled down to the normal everyday routine, helped by the fact that a few of the teachers seemed to take a shine to me, especially Mr Reece, my woodwork tutor. He did such a good job of nurturing my woodworking skills, I ended up winning the school prize for woodwork every year I was there.

One teacher, though, had it in for me from day one, seemingly on a mission to make my life as miserable as possible. It all came to a head one afternoon when he was in a particularly grumpy mood.

"And Morton – what do *you* want to do when you leave school?" he asked.

"I want to be a professional speedway rider, sir."

But as my three classmates had previously answered "astronaut", "brain surgeon" and "gynecologist", he was in no mood for anymore tomfoolery and exploded with rage – even though

I had been the only one who had been totally honest.

I looked forward to the summer holidays, which meant at least five weeks playing down on the farm and a week away at the seaside. Family holidays were usually taken in Wales, with Rhyl or Llandudno the preferred destinations. One abiding memory from one holiday in Llandudno was when Randolph Turpin, the famous boxer, who had purchased a pub on the summit of the Great Orme (which I believe is still there), lifted me out of the crowd.

Another Wales adventure saw me and Chris spend all our weekly holiday allowance in the first morning after being lured into the amusement arcade. This was definitely a lesson learnt. I rarely gambled again, especially on slot machines.

We spent the rest of our break from school at the farm, as there really wasn't much else to do in the village. There was a youth club and for a time I tried the Boy Scouts but the farm was our playground and we would often be there first thing in the morning and only return home when it became too dark. We would race our pushbikes around the various tracks and would also compete in small go-karts.

When we became a bit older the pushbikes were replaced by old scooters and motorbikes – basically anything we could chop down.

As I lived just down the road from the farm, we used to push our motorbikes off our small estate to where the River Mersey used to flow before the ship canal was built. Here we would ride them up the hill which led to the back of the farm. One of the tracks we built was constructed on the old river bed.

Among the lads who would ride here and on the farm were Dave Trownson, Wayne Hughes, Geoff Rogers and Neil, Phil, Steve and Les Collins, who would all become professional speedway riders.

On the rare occasions that we weren't tearing around the fields, we would amuse ourselves at the back of the farm by hurtling down an 80-foot railway embankment on an old upturned car bonnet. Three-quarters of the way down, a small ridge sent us airborne, so the aim of the game was to hang on for grim death. It was a great adrenalin rush and another activity that earned us a few bumps and bruises.

Saturday nights from March until October were spent at Hyde Road, famous home of the Belle Vue Aces. The track was in the grounds of the Belle Vue Zoological Gardens which in the mid-60s attracted thousands of visitors a week, especially on Bank Holidays. As well as the zoo and gardens, there was a funfair, with rollercoasters, swingboats and shooting galleries among the many attractions.

The 'Bobs' rollercoaster was arguably the most popular ride of all, so named because it cost a bob (shilling) for admission. It had an 80-foot drop at a 45 degree angle, which the cars travelled down at 60 miles per hour. It was a magical place for us youngsters.

Most of us arrived at the stadium with our parents but the gang soon joined up to watch the racing on our own, away from the gaze of the adults, so we could basically get up to no good. As PC has written in his foreword, we used to vault the safety fence when each heat was concluded to collect the discarded goggles and one night a helmet cover came off near to where we were standing.

This was too much of an opportunity to miss, so with the race still in full flow, I ran onto the track and back over the fence before the security track officials could react. They gave chase but I was a very quick runner as a youngster and escaped via the back of the stands, where I hid until they gave up.

We were generally always up to no good while at Belle Vue and after one meeting, we found ourselves in the stadium bar, waiting on the balcony for the riders to arrive so we could get their autographs. In walked Soren Sjosten and in the rush to get down the stairs, PC knocked over a table of glasses. They smashed all over the floor, with beer soaking the carpet through and broken glass everywhere. As you can imagine, we failed to get any autographs that night and made a quick getaway, laughing our heads off as we ran away.

I had my first actual motorbike experience when I was about nine-years-old. My dad, George, had a Matchless 500 which he used for work, and I would ride pillion. He also had a Capri 80 scooter and this was the first that I rode solo, around the yard where Dad worked repairing cars in his spare time.

Chris, like younger brothers often do, thought that anything big brother could do, so could he. So he had his first ride on the same scooter but crashed it into one of the garages in the yard. Apart from a few bruises, his pride was hurt more than his young body, but it was another valuable lesson learnt on the road to a speedway career. Motorbikes were dangerous when handled incorrectly and falling off bloody hurt!

My boyhood hero, the late Cyril Maidment, in his Belle Vue heyday. In 1963 he was the uncrowned 'World Champion'!

Talking of falling off, when Dad had given up riding to work, I had his Capri scooter as my first road bike. I was 16 and one day I had been to see my girlfriend, Shirley, who was staying with her mate just down the road in Carrington. I was on my way home when a car, travelling too fast around a blind bend, hit me side on, just as I had pulled out of the junction. Fortunately, with the scooter being open platform, I was scooped on to the bonnet, over the roof and crashed down on the road behind. I lay dazed for a few moments but when I tried to sit up, I realised that I had broken my collarbone – my second break and I hadn't even started racing yet!

Sitting in the road, minus my shoe (I never did find it), the double-decker bus to Partington passed by. On it was my mate Gary Quayle, who went straight round to tell my parents about my accident. I felt a little silly when they arrived at the hospital to pick me up but despite the pain in my shoulder, I felt quite lucky to be alive.

I left school in 1969 and started almost immediately at Shell Chemicals in Carrington. Gaining an apprenticeship was the sensible thing to do, as I needed something to fall back on if my racing career failed to get off the ground. Unlike today, jobs in the Manchester area were plentiful and although I had three or four different offers on the table, the lure of qualifying as a fabrication fitter at the end of my apprenticeship with Shell, who paid twice as much as the other jobs, was the hook. PC and our Chris also chose the same path at Shell but, due to riding commitments, didn't complete their training.

On the racing side, the need to go as fast as possible saw most of the gang join 'The Bar None Club' in Cheshire, so we could compete in grass-track racing. For anybody not in the know, the sport is, literally, speedway on grass. I had attended grass-track meetings for years and followed Chris Pusey, Johnny Cox and the Baybutt brothers, Chris and Dave, who were among the top riders in Cheshire and Lancashire.

I can remember as if it was yesterday when PC acquired his first grass bike – a 250cc Hagon BSA C15. He would ride it around his dad's farm, and it seemed a big step up from our small-engined machines. He had been racing in meetings for about 12 months and was sponsored by Chris Pusey's backer, Jim Rowlinson. I couldn't wait to get a bike of my own so that I, too, could compete.

Dave Morton
November, 2015

My first competitive grass-track rides came at the Shevington circuit near Wigan. The adrenalin rush and some decent results whetted my appetite for speedway. Above: Brother Chris is about to push me off to the start. That's our dad's Mini parked on the right, hooked up to a trailer made out of a Mini car subframe.

Chapter 1

Comfrey leaves cure

MANY speedway riders of the time had graduated to the sport from grass-tracking, so it seemed a natural progression for me to start on the grass before making the move to shale.

After Dad promised to loan me the money for my first bike, I spotted a 500cc Hagon-JAP for sale in *Motorcycle News,* so we travelled up to Selby in Yorkshire in his mini, towing a trailer to collect it. It had belonged to Alan Bradley, who was one of Yorkshire's finest grass-trackers, so I knew the bike was a good one. We paid £145 for it, which was a small fortune in 1971.

I also had a few quid left to acquire my first set of leathers, from TT Leathers at Barnard Castle in Durham. They were specially designed and were mainly orange with white arms and a green stripe down each arm.

PC had already progressed to the bigger national meetings but after learning to handle the JAP, I started competing in the local club meets in Lancashire and Cheshire. In grass-tracking you had a race number but I didn't want any old number. Even though I wasn't really superstitious, I wanted my lucky number, three, or any multiple of it. As many of the early numbers had already been taken, I plumped for No.39.

My first competitive meeting was at Shevington, near Wigan, in a field just off the motorway. Although the track wasn't a regular size (it had a small jump just before a tight corner), it gave me the opportunity to try out my skills and the chance to open up the throttle. The adrenalin rush from competing, even at this level, was incredible and I did well enough to make the 500cc final, where I finished second. A few weeks later I went one better and won the 500cc final at Pilling in Lancashire.

There were always plenty of meetings around the area organised by a number of clubs, so you could race almost every weekend. Admittedly, there wasn't a lot of prize money on offer but with the varied tracks and the bumpy conditions, it proved valuable experience in riding a motorcycle similar to a speedway bike.

During my early days on the grass-track scene, I remember one particular weekend when I was racing on both the Saturday and Sunday. On the first day, I again made the final but crashed and injured my shoulder and neck. Nothing was broken but I was very sore and stiff, and could hardly move my arm or turn my neck.

When we got home I realised I would be a big doubt for Sunday's race but Mum had other ideas and collected some comfrey leaves from the garden, put them in a big pan on the stove and boiled them up. She added them to some liniment and wrapped the hot wet poultice around my injured shoulder and neck, just before I went to bed. The next morning, I awoke and, as if by magic, no more aches and pains. The 'miracle cure' worked wonders, because I won the final. So since then, I have always sworn by the healing powers of comfrey leaves.

The holy grail for me, however, was to be a full-time speedway rider and earn a living from the sport, so I started to attend the Belle Vue training school, which took place during the off-season on Monday evenings and Saturday mornings. Dent Oliver – team manager of the Aces – used to run it, along with a few members of staff and first-team riders. Many of the grass-track boys attended, including Chris and Geoff Pusey, Keith Evans, Wayne Hughes, Dave Baybutt and Dave Trownson.

Mum's healing remedy got me going on the grass in 1971.

Another shot from Shevington later in my first season, this time wearing an open-face helmet.

I had saved hard during my time at Shell, and this gave me the money to buy my first speedway bike (a 500cc Jawa), which I bought from Alan Knapkin's shop in Eccles. Alan rode for Bradford Northern and it was one of his old bikes that I decided to buy – another tried and tested machine.

Despite the thrill of riding at the training school and around the famous Hyde Road circuit, the next goal was to earn a place in a second half race. These races were an opportunity to get yourself noticed and earn a contract. PC was the prime example. He had impressed the hierarchy during the training school days and in a few second half races, which earned him a deal with our local club. He was then immediately loaned out to Division Two outfit Rochdale Hornets (Belle Vue's nursery club, who the previous season had been the Belle Vue Colts) to gain further experience.

His rapid rise to the professional speedway ranks was all the inspiration I needed and I was desperate to do the same. But how could you prove yourself when those elusive second half slots at Belle Vue were so few and far between? Fortunately, fate would play its part one cold and rainy night at Hyde Road.

"Why don't you try and get a ride at Crewe?" suggested Fred Jackson, whose son John had joined the Kings the previous season after impressing during their second half events. As it was only about 30 miles up the road, I decided to act upon Fred's advice that would kick-start my speedway career.

New Zealand rider Colin Tucker built the Crewe track virtually single-handedly in 1969.

Chapter 2

In the blink of an eye

CREWE was run by a small group of experienced promoters calling themselves Allied Presentations Limited (APL). The APL was formed during the close season of 1967-68 following the decision to introduce a second tier of league racing to British speedway, which gave talented up and coming riders the chance to gain experience before making the step up to Division One.

The company consisted of five directors: Reg Fearman (who was promoter at Halifax), Len Silver (Hackney), Danny Dunton (Oxford), Ron Wilson (Leicester) and Maurice Littlechild (King's Lynn).

Their idea was to each operate a Second Division track to feed the best riders into their respective senior outfits. Maury formed Crewe Speedway in 1969 – the second year of BL2 – even though they didn't yet have a track ready to race on. Kiwi Colin Tucker, who had ridden for Len Silver's Rayleigh in 1968, was employed to convert the town's London Midland Railways Sports Ground into a venue suitable for speedway, a task he managed to complete in just 16 weeks. And what a track he produced.

The circuit with banked bends measured a colossal 470 yards (it had been built around a cricket pitch) and soon had a reputation of being the biggest, fastest and most feared in the country. Certain visiting promoters cruelly labeled it the 'Wall of Death' or 'Devil's Bowl'. During the opening meeting of the 1970 season, home rider Barry Meeks flew round in a time of 70.4 seconds – the

'Tuck' testing out the Crewe track. From this angle you get a sense of how wide it was.

fastest average speed (54.62 mph) recorded on a speedway track and a feat that earned him a place in *The Guinness Book of Records*.

However, later that season, the management decided to reduce the track length by approximately 40 yards, thinking it would encourage more evenly-contested matches. The majority of visiting sides had been on the receiving end of heavy defeats.

Another factor in the shortening of the circuit was that it would also help Crewe riders adapt to riding smaller away venues. Despite the alterations, the track continued to maintain its fearsome reputation, with many visiting teams beaten before the first heat.

Even though I had never been to the old railway town, I had heard how fast the Crewe track was from Fred Jackson, who informed me that due to the high banking on the corners you could basically go flat out for the four laps.

It was an exciting thought as I travelled with Dad and our Chris down to Crewe, after finishing my shift at Shell on Monday, August 2, 1971. Dad transported us in his Mini with my bike on the back of his trailer, in the hope of a chance to show what I could do, even though I wasn't programmed to ride in the second half. As we stood on the back straight watching the Kings take on Boston, I soon realised that everything that I'd been told about the place was true, as the riders shot past in the blink of an eye.

During the interval we managed to persuade the management to let me have a ride, although I believe that Fred had already put in a good word for me. So an extra race was pencilled in at the end of the programme with myself, Stuart Riley and Don Beecroft coming to the tapes, in what was effectively a third-half race. With only a few minutes to set-up my bike and having received no advice on how to race this 'monster', it was no fairytale beginning. But despite being extremely nervous, I obviously did well enough to be asked back a fortnight later (there was no second half the following week due to the track staging an international match).

I hardly remember my debut outing at Crewe. The one thing that does stick out in my mind more than anything, however, was the strange-goings on after racing had concluded. Normally, following the end of the main meeting, a fair portion of the crowd would make an early exit for home or go for a post-meeting pint – many weren't interested in watching second rate second half races, consisting of first teamers, trialists and juniors.

But this night was different.

Attendances at the track had been steadily declining since the opening season, when crowds had reached as high as 6,000, so in a bid to entice more punters through the turnstiles, Maury Littlechild had booked a side attraction. It consisted of a madcap, high-dive artist named Stan Lindbergh, who was attempting to jump from an 80-foot tower into a tiny tank of water only six feet deep . . . while blindfolded and on fire!

I overheard two young supporters, both clad in red-and-white scarves and bobble-hats, discussing the act, with the older boy saying:

"Do you thing he might get killed?"

"I hope so," said his mate.

But despite the slightly windy conditions and the failing light, the act was performed without a hitch, much to the disappointment of the young Crewe fans.

So a long, drawn-out fortnight elapsed before my next competitive ride, which took place after the Speedway Express KO Cup semi-final, first leg encounter between Crewe and Rochdale – which the Kings again won easily, despite a fine 13 points from PC, who had also starred at Earle Street a week previous in the Young England versus Young Czechoslovakia Test.

My race – in the 'Future Stakes' – was not nearly as prestigious. I must admit, it was quite a proud moment to see my name in the programme, and they even spelt my surname correctly (unlike

The Crewe team before their match at Canterbury in 1971. Along with the absent Jack Millen, these were the men I wanted to emulate in my first season of speedway. Left to right: Dave Parry, John Jackson, Dai Evans, Gary Moore, Ian Bottomley, Barrie Smitherman. On bike: record-breaker Barry Meeks.

Up the workers! PC and myself at Shell, where we both began our working lives, after he had been crowned British Grass-track Champion in August 1971.

in future editions when they spelt it *Moreton*). I was even approached in the pits to sign a few autographs.

In this race, however, I had set my bike up properly for the track, courtesy of Crewe riders Dai Evans and Jack Millen, who had both been more than helpful since my arrival. In fact all the Crewe lads were more than willing to pass on a few trade secrets, some of which had been passed down to them.

For example, in 1969, the late, great Geoff Curtis (who tragically died after a fall at Sydney Showground in 1973) had shown Kings skipper Colin Tucker how to protect his inner tubes, by placing them in an old cut-up one. As the tyres were run on such a low pressure (around 10 psi), they were prone to punctures as the tubes chaffed on the tyre when cornering. Tyre clamps were also a must to prevent the tyre moving around the rim.

At Earle Street, the bike had to be set up with a higher gear ratio. An 18-tooth engine sprocket and changing the rear wheel sprocket would cover most tracks but here at Crewe you had to go up one tooth on the engine sprocket (a 19 tooth engine sprocket was unique to Crewe) with a 57 sprocket on the back wheel (others would use a 58). It was all worked out with the counter shaft sprocket, clutch sprocket, engine and rear wheel sprocket and a little bit of mathematics. Easy when you knew how!

Apparently, Taffy Owen, the Workington rider, who also specialised in bike parts, made a killing when riders rode at Crewe, because they had to purchase a 19 tooth engine sprocket off him.

The whole set-up was a science in itself, and it was rumoured that Ivan Mauger used to have his sprockets stamped incorrectly (on purpose), so rival riders would set their bikes up wrongly when trying to copy his settings.

My race was won by second-half regular Charlie Scarbrough, who had ridden Earle Street many times, but I managed to nick second spot. Although pleased with my efforts, when analysing my time I realised I still had a considerable amount of improvement to do – I had trailed in a full seven

Crewe boss Maury Littlechild offered me my first speedway contract in 1971. I tried to act cool but was bursting with pride and excitement inside.

John Jackson, the rider I replaced for my Crewe debut at Sunderland. Jacko's dad, Fred, was the one who first suggested I should try to get rides at Earle Street.

seconds slower than Jack Millen's Heat 1 time in the main event. But I wasn't being over-critical. After all, I'd only ridden the track twice and had already improved on my first outing.

By the end of August, I heard rumours that the Crewe management were about to offer me a contract but was still a little surprised when team manager Ken Adams approached me about signing. At the start of the 1971 season, Crewe had tried to sign PC, after he had starred in a couple of second half outings there, but when he declined their offer and then put pen to paper at Belle Vue, Crewe's supremo Maury Littlechild was furious on missing out, especially when PC was then loaned out to Rochdale, who were at that time Crewe's biggest rivals.

So when Maury got wind of me being PC's mate and knowing I had been at the Belle Vue training schools, he decided to act quickly, to prevent Dent Oliver from 'poaching' any more of his teenage prospects, even though Belle Vue had not shown any interest.

"So lad, how would you like to sign for the Kings?" Maury asked, sat in a battered brown leather chair, in a dusty old room by the pits which acted as his office. I tried hard to keep my emotions in check by delaying my answer but this lasted all of about two seconds before I replied: "Yeah, of course I would."

As far as I can remember, it was over in the blink of an eye – a quick scribble of my signature, a handshake and that was that. I had signed my first contract. I walked out of the office feeling that all my birthdays had arrived at once. I had achieved my dream of becoming a professional speedway rider, albeit a part-time one. All those years of riding on the farm fields, the bumps, scrapes and bruises on the grass-tracking scene, had all been worth it. Now for the hard work.

If I showed continual improvement, Maury had promised me a first-team outing before the end of the season. But as the 1971 campaign was nearly over, I didn't really imagine it would occur before the conclusion of the season, especially with the likes of Phil Crump, John Jackson, Barry Meeks, Jack Millen and Dai Evans in the home line-up, plus a crop of up-and coming youngsters.

However, Ray Hassall had signed around the same time as myself, with the same promise from Maury, and during the home double-header versus Berwick and Sunderland in early September, Ray made his debut in the second match – and did well, scoring six (plus two bonus points). Now I had beaten Ray on several occasions during my second half rides, so I knew that if he could ride for the first-team, then so could I.

Even though I hadn't ridden during the double-header (there was no second-half), I still attended the meeting, to try and pick up some tips and tricks from the more-established riders. I was just about to make my way home with Dad when team manager Ken Adams pulled me to one side and said: "Dave, don't make any plans at the weekend."

Being a bit naive, I hadn't a clue what he was on about, until he said: "Your riding at Sunderland, Sunday afternoon, in the return league match."

"Okay, thanks Ken," I replied, trying to be cool and nonchalant.

"Dad, are you working Sunday or doing anything else?"

"No, why?"

"Well, you are now – you're driving me to Sunderland."

The rest of the week at Shell was hard work. Not because it was strenuous, but because I couldn't concentrate properly on what I was doing. I told all who would listen that I was about to make my debut for Crewe, although many of my workmates showed not the slightest bit of interest.

On the Saturday evening, I don't think I slept more than a few hours. After a good breakfast, we set-out early that morning of Sunday, September 12 for the long trek to the north-east, in Dad's trusty Mini – a journey that seemed to last forever. Finally, we saw signs for the Sunderland Greyhound Stadium in East Boldon, and this was when the nerves really kicked-in. We had arrived in good time, and there were a few home supporters milling about outside.

TEESSIDE / RAYLEIGH / READING / CREWE / PETERBOROUGH / SUNDERLAND	Date *18 Sept 71*				TEESSIDE SPEEDWAY, Stockton Road, Middlesbrough *Tel.* 47381—Markfield 2841 RAYLEIGH SPEEDWAY, Rayleigh Weir, Essex *Tel.* 5498—Romford 60065 READING SPEEDWAY, Oxford Road, Tilehurst *Tel.* 27151—Henley-on-Thames 3709 CREWE SPEEDWAY, Earle Street, Crewe *Tel.* 56806—Waltham Cross 28338 PETERBOROUGH SPEEDWAY, Showground, Peterborough *Tel.* 5868—Chesham 5353 SUNDERLAND SPEEDWAY					

ALLIED PRESENTATIONS LTD.
Registered Office:
HACKNEY WICK STADIUM, Waterden Road, London E.15
Telephone 01-985-9810 — 01-985-9822

TEAM/RIDER'S NAME *Dave Morton*

DATE OF MEETING					*13 Sept*					
RIDER/TRACK	*Sunderland*				*Crewe*					
MATCH STARTS	*3* *2.25*									
MATCH POINTS	*3*									
BONUS POINTS	*2*									
TOTAL POINTS	*5 5·00*									
MATCH RACE										
S/H STARTS	*1 ·75*				*2 1·50*					
S/H POINTS	*—*				*0*					
TRAVEL EXPENSES	*5·00*				*1·00*					
GUARANTEES										
GROSS TOTAL	*10·75*				*2·50*					
FUEL OIL										
INSURANCE	*-60*				*(2) 30*					
SPARES										
ADVANCES										
DEDUCTIONS TOTAL	*-60*				*30*					
NETT TOTAL	*10-15*				*2-20*					

ENCLOSED PLEASE FIND CHEQUE £ *12:35:*

Pay-sheet sent out by Allied Presentations Ltd showing earnings from my first meeting for Crewe at Sunderland, plus second-half at Earle Street the following night. The pay rates were 75p per start, £1 a point, with 15p per start deducted for insurance. The North-East was a long way to go to earn £10.15 but I wasn't doing speedway for the money.

Sunderland was a small, tight track, where passing was difficult. It was only 310 yards in length, a colossal 120 yards shorter than Earle Street.

Dai Evans was there to greet me and soon put me at ease with some calming words while helping me set-up my bike with the correct sprockets, etc. Jack Millen also gave me some tips on how to ride the track, having been a Sunderland rider at the start of the season. It was only then I learnt I was in the team as a replacement for John Jackson, who for whatever reason had not made the trip. So I was making my debut at No.3 – as a heat leader!

'Jacko' had been riding in the Young England versus Young Australasia series, so I figured that the Crewe management had decided to rest him. Crewe were unlikely to win the match, despite the Stars being bottom of the league (they had won away only twice in Division Two in nearly three seasons).

The meeting however, started well, with the Anzac pairing of Crump and Millen romping home. My first ride came in Heat 4 and I was paired with Barry Meeks, another rider who had progressed from grass-track. I gated quite well and tucked in behind 'Meeksy' as home rider Peter Wrathall streaked away from us both. When Gerry Richardson fell on the third lap, I managed to hang on without any major mishap to earn my first point in British speedway – with a bonus point to boot.

For my final two rides, I was paired with Aussie Gary Moore and secured two more third place finishes. I had scored in all three of my races and was quite happy with my performance. But despite

Phil Crump's maximum, we just failed to bring home the points, losing 40-38.

The score was a perfect example of why Crewe had so far failed to win any silverware. Riding at home on that massive track was all fine and well, as they had proved just six days previous when trouncing Sunderland 61-17, but it was adapting to the smaller tracks that was the real problem.

With my league debut under my belt, I rode again at Ipswich on September 30, in what would be a dress rehearsal for the KO Cup Final held a few weeks later. My two rides yielded no points but riding against some of the top riders in the league only added to my experience and I was confident that, with a few more outings, I could make the grade in this division.

My rides for the remaining weeks of the season were limited to second half appearances and a challenge match at Workington, where a makeshift team included Reg Wilson, who would become a team-mate of mine at Sheffield in later years and a good friend, guesting for the Kings from Hull. Torrential rain made racing treacherous but we managed to secure a rare away win, despite the efforts of Lou Sansom – the 'Mini-Mauger' of Division Two.

The season wound up with the Chester Vase individual meeting at Earle Street, with a whole host of lower league stars invited to ride, including John Louis, Reg Wilson and PC. I managed to nick a reserve spot and in Heat 15, after two pointless outings, found myself lining up against Taffy Owen, fellow reserve Ray Hassall and, you've guessed it, PC.

Now we both loved big, fast tracks, and on the farm fields had ridden against each other many times, but this one was for real, even though my chances of success against my old mate were slim. PC was riding a really fast bike and had done so well in 30 matches for Rochdale that he had been promoted to the Belle Vue Aces' British League First Division line-up and appeared in the top flight 11 times.

PC didn't disappoint but I did give him a run for his money when finishing third behind Taffy Owen. Only a fall in Heat 17 prevented him from winning the coveted trophy, won by Crewe's new up-and-coming star Phil Crump.

Looking relaxed on parade at the start of 1972, my first full season, with Dai Evans beside me.

Chapter 3

Pain and glory

CREWE were installed as one of the favourites to win Division Two in 1972, so I was delighted when team manager Ken Adams contacted me about six weeks after the '71 campaign had concluded about returning to Earle Street for the new season.

I kept my eye in during the close-season with regular trips to Hyde Road – one of the very few northern tracks that was open during the dark, cold winter months. It was again supervised by Dent Oliver but it wasn't really a training school. It was frequented by newcomers eager to be recognised and earn a second-half slot but also by many of the top riders, including Jim McMillan and Bobby Beaton, who travelled all the way from Scotland for a spin around the famous Belle Vue circuit. All the riders were charged £1 for the privilege, which included a gallon of methanol and a quart of castor oil.

I had spent a few quid on new parts for my bike and equipped it with a new engine, and it performed well during practice.

Just before the season, Jack Millen returned to Sunderland. Not only had the team lost a damn good rider, I had lost a mentor and friend. However, I had noticed during the latter part of the 1971 race term that things didn't seem quite right in the Kings camp between skipper Dai Evans and Jack, and I think a clash of personalities was the reason. Something had gone on, although I never found out what.

But the Crewe management had not been idle during the close-season, and had persuaded another young Aussie scrambler to join the team, Melbourne's Garry Flood, who had been recommended by Phil Crump and was keen to show what he could do. This was a shrewd signing and completed a

With Crewe's young Aussie signing Garry Flood.

Phil Crump and promoter Maury Littlechild.

John Jackson and me grabbed our opportunity to shine in the Halifax Shaytona.

formidable line-up – a good mixture of experience and youth.

I was handed the No.2 jacket, deemed to be one of the hardest positions in the team to fill, but being paired with Phil Crump would be a massive bonus for me. 'Crumpie' was the league's hottest talent and had turned down a chance to ride in Division One to continue his racing apprenticeship at Crewe. During the campaign, he would show me the art of team-riding, pass on tips and tricks and, despite his No.1 star status, would often give me choice of gates.

The season began with a challenge match at Workington and in the first heat, I secured my first win in Crewe colours. The track was big, but narrow, so passing was difficult. However, the rest of the meeting proved pointless, thanks mainly to spark plug issues.

Now as I had mentioned before, Crewe were among the favourites for league honours, so it was quite a shock to find the team bottom of the Division Two table after three matches, which included a shock home defeat to title rivals Peterborough, who became the first team to win a league match at Earle Street since Belle Vue Colts in July 1969. This match was my home league debut but there was little to write home about after collecting just a solitary point from three outings.

The team's fortunes slowly improved and, more importantly, there were away wins at Ellesmere Port and Sunderland, which seemed to quash the theory that Crewe could only perform at Earle Street.

But one thing that had gnawed away at me from my very first league encounter was the fact that I had yet to win a heat in a competitive race (KO Cup or league). Okay, for the vast majority of my early outings, I had been paired with Crumpie and not many riders were going to beat him that season.

That first elusive win, though, came in the home meeting with Birmingham – my 10th competitive match (including 1971 outings). After being paired with Crumpie in my first two races (where I followed him home on both occasions), my first triumph occurred in Heat 8, beating Mike Gardner, with team-mate Gary Moore third. Although it was a huge relief to get that first victory, all I can remember of it is coming into the last bend praying I would stay upright and my bike would not let me down.

With my first victory under my belt, and a huge weight lifted off my shoulders, it was time to enjoy my racing and further contribute to the team's title and cup aspirations. The Kings were in a tremendous run of victories and although the title was certainly on the radar, it was the KO Cup that our promoter Maury Littlechild craved the most, and on Sunday, June 4, we travelled to Scunthorpe for a second round, first leg, tie with confidence sky-high.

The Saints had been struggling in the league but while preparing for the meeting, I sensed that something special was on the cards. Over 500 Crewe fans had travelled to cheer us on, including a group nicknamed 'The Cats Choir' who followed us everywhere and orchestrated the singing. The large, slick Quibell Park track suited us down to the ground and I followed home Crumpie in Heat 1. And when Dave Parry and Gary Moore did the same in the next, a big away win looked on but not even I could have envisaged the size of the winning margin. Crewe riders won every heat and gated superbly – the result making the second leg a mere formality. We had won 59-19, later deemed the biggest ever away victory in British speedway history.

The scoreline was repeated the next night and I achieved my first paid maximum, which not only improved my average but my bank balance as well. The poor Saints had been hammered 118-38 on aggregate – another record.

A big away win at Long Eaton kept the double dream alive but Boston, Peterborough and Eastbourne were also vying for the title. However, when Eastbourne arrived at Earle Street on June 19, their hopes were all but extinguished when they were thrashed by 40 points.

Eastbourne's manager Dave Lanning was less than complimentary about the Crewe track and

At a supporters' function with brother Chris (standing to my right) and our dad.

during his post-match comments complained bitterly that we had an unfair advantage riding on this 'wall of death' circuit.

Now don't get me wrong, we did have a big advantage but all teams had the upper-hand when riding at home. There were tracks that we didn't like, including Eastbourne, which was always slick and hard to pass on if you missed the gate. As for Lanning's comments, many a visiting rider enjoyed riding Earle Street – ask the Workington trio of Taffy Owen, Mitch Graham and Lou Sansom, who always seemed to do well in South Cheshire. Funnily enough, the riders who did complain about Earle Street were generally those from the smaller track outfits.

Crewe's circuit was subject to much criticism from rival promoters and riders during the seven years of speedway there but, believe me, it was no green-eyed monster. If your bike was set-up correctly and you were properly prepared, then it was an exhilarating experience.

My pre-meeting routine at Earle Street was always the same. I would arrive at the stadium about two hours before the off, just as the track staff were completing their last minute preparations. usually had a walk around the track to see how slick it was going to be, or to spot where the deeper patches of shale were. This would determine what gear ratio to start the meeting with, and with that decided, I would go for a cup of tea.

After unloading my bike and equipment, I would head for the pits and off-load in my designated spot, which was the same every week.

In the changing rooms fellow riders would discuss conditions and what gearing they were using then around half an hour before the start, I would change into my leathers.

Meanwhile, my bike was started and warmed up for about 10 minutes to get the engine up to racing temperature, then it was time for the parade. At Crewe we came out to *Entry of the Gladiators,* which was the tune associated with the circus. At this stage my adrenalin was pumping, as I was usually in the first heat.

Every Crewe rider had a similar way of riding at home, and I suppose my approach was no different. With Earle Street being such a big track and pulling a high gear ratio, you had to slip the clutch from the start to get to the first corner without losing engine power. Your aim was to head for the banking as near to the top as possible, so you could generate plenty of speed when coming off the corner and down the back straight and into the next bend.

The idea was to try and keep your wheels more or less in line for going into the next (third) bend again heading as near to the top of the banking while being careful not to collide with the boards (which were six-inch thick railway sleepers).

Of course, it was a shorter distance around the inside of the track but you didn't have the same speed as a rider coming off the bank.

Then you would ride it flat out, without shutting off the throttle until you crossed the line.

Gating was also key. Being ahead at the first bend meant you could decide your own racing line so knowing the referee was also important. Certain referees were easy to work out and I would always count the number of seconds from the green light going on to the release of the tapes. Some refs would be quicker than others and release the tapes as soon as the green light came on. It became quite an art and I always ensured (unlike in today's racing) that I was on the move just before the tapes went up, even if I was going backwards, because any sort of momentum would get you away quicker than a stationary rider.

As the season progressed my partnership with Crumpie continued to flourish. He racked up the maximums while I averaged around seven points per meeting. With John Jackson also scoring regular double-figure totals and Garry Flood winning more than his fair share, it was no surprise that we were in the mix on both fronts.

The next round of the KO Cup saw us drawn against Jack Millen's Sunderland. In the first leg we won at Earle Street by 28 points but before the second leg four nights later, the team received some devastating news. Maury Littlechild, the main driving force and founder of the Kings, and the man who had given me my first chance in professional speedway, had died of cancer.

Maury rarely missed a home meeting, so when he was absent from the Sunderland match, we realised that something was not right, as he had not been well for a number of months.

He had been a terrific promoter and never meddled in team affairs, leaving it all to Ken Adams and Dai. He just took a back seat and paid the wages but was fully-committed to Crewe and King's Lynn.

His death not only stunned the team, officials and supporters, but left us in a dilemma. We all wanted to attend the funeral but Crewe were due to ride at Hull in the league on the same day and Maury's send-off was down south in the rural Essex village of Upshire. Dai held a team meeting and we decided that Maury would not have wanted us to postpone the meeting, so we reluctantly agreed to ride, while Ken Adams represented the club at the funeral.

The Hull meeting gave Crewe the chance to pile further pressure on our rivals but the Vikings had recently appointed Colin Tucker as team manager and he was in the mood to put a dent in our title challenge following his dismissal during the early stages of the 1970 season, following an incident with fellow Kiwi Paul O'Neil. It mattered little to Maury Littlechild at the time that Colin had built the Crewe track and was the skipper. O'Neil was No.1 at Earle Street, so there was only ever going to be one winner there.

But 'Tuck' put his track-building knowledge to full use for this particular meeting. He prepared parts of the surface that only the home riders knew about, where extra grip and momentum could be gained. He did this by preparing three 15 foot-long strips about a foot wide. After the track had been watered, these strips received an extra dousing, so instead of around two inches of wet shale, these doctored areas were around four inches deep.

I was gutted to miss out at the end of the '72 season due to injury but the lads made me feel involved. This was taken after the second leg of the KO Cup Final at Peterborough, with me and Dai Evans holding the trophy. Standing (left to right): Dave Parry, Gary Moore, Ken Adams, John Jackson, Phil Crump, Garry Flood and Peter Nicholas.

Crewe's double success in 1972 did the Cheshire town proud – and don't the Mayor and Mayoress look pleased!

Before the off, he walked his riders around the track and secretly pointed out these strips, with two of them positioned just as you came off the bend, in relation to the inside line.

Despite our best efforts, and the majority of us wishing we were somewhere else, the ex-Kings skipper got his wish as we lost narrowly 41-36.

On July 15, I accompanied John Jackson to Halifax to take part in the Shaytona, an individual event exclusively for Division Two riders. Halifax was similar to Crewe, was fast and banked, so it was no surprise that we did well, with 'Jacko' winning the meeting and myself a close second.

What surprised me more was my time in Heat 4 – 66.6, which I was later informed was only two-fifths of a second outside the fastest time recorded by a Division One rider at the West Yorkshire track all season.

We also learnt that a number of Division One promoters were in the crowd that night and were impressed with the way we had handled ourselves.

Crewe continued to sweep all before them at home, while away wins at Teesside and Cheshire rivals Ellesmere Port (which put the Kings top) kept the double dream alive.

A finger injury, however, kept me out of three matches following a fall at Earle Street in a league match with Long Eaton. It occurred in Heat 8 and as I hit the shale, my finger caught under the handlebars. It wasn't until I reached the pits and took off my glove that I realised I had broken my finger.

It was cleaned and strapped up and I was told it would be a few weeks until it healed. I was hoping I could still ride but after scoring only one point at Teesside the following week (it was painful when trying to pull the clutch in), I decided that the doctor knew best and took some time out.

The war of words had continued with Eastbourne's Dave Lanning, so it was sod's law we would draw them in the semi-final of the KO Cup. There was a growing feeling in the camp that is was our destiny to win the cup for Maury, so this grudge match was not what we wanted at this stage of the competition. The first leg was at the Arlington raceway and trouble started even before the first race, when the Crewe management refused permission for the track to be watered, resulting in the match being played out in a cloud of dust.

It was a damage limitation exercise in the first leg, so a 10-point deficit was a satisfactory result, thanks mainly to a 14-point haul by Phil Crump and two heat wins by John Jackson, who were by now one and two and in the Division Two averages.

The following night I returned from injury to complete a full-strength Kings line-up for the second leg. The Crewe public had taken the competition to heart and the stadium was packed well before the off.

But Eastbourne had learnt valuable lessons following their earlier drubbing and were still ahead on aggregate after Heat 5, thanks to a Bobby McNeil/Malcolm Ballard maximum. Our cause was not helped by mechanical problems for Dave Parry, Garry Flood and Gary Moore but when I beat Ballard in Heat 8, we led by 14 – an advantage we took into the final heat, where John Jackson prevented any hopes of a shock.

We were in the final, much to the delight of the home crowd, the team and management, but especially Dai, who had vowed to win the cup for Maury.

It was my first full season in British speedway and to reach a final was a real bonus. But just as things seemed to be coming together, disaster struck.

Berwick were the opposition at Earle Street and were in no mood to be rolled over. The night had not started well for me and a fall in Heat 1 on a heavily watered track left me unable to ride until Heat 8.

Determined to make up for my earlier spill, I streaked away from the tapes and had a big lead approaching the pits bend on the second lap. Again, I misjudged how slippery the track was and my bike spun round and I was dumped to the floor. The first two riders sped past, easily avoiding me, but the back-marker seemed not to even notice me as I lay on the floor. Now whether he didn't genuinely see me, or didn't know how to put down his bike, he continued without deviating.

I thought, 'my god, he's going to hit me', so I put up my left arm to offer some sort of protection, just as he ploughed into me, which took the full impact from his engine.

Shocked and stunned but in little pain, I walked to the pits holding my arm as though in a sling. The St. John's men carefully took off the top part of my leathers so they could assess the damage, and it revealed the bone had penetrated the skin. They immediately took me to the local hospital at Leighton, where they operated the next day, screwing a plate onto the bone to hold everything together. I spent a full week in hospital before returning home.

My season was over.

Not being involved in the run-in was hard to stomach. Gutted wasn't the word – I was pig sick to be watching the boys instead of being in the thick of it. Thankfully, money wasn't an issue – I was still living at home and receiving sick pay from work – but I was still rather humbled when the supporters' club organised a collection at the home meeting with Rayleigh, which raised a £60 bonus for me. It made me realise that the team and the supporters were in this together, and we were nothing without their support.

I travelled with Ken Adams to as many away meetings as I could get to but as the season reached its climax, things tightened up at the top following a surprise defeat at lowly Barrow.

During this spell my brother Chris had taken his first steps on the speedway ladder when he had a few second half races at Earle Street and I remember his very first outing. He had borrowed my

Dai Evans and Ken Adams receiving the Division Two championship trophy from the great Johnnie Hoskins, with BSPA chairman Reg Fearman (one of the APL consortium) also present.

Well, everyone had long hair in 1972, didn't they?

bike and was determined to put on a good show. I stood by the starting gate to get a good view but as the tapes went up, he flipped my bike clean over and fell with an undignified bump on his bottom on the wet shale. Thankfully, only his ego was bruised but he had bent the handlebars and broken the mudguard on my bike.

Chris continued to appear in second halves until the end of the season (including a run-out with the Crewe junior team at Wolves, where he top-scored), and the Crewe management must have noted his potential after he won his fair share of races.

On September 4 a full-house at Crewe gathered for the first leg of the KO Cup Final, with Peterborough the opposition, but it could not have started any worse. Kings' junior Pete Nicholas had been drafted into the team to take my place but could do little in Heat 1 when Phil Crump suffered a rare retirement.

However, by Heat 5 we had sailed into a 10-point lead, before a 'Jacko' maximum and three heat wins by Phil Crump resulted in a healthy 51-27 victory. Barring a disaster, the KO Cup was ours.

The second leg took place the following Sunday and even though we held a big lead, it was still a nervy affair, especially when the Panthers went eight points clear after seven heats. Crumpie was in no mood for a close affair, however, and when he and Gary Moore won the next, it was all over bar the shouting. John Jackson confirmed victory in the next.

Despite not riding in the final, I had won my first trophy – a silver tankard. If only Maury had been there to witness the fruits of his labour. But we had no time for sentiment. We had a league title to win.

So far in the league campaign, Phil Crump and John Jackson had received the plaudits for their consistent performances throughout the season but one of the unsung heroes was skipper Dai Evans. He was a very good captain who helped others, including myself. As soon as I had arrived at Earle Street he and his wife Trisha looked after me like a son.

Dai would be continually geeing up the riders and many a time would tell us that such and such a rider wasn't riding very well and was beatable, even if the rider in question had won all of his previous races!

He would also lend out various items of equipment and his bike if any of the team had a sick motor. As Crewe had a number of youngsters riding, it was great to have Dai in charge. He was not only a good rider, but an unselfish one at that. This became apparent at the end of the season when his team-riding earned him 49 bonus points – more than any other rider in the league.

After a draw at Berwick and a narrow win at Canterbury, Kings had the chance to secure the league title at Eastbourne. But a four-point defeat in Sussex meant that Crewe had to beat old-foes Workington at Earle Street the following night to secure the coveted double. It was the third meeting in three days and before another big crowd, we made a nervous start. As mentioned before, the Workington lads were comfortable riding on the big tracks and Mitch Graham and Lou Sansom won heats two and three.

But that was the last victory they would register, and it was fitting that John Jackson – Mr Crewe Speedway – won the heat that secured the title. The whole stadium erupted in a sea of red-and-white, with the deafening sound of air horns being blown all around the stadium just about drowning out the cheering. Unfashionable Crewe had won the double – and deservedly so.

After a number of end-of-season challenge matches, myself, Dai, Gary Flood and Ken Adams travelled to Wimbledon to cheer Crumpie on in the Division Two Riders' Championship. Now the Plough Lane track was only a shade over 300 yards in length and I was a little apprehensive about Phil's chances, even though he could adapt to any track conditions or length.

A retirement in his first outing confirmed my worries but he won his remaining four heats, then defeated Boston's Arthur Price in a run-off by a good 40 yards to confirm his status as the best rider in the second tier.

With the season concluded, I learnt that Crewe had filed for a place in Division One, in what would be a massive step up in class. If this was to happen I knew I would have to invest in better equipment. And although I felt I could cope at Earle Street, I was unsure whether I had the experience to ride week in, week out in the top flight, and another season in Division Two would probably be the better option, if Crewe did make the step-up.

Looking back on the 1972 campaign, Crewe succeeded simply because they had the best team. Both Phil Crump and John Jackson had averaged double figures but throughout the season, all the squad had done their bit. Even though my contribution had been punctuated by injury and mechanical problems, I had still scored over 150 points, averaging a shade over 6.5 points per match, which included three paid maximums.

Another telling factor was the tremendous team spirit in the club. I can honestly say that throughout the campaign, hardly a crossed word was said between us. Everybody got on together.

To prove the point, after the conclusion of the 1972 season I enjoyed my first foreign holiday in Lloret de Mar with girlfriend Shirley, John Jackson and his partner Sue, plus Kings junior Ray Hassall and his girlfriend.

Above: Finding the right lines on the new Chesterton track that opened in early 1973.
Left: Ivan Mauger with Peter Collins at the 1973 European Final. I picked up a few tips from Ivan at his Chesterton training school, while PC was another youngster who learned from the Kiwi maestro during his early days in the Belle Vue team.

Chapter 4

Turning point

IT was quite a proud moment in the Morton household when Chris announced he was signing for his beloved Belle Vue Aces in 1973. Just 18 months previous, myself, Chris and PC were dreaming of emulating our speedway idols. Now we all had a chance of writing our own names in the history books.

PC had established himself in the Aces' senior team and had helped them to the Division One title in 1972 but Chris would have to wait for his chance to shine at Hyde Road. In April, to gain some much-needed experience, he was loaned out to the Division Two outfit Ellesmere Port, who were Belle Vue's feeder club, following the demise of Rochdale at the end of 1971.

I know for a fact that Crewe were interested in Chris and it would have been fantastic to have had him in the Kings line-up, but Dent Oliver moved quickly to sign him up. So instead of being team-mates for the 1973 season, we were rivals, following news in early January that Crewe had failed with their application to join the British League first division.

Again I frequented Hyde Road during the winter months, and then signed up for Ivan Mauger's training school at Chesterton – a newly-built track, just 13 miles from Crewe – along with fellow Kings riders Dave Parry, Ray Hassall and Pete Nicholas.

Ivan passed on many valuable tips and advice on different techniques and although the majority of riders attending did their best to follow his instructions, 'Mad' Jack Millen basically did what he wanted. In one exercise, we were shown the art of weaving in and out of cones strategically set-up on one of the Loomer Road bends but Jack decided to do it his way – and ploughed through the lot!

At Earle Street, the team assembled for the new season was unrecognisable from the one that had won the double. Phil Crump had signed for Division One outfit King's Lynn, Garry Flood returned to Australia just two meetings into the new season and fellow Aussie Gary Moore disappeared from the face of the earth, just as the season's league fixtures were about to commence.

There were also changes in the management set-up at Crewe, following a shake-up at Allied Presentations. In came Len Silver, who had delegated most of his duties at second division Rayleigh to Peter Thorogood but was still running British League Hackney, with Tudor Blake brought in as our new team manager.

They moved quickly to plug the gaps in the line-up by signing former Division Two Riders' Champion Geoff Ambrose, who ran a successful motorcycles business in the town, and 16-year-old British schoolboys scramble and trials champion Keith White, whose father Vic was team boss at Leicester. The squad would be further strengthened during the first few months of the season with the arrivals of Aussies Glyn Taylor and Wayne Forrest, plus Halifax junior Ian Cartwright.

John Jackson signed for Halifax as their No.8 but this allowed him to continue riding at Crewe. There was also a tentative enquiry from the Yorkshire outfit for me as well, plus interest from Sheffield and Poole, but I was more than happy to continue – for another season at least – in Division Two, where I was confident I could become one of the top riders.

Crewe's biggest loss, however, was skipper Dai Evans, who announced that he was hanging up his leathers after riding in our first meeting at Workington. Dai had helped me so much when first arriving at Earle Street and I was sad to see him go. On reflection, I think he was no longer enjoying

Oh brother! Chris and me in 1973, his first full season. Races between us were always ultra competitive.

racing and the travelling involved. Also, Dai had been comfortable with the old regime at Crewe, so the arrival of Len and Tudor and their different way of doing things prompted him to call time on his riding career.

The only rider left from the original 1969 line-up was Dave Parry but he too would also retire from speedway mid-season, although that would not be the end of his time at Earle Street.

With Crumpie now gone, my first objective was to challenge Jacko, who was appointed our new skipper, for the No.1 jacket, but this challenge would have to be done on a modified Earle Street track. The banking angle on both bends had been significantly reduced, in the hope of providing more evenly-contested meetings.

Now this was all well and fine if we'd had a chance to practice on the new track but as the work was completed only days before our first home meeting with Workington (in the Cheshire/ Cumberland Trophy), the advantage of powering off the top of the bank was now gone, plus the fact that we had new riders who had little experience of riding the Crewe track anyway. This became apparent, when just three heats into the meeting, we found ourselves 14-4 down.

Despite the shock 45-33 defeat, I secured 13 points from five outings, to easily top-score for the hosts. I had quickly adapted a new style of riding the modified track, adopting a new racing line, which meant staying much closer to the inside line.

After the meeting, Len Silver called me into his office and said that he wanted me to gain some Division One experience by riding for his Hackney outfit. And what excited me even more was the fact that the Hawks' next meeting was at Belle Vue, where I would be pitting my wits against riders I had watched from the terraces and once tried to imitate on the farm fields.

I got on with Len from day one and straight away realised that he was nuts about speedway. He knew I was ambitious and had some experience of riding the big open spaces of the Hyde Road track and I couldn't thank him enough for the opportunity. But when Saturday arrived, I was both excited and nervous at the prospect of fulfilling a life-time dream, although my recurring dream involved me riding for the Aces, not against them.

It was a surreal moment when we went out on parade. The stadium seemed different, almost alien to me, and spotting old faces in the crowd only made me more nervous. Could I hack it riding with the big boys, or would I fall flat on my face?

My first two outings, in Heats 2 and 6, confirmed my initial doubts when I finished last in the first (to Mitch Graham, Paul Tyrer and Terry Kelly) and then trailed behind Chris Pusey and Alan Wilkinson after my team-mate Dave Kennett had retired.

After racing against one of my idols, Pusey, I lined up against another in Heat 9 when Soren Sjosten appeared for the Aces. Now this would be a scalp-and-a-half, I thought, as we approached the tapes. But despite tucking in behind him after the first lap, the race came to a premature end when Barry Thomas fell and was excluded. In the re-run, I made the gate but Soren came past me on the inside of the first corner, taking advantage of the tiniest of gaps, but I wasn't losing any ground and tried to pass him on several occasions.

I was aware of Eric Broadbelt just behind me, so instead of risking everything, I consolidated my position and shut the door on Broadbelt to ensure second place. Three points from three rides in my first Division One outing was a fairly satisfactory total despite Hackney's heavy defeat.

After my debut top flight appearance, I was in a confident mood for Crewe's league opener with Peterborough two nights later. Having ridden against riders that were so much faster and more professional, I felt my riding level was a notch higher than the previous week, and to prove the point, I secured my first full maximum by winning all my five rides, in a close contest that we just edged.

The new track layout now had us competing on a more level playing field and for a change there were positive comments regarding the track from the opposition. These more competitive matches

1973 Kings. Left to right: Myself, Glyn Taylor, Wayne Forrest, John Jackson (on bike), Keith White, Ian Cartwright, new promoter Len Silver and Geoff Ambrose.

would also be appreciated by the home crowd – after all, who wanted to watch a one-sided affair every Monday night, when the meeting was as good as over by Heat 7?

A neck injury kept me out of the next three Crewe meetings. I had ridden for Hackney at Ipswich in the Spring Gold Cup on April 20 and injured my neck in a Heat 2 fall, with Witches' Mick Hines also breaking his collarbone in the process. Unable to complete my programmed rides, it meant I had endured a 450-mile round trip for 30 seconds of racing.

By this time I was now travelling to meetings on my own. After passing my driving test when I was 17, my first vehicle was a Morris Minor van. But for the 1973 season I decided to splash out and paid £800 for a gold Cortina 1600E from a garage next to where Shirley worked as a hairdresser, in a salon owned by Manchester City chairman Peter Swales. She said he would frequent the salon on many occasions, having his comb-over trimmed! My new car, with its specially made bike-rack which Dad had constructed on the back, was the perfect way to travel to meetings.

I had recovered enough to travel to Boston nine days later to compete in the preliminary round of the World Championship, scoring enough points to qualify for the next stage. Everything seemed to be falling into place for me. My mechanical faults were minimal and my new-found confidence saw me top-score at Peterborough and then get 13 at home against Bradford. Although my World Championship campaign ended at Poole and Halifax, I continued my Division Two scoring spree with 10 points at Eastbourne.

However, during the second-half on a greasy surface, I locked up coming into the pits bend and collided with Bobby McNeil. We both crashed to the ground, and I struck the small of my back on the engine of my bike. Although winded, I got changed but didn't feel like driving the long way home, so asked my mate Jack Bassett to drive while I sat in the back with Shirley.

As we stopped for fuel just down the road, I decided to spend a penny. But things weren't all right. All I did was pee blood. The pain in my back was excruciating and I couldn't stand up properly, so we headed off to Panbury Hospital, where, after an X-ray, they confirmed that I had damaged my kidneys.

I spent the next week lying on my back while they settled down, and another week while further checks were carried out. When I was allowed home, it was subject to further examinations at my local hospital, where the consultant informed me that I had a defective kidney – basically, one was doing the work of two, so I needed to have an operation to remove the defective one, and it needed to be done straight away.

But because I felt okay, I informed the consultant that I would have it done at the end of the season. In no uncertain terms the consultant told me I was being very foolish and said I was risking serious damage, or even kidney failure, if I crashed or received a further blow to the lower back.

In all, I missed 11 meetings for Crewe and was unable to compete at Canterbury in the Junior Championship of the British Isles, incidentally won by PC. While I was out of the team, Crewe had been knocked out of the KO Cup by Boston and received hammerings at Sunderland, Birmingham and Bradford Northern. One thing was certain, we wouldn't be retaining our league title.

For me it was imperative to return to the team as quickly as possible and I declared myself fit for the home meeting with Ellesmere Port. After all, I wasn't going to miss the opportunity of riding against Chris, who was by now sponsored by Jim Rowlinson and had started well in his first season.

During the week leading up to the meeting, we ribbed each other at home and at work about the forthcoming league encounter and how we were going to beat each other – even when travelling down to Crewe together!

We both started well. Chris won two heats and I won all of my first three rides but we had still to ride against each other – in the final race. I was more than confident that I could beat Chris – he was riding on my patch and I had won 12 of my last 13 outings at Earle Street.

Warming-up in the Earle Street pits before a match against Workington.

Last-minute preparations at the gate. Studying the different routines of referees was important.

But Chris too enjoyed riding the big tracks and was on a really fast machine, so I had to start well to ensure the family bragging rights belonged to 'big brother'. In fact we both wanted to beat each other so much, we virtually blanked each other in the pits.

As we lined up at the tapes, I knew Chris wasn't the greatest of gaters, and had earned a reputation of battling from the back. I had already worked out the referee, who was releasing the tapes around a second after the green light.

I was paired with Geoff Ambrose, with ex-Kings No.1 Paul O'Neil partnering Chris. I timed the start to perfection, leaving the other three standing, but as I hit the first bend, a loud crack brought my race to a premature end – my chain had snapped. Geoff won the race and Chris followed him home. Even though Crewe had secured the points with a narrow victory, I was a little disappointed about the outcome.

Our next away meeting was at Scunthorpe and the previous season's big win there was in my thoughts when I travelled north on Sunday, July 1. However, the Saints had made a couple of shrewd signings in the close season and it was a perfect example of how much they had improved and Crewe had fallen down the packing order when they thrashed us 55-23, and then just failed to take home the points the next night in the return clash at Earle Street.

At this stage of the season, I was starting to have my fair share of bad luck regarding mechanical problems. But just as I started to despair over my equipment, events would take a turn for the better.

On July 16, Long Eaton were the visitors to Earle Street and in Heat 5, I managed to break the track record with a time of 71.2 seconds – the previous time being set by John Jackson some 15 months previous. This was an important moment for me, as it not only confirmed me as the record holder, but it was another feather in my cap regarding being No.1 at Crewe.

All speedway riders love to ride in front of a big crowd, so I looked forward to Crewe's away league fixture at Chesterton (Stoke) – by now regarded as our 'local derby' meeting. The Kings' management had originally objected to Chesterton's application to join the league, fearing that attendances at Earle Street would fall significantly. Many former Stoke supporters, who followed the Potters in their Provincial League days of the early 60s, regularly attended Crewe meetings, being the only speedway track in the immediate area. But a change of heart saw Crewe withdraw their objections, allowing Chesterton into the league from the start of 1973.

The whole set-up at Loomer Road was brand new and I had knowledge of the track after attending Ivan Mauger's training school, so went into the meeting relishing the night's racing. I arrived about an hour before the off and already there were several thousand fans queuing to get in, and by the time we paraded, there wasn't an empty space in the stadium. The atmosphere was electric but despite a combined 30-point haul from myself, Jacko and Geoff Ambrose, the lower order again failed to deliver, so we just fell short.

On Monday, August 6, Crewe met championship favourites Boston, who had stormed to the top of the table, some distance ahead of Workington. We had lost 44-34 at Boston 24 hours earlier in atrocious conditions, with heavy rainfall causing many falls and retirements, so the Barracudas knew they had to ride well at Crewe if they were to maintain their stranglehold on the league.

The tactics they adopted however, didn't go down too well with the home riders or supporters. Don't get me wrong, they had a team packed with talent and we knew we were in for a match when Arthur Price equalled my lap record in the first heat.

I won my first outing in Heat 3 but two races later I ended up crashing into the boards, when Price barged into me after losing control. Whether it was a deliberate act, I don't know, but when we returned to the pits a number of riders from both teams joined in the debate, and for a moment things got out of hand.

Worse was to follow in the penultimate heat, when Carl Glover barged past Crewe youngster Keith White, who just managed to avoid the safety fence. This proved too much for Wayne Forrest in the pit area. When Glover came in, Wayne slugged him, with the warring pair eventually broken up by fellow riders, pit crew and staff.

We held on for a narrow victory but the fighting spirit in the Boston team would see them win their own double that season.

Fighting in the pits or even on the track did happen now and then but it was all part and parcel of the sport, especially when adrenalin was running high. If you thought that you had been on the wrong end of a spot of dirty racing, you made a mental note of who it was, as your turn would come at a later date.

On August 18, Len Silver had me pencilled into his Hackney team for a BL1 match at Swindon. I had ridden there twice earlier in the season but hadn't exactly torn up any trees, scoring five and nought. In this encounter, my first outing (in Heat 2) brought about my first victory in the top division when partnering home Hugh Saunders. I was elated by my success, and it got even better when winning Heat 4. After two third places in Heats 8 and 10, the final heat saw myself line-up alongside Swedish star and former World No.2 Bengt Jansson, with Hawks 37-35 up.

I had been nervous before in my short speedway career but nothing had compared to this. Fortunately Bengt took the pressure off by winning the heat, but I played my part when finishing third and preventing Edgar Stangeland from threatening the front. It was great to win the league points and for me to play more than a bit part in the unexpected victory.

On the way home I felt I had turned the corner in my speedway career. I was now convinced I could compete in BL1 and was already contemplating that the remaining meetings in Division Two would be my last.

Crewe's '73 season so far had been one of disappointment. There had been some highs but far too many lows, which included some very poor away performances. But the one record we had kept

Hardly any elbow room as Ellesmere Port's Barry Booth and me arrive at the first bend locked together, with my team-mate Wayne Forrest forced to go wide.

intact during the campaign was our proud unbeaten home record, which now ran to 28 successive league victories, stretching all the way back to the start of the 1972 season. Chesterton's promoter Russ Bragg, however, was intent on ending our sequence, and reported in the Potteries press that his team was about to end it in the return league match at Earle Street on August 20. This added extra spice to the derby match, and as we marched out with 'the enemy' we were determined to make Mr. Bragg eat his words.

Potters riders Alan Bridgett and Mike Broadbank won the first heat 5-1, much to the joy of the large travelling support, and when visiting rider Nigel Wasley won Heat 2, I thought that maybe Bragg's idle boast was not so idle after all.

But home riders took charge from then on, winning all the remaining 11 heats as we thrashed them 53-25.

To rub their noses further into the shale, Geoff Ambrose capped off a great night when snatching the Silver Helmet from the veteran Broadbank. The meeting passed off without incident, apart from when 'Broady' complained to the referee about the state of the track, after heavy rain fell during Heat 11, in which he'd finished last.

It had been my ambition to win the Silver Helmet and the opportunity came during the home meeting with Rayleigh at Earle Street on September 10. The week before the match, I was informed that I had been picked for the Division Two England team in the Test decider against Australasia at Hull, so I arrived for the league encounter brimming with confidence. I won all my four outings and as the top-scoring home rider of the night, earned the right to challenge current Silver Helmet holder

Trevor Barnwell, who I'd beaten by nearly half a lap in Heat 3. Furthermore, Barnwell had endured a wretched night, scoring only three from his four rides, so to say I was confident of winning the helmet back for Crewe was an understatement.

Barnwell won the toss and chose gate two but even then I wasn't concerned because I'd gated well all evening. The tapes went up and Barnwell just beat me to the first bend, so I tucked in behind waiting for my moment to strike. I tried everything to get past but he rode the track superbly, keeping to the correct racing line for all four laps, and deservedly kept his crown.

I had been too over-confident. I was shocked and extremely disappointed to have been beaten, especially on my own track, but it was a valuable lesson learnt. For the rest of my speedway career I would never take another race for granted, no matter who the opposition was.

As the season headed towards its conclusion, I rode one more time in Division One, but not for Hackney. As Reading were also an Allied Presentations outfit, they asked me to guest for them at Belle Vue on September 8, which was convenient for both parties. It was just five minutes up the road for me and saved Reading money on travelling expenses.

By this time Chris had continued his incredible progress in the sport, earning a place in the Aces' line-up. Around Hyde Road he was very quick and he easily won Heat 4, with me last. To complete a miserable night, PC also streaked away from me from the tapes to take the chequered flag. In that final heat I partnered former Australian international Geoff Curtis but, again, without success.

Pulling on the England race jacket four days later was a proud moment, when I rode in the Test decider versus Australasia at Hull. I scored four points but we were no match for the colonials, who gave us a speedway lesson.

A few weeks later, however, I received the ultimate accolade when I was chosen to captain England in the second Test against Sweden at Earle Street. We were represented by a really strong line-up, including home riders John Jackson and Geoff Ambrose, and even though Crewe lads scored 40 points of the total, it was Peterborough's John Davis who stole the limelight with a magnificent performance. It was no surprise that the tourists were hammered in a one-sided affair, with only Tommy Nilsson winning a heat (twice).

After pocketing £100 at Peterborough in the K.R.C. Trophy meeting (nearly four weeks' wages at Shell) on September 21, I competed several times against Chris, with mixed fortunes. On September 24, Crewe faced the Stars of the League team at Earle Street, and we met in Heat 4.

Now Chris had taught me a lesson at Hyde Road a few weeks previous but he was not going to show me up in front of the Crewe public, and I exacted my revenge with a super-quick start and built a big lead by the end of the first lap, which I didn't relinquish. Chris trailed home in third behind Geoff Pusey.

Next night, Crewe were at Ellesmere Port in the final league meeting of the season. The Kings had failed to win a single away league match all season (our only point being a 39-39 draw at bottom club Rayleigh), so we were desperate to end the sequence.

My first ride was in Heat 3, where I faced Chris and Gerald Smitherman, with the scores tied. Once again I found myself ahead at the first bend but turning into the next, Chris came underneath me, but somehow we avoided touching. I moved off the racing line to avoid any contact but inadvertently lost control and fell heavily.

To all who were there, it looked as though Chris had brought me down and when he was excluded, I decided to inform the referee that Chris wasn't responsible – so he excluded me instead! Chris won the re-run but, looking back, I should have kept my mouth shut, as my honesty cost us the meeting.

Since I had been at Crewe I had longed to ride in the Division Two Riders' Championship held at the end of the season at Wimbledon and emulate Phil Crump's victory in '72. At the season cut-off point, Geoff Ambrose shaded the averages from myself and Jacko (who had since retained his track record) but Geoff was not chosen by the Crewe management. He had missed several away meetings during the season, which effectively gave him with a false average. It certainly helped my cause that Len was in charge and he informed me that I was to represent the club on October 6.

It was another terrific honour and to be chosen ahead of Jacko was another plus. John had tried his hand in Division One at Halifax but with limited success, so returned to Division Two where he earned a more than decent living. Jacko would ride in the lower league until the early 80s and it is hard to pick a better, more consistently successful second tier rider during this period.

Wimbledon's Plough Lane stadium was not my sort of track at this stage of my career (although I would win a few individual meetings there later on). It was tiny compared to Earle Street or Hyde Road. Among my opponents on the night were Lou Sansom (Workington), Mike Broadbank (Chesterton), Bobby McNeil (Eastbourne) and meeting favourite Arthur Price (Boston).

There was a terrific crowd and a fantastic atmosphere, and as we walked out for the parade I spotted quite a number of Crewe fans around the terraces, which made me even more determined to put on a good show.

Holding the inside line against Eastbourne. Our battles with the Eagles were usually tense and lively.

Another team photo from '73. Standing (left to right): Keith White, Geoff Ambrose, Peter Thompson, Ian Cartwright. Glyn Taylor and myself kneeling, with John Jackson on machine.

My first ride, in Heat 2, resulted in a second place, after just being edged out by Dave Baugh of Bradford in a fiercely contested heat, with Barney Kennett in third and Tom Owen bringing up the rear. What I needed in the next was a three-pointer but after making a poor gate, I came third, just holding off Sunderland's Jim Wells, whom I knew from Crewe, as he was working there on track maintenance with Jack Millen.

There was little chance of me making a podium place now but after trying a little too hard in Heat 12, I ended up colliding with Bob Young (Rayleigh) and was quite rightly excluded. Furthermore, I caught my finger under the clutch lever, and it proved impossible to pull in the clutch for my next heat, so my night was concluded early. I watched the remaining races from the pits, with Arthur Price winning the title after a run-off against Bobby McNeil.

Despite my injured digit, I top-scored in Kings' 'Revenge Challenge' match with Chesterton two nights later. But when I had it checked out at the local hospital next day, it was confirmed that it was broken. The finger was set and strapped up and another injury had ended my season prematurely, so I booked myself in for my kidney op.

There had been a marked improvement on my previous season's average, which I'd raised from 6.5 to 8.5, having won nearly half my rides in the league and KO Cup. Now I had a decision to make. If the call came, was I ready for Division One, or should I have another season at Crewe to try and establish myself as one of the top riders in the division before my step-up?

Chapter 5

Snubbed by Ole Olsen

A T the end of November 1973, I entered hospital for my kidney operation, much to the relief of my parents and doctor. Fair play to Mum and Dad, they had never pressured me into surgery after the fall at Eastbourne. They knew it was my decision alone, and realised I wouldn't have listened to them anyway. They knew speedway was my world, and sometimes in life you have to take a gamble or two to try and succeed in your profession – even though my doctor thought I was extremely foolish for not having the procedure straight away.

The op' meant a prolonged stay in hospital and a scar which stretched almost half way around my body. I was left very sore for a while and Christmas was celebrated quietly, and it wasn't until February before I felt well enough to resume riding.

It was around this time that I heard rumours that Halifax were interested in signing me. Now Halifax was a track I really enjoyed riding and I probably would have signed if the interest had turned into a concrete offer.

In the Hackney pits, where they had their own workshops, in 1974.

But, for whatever reason, the season resumed without any further word from the Yorkshire outfit, so I resigned myself to another season at Earle Street, with the hope of adding to my brief top flight experience.

Hoping to start the season on a high, I decided to purchase a new machine (another Jawa), following the previous mechanical failures of my old bike, so I got in touch with Barry Briggs, who was the sole importer from Czechoslovakia, and he fixed me up within a few weeks.

Dave Parry returned to Earle Street but in his new role as team manager. I got on well with Dave. Not only had I ridden with him in the Kings team, but he was a great man-manager and was also determined to succeed in his role – a drive and determination which eventually saw him become an extremely successful businessman, after setting up a coach travel company (Parry's International), which continues to flourish today.

On the rider front, my old mate Jack Millen returned, after his two seasons at Sunderland, and the Crewe management hoped that the colourful Kiwi could address the falling attendances. Jack's appearance and often outrageous antics usually guaranteed to add a few hundred to crowd figures wherever he rode. It was during his time with Sunderland that the 'Jack and Frankie' wars had taken place. The spats between Teesside's Frank Auffret and Jack would go down in speedway folklore. As lifelong Sunderland fan Bob Ferry once wrote: 'The local derby meetings against Berwick and Teesside were something special – especially Teesside, when the Jack Millen/Frankie Auffret hostilities were raging. For Frank it was hatred but to Jack it was all showmanship and to generate excitement with the fans, whip them into a frenzy, leaving them wanting to come back for more when the SHOWMAN was in town. Crazy Jack's mantra was to give the fans something to cheer, jeer, boo, hiss – anything to get them on their feet and exercise their vocal chords'.

Another rider to join the team was Mike Gardner, who had the distinction of winning the first ever heat at Crewe in 1969 while riding for Rayleigh. Mike had then moved on to Cradley and Birmingham but his stay with Crewe was a short one, due to an incredible run of mechanical bad luck. On one occasion at Earle Street, following yet another break-down, he wheeled his stricken bike onto the centre green and proceeded to kick the living daylights out of it.

Rather ring-rusty, the 1974 season began with a four team tournament at Ellesmere Port on March 26 and after a rather tentative start, I slowly began to find my form when the league matches started in May. I top-scored in the opening encounter with Eastbourne, just missing out on a maximum when team-mate Keith White pipped me on the line in Heat 9.

Five days later, I took part in the Halifax Best Pairs alongside Mick Newton and although we didn't threaten a podium place, I beat some decent riders and rumours resurfaced that the Dukes' management were poised to offer me a deal. Whether this had a bearing on what happened next, I don't know, but following the home meeting with Long Eaton, Len Silver called me into his office and asked if I was interested in signing for Hackney.

I asked for a few days to think about it. Even though I was excited at the prospect of moving up to Division One, the travelling side of the deal didn't exactly have me jumping for joy. However, Jack Millen convinced me that the move would be good for my career, so I decided to sign. Unfortunately, I didn't receive any sort of transfer fee, although I do believe Jack got a backhander for persuading me to put pen to paper.

Had I made the right decision? I later thought that if I had continued to perform well in Division Two, a northern track would eventually come calling but when that failed to materialise, the Hackney deal gave me the opportunity to fulfil my dream of riding in the top flight on a regular basis.

I was to continue to ride at Crewe (on loan) until a suitable replacement could be found but I was confident I could do a doubling-up job until the end of the season, which would mean a great deal of travelling but double the pay packet.

The idea to double-up was in fact Len's. He knew the British League was going to be tough for me at first, so going back to Crewe would be a good way of building up my confidence. Riding in both leagues also meant that I had to utilise my holidays at Shell for the away trips. As I was still an apprentice, they were a little more flexible with my time off, often letting me leave early for the longer journeys. Hackney rode on a Friday night, so I'd leave work at around 2.30pm, and arrive at Waterden Road in plenty of time for the 8.00pm start, then be home for about 3.00am – a round trip of 400 miles for home meetings.

As a full-time Hawk, I made my debut at Poole in the KO Cup, scoring two, but it was the following week before I made my bow in front of the Hackney supporters in a match versus Hull. The East End fans gave me a tremendous welcome and I immediately felt at home.

I made a good start in Heat 2, leading home Laurie Etheridge. I took an initial liking to the track and although it wasn't as big as Crewe, the whole set-up was much more professional – they even had a workshop, run by resident mechanic Terry 'Bert' Busch, behind the pits where you could prepare your bike. My fellow Hackney riders were also more-than accommodating, especially Barry Thomas, whom I struck up a great friendship with straight away.

On May 25, I rode for the Hawks at Halifax and wanted to show the Dukes what they had missed out on. But sometimes being over-determined doesn't always guarantee success and I fell flat on my face, scoring only one point from my two outings. Two nights later I was back at Crewe in a league meeting with Birmingham. I do remember before the first heat that Jack Millen wasn't his usual

Riding for Hackney at Waterden Road, with a Crewe Kings fork cover, in 1974.

self, and it was Jack that lit the touchpaper to an explosive affair after bringing down Carl Askew. Jack was excluded from the re-run but when Askew put Ian Cartwright into the boards, tempers got the better of both sets of riders and punches were thrown, which included a good dust-up between Cartwright and Askew.

The following night we rode in the return and, again, Jack was in trouble. Now Jack had a particular hatred of Arthur Browning and unlike his 'war' with Frank Auffret, he seemed to take exception to anything Browning did. To prove the point, in Heat 1 Jack deliberately put Browning into the boards, much to the derision of the large home support. I thought, 'Oh no, here we go again!'

Birmingham, inspired by maximums from Browning and Phil Herne, easily won the contest but Ian Cartwright and Askew decided to have another bust-up in the pits, which earned 'Mousetrap' a fine.

Up to this point, I hadn't exactly set the Division One scene on fire, scoring 2, 6, 1, 3 and 3 from a reserve berth, but this all changed on June 7 when I rode against Swindon at The Wick. Everything went right that night, when I gated as well as I had done for ages, winning all of my three outings, partnering Laurie Etheridge, Geoff Maloney and Dag Lovaas. Just to prove a point, I then won the 'Stratford Scorch' second-half final, to remain unbeaten on the night.

It was one of those defining moments in my career. Another one would be just around the corner.

Hackney Hawks of '74. Standing, left to right: Bert Busch (team mechanic), Colin Pratt (coach), Barry Thomas, Dag Lovaas, Dave Erskine (team manager), Dave Kennett, Laurie Etheridge and Len Silver (promoter). Kneeling: Geoff Maloney and myself, with Hughie Saunders on machine.

On June 29 Chris won the Junior Championship of the British Isles at Canterbury with a 15-point maximum. Although I couldn't be there to witness his triumph, I did my bit when passing on a few tips about the Kingsmead track, as he had never ridden there before.

Despite being a Division One rider finding my feet, I still looked up at the top riders, especially the big two at the time – Ivan Mauger and Ole Olsen. So to beat any of these riders this early in my career would be a big scalp – and the opportunity came when Wolves came to Hackney on July 5.

By this time I had developed a riding style at Waterden Road not too dissimilar to the way I rode at Earle Street. The Hackney track was fairly big, about 360 yards, and was constructed inside the dog track. But it had long straights and tight corners – too tight really for the length of the straights. The bends were wide and slightly banked, so the majority rode around the inside-to-mid-track.

But when I first rode it, I found that you could race around the top of the bank as near to the fence as possible and pass riders coming off the bend, either around the outside, or up the inside when coming off the top of the bank half-way around the bend. Fence-scraping, if you like.

Even when the track was slick after a few races, there would be plenty of dirt around the bottom of the safety fence, so you would use this to gain that extra momentum. It was more risky, because you had very little room for error riding so close to the fence, especially when going flat out entering the bend. A few other home riders soon adopted a similar style, including Barry Thomas, but the majority preferred the relative safety of the 'inner sanctum'.

I started well in the Wolves match, winning my opening ride thanks to some fine work from Hughie Saunders. In Heat 5 we again teamed up but this time our opposition included the Great Dane, Ole Olsen. I had studied Olsen in the pits, and everything he did personified class – even his leathers, which were spotless, seemed to be better than what all the others were wearing.

Just before the tapes went up, I told myself that I had to beat him to the first bend – I had to outgate him to have any chance. But it didn't turn out that way, when he stormed out of the gate and left me swallowing his dust.

I tracked him for the first two laps as he rode mid-track, then I made my move and swooped off the top of the bend with a tremendous amount of drive and easily took him on the outside. 'Bloody hell!' I thought, 'I've just done one of the world's greatest speedway riders' but the manoeuvre would mean nothing if I couldn't hold him off, and I had no help from Hughie as he trailed in last place.

'Concentrate, Mort . . . concentrate', I told myself over and over again but my lead was too big for Olsen to claw back and as I crossed the line I punched the air in delight.

That Heat 9 win meant I went into the final race of the meeting with a chance of recording my first Division One maximum . . . but Olsen stood in my way and he was spitting blood after being upstaged by the young upstart. It proved to be the race of the night.

I got to the first bend in front, with 'Thommo' guarding my rear. Now Olsen wasn't one of the best for nothing and he tried every trick in the book to split us, before procedes finally forcing his way past Thommo on lap three, only for Barry to fight back in typically thrilling fashion to help earn the 5-1 and my first maximum in the 49-29 victory.

The crowd went berserk and I was thrilled to bits when I came back into the pits, where I was greeted by a jubilant Len Silver, who seemed even more pleased than me!

A few seconds later, Olsen followed me through the pit gate on the fourth bend but completely blanked me. No pat on the back, no 'well done', or even a wink of recognition. Nothing – it was a complete snub. It would have been nice to have shaken hands and exchanged pleasantries but the Wolverhampton and Denmark No.1, who had won the first of his three individual world titles in 1971, walked straight past me as if I wasn't there.

I drove back up the M1 that night with plenty of time to reflect on what I had just done. I was no rookie anymore and from now on my card would be marked.

On Monday, July 8, I appeared in the England versus Poland second division Test at Crewe. The hosts were 2-0 up in the series but England team manager Joe Thurley had picked a team that were all more than competent around the Earle Street bowl, including John Jackson, Keith White, Graham Drury, Carl Glover and Mitch Graham. The result was never in any doubt and although Cieslak and Nowak mustered 22 points between them, we thrashed the Poles 74-34, with myself top scoring with paid 15.

It was no secret among the Crewe riders that the club were struggling financially. Attendances had plummeted to around the 2,000 mark – barely enough for the club to break even. It was up to the promoter to try all the tricks in the book to create revenue, so Len arranged a 'Race of the Century' between Crewe old boy Phil Crump, who was now riding at first division Newport, and Ole Olsen. After initially being washed out, it was re-arranged for July 15, to follow the Crewe v Sunderland league match.

Whether the whole event was stage-managed, I don't know, but Ole won the first, with Crumpie levelling it up to set up the decider, which was won by the home favourite. Just to even things up, Ole won the Rider of the Night final, so everybody went home happy – apart from Len, who lost a few quid due to a disappointing turnout.

By the end of July, all the travelling involved in riding for two clubs really started to affect me, even though I still scored enough points to make it all worthwhile financially. The long hours on the road started to put a strain on my relationship with Shirley, even though she would travel with me as much as possible.

Consider this seven-day spell involving five meetings: On Wednesday, July 24, I took the long journey to Poole in Dorset, followed 24 hours later with Hawks' London derby trip to Wimbledon. On Friday, Hackney had a home match with King's Lynn, and then after riding in Crewe's home fixture against Stoke on the Monday, I made the long haul back down to the south coast for the Kings' match at Weymouth the next night. At least I had the weekend to recuperate.

Apart from tiredness from spending so many hours on the road, there was no doubt that the experience gained from riding for Hackney made life a lot easier when returning to Crewe, where I started wracking up maximums, especially at Earle Street. In my quest to become No.1 at Crewe, I equalled Jacko's track record on August 5 during a big win over Coatbridge. But in the pits afterwards I was given a piece of advice which would earn me a place in the record books.

We were one big happy family at Crewe and I had a great relationship with track electrician Alan Corbett, who had noticed that when winning races by a distance, I would shut off well before the chequered flag and coast over the line. 'Mort, keep it screwed on until you cross the line', he said, so the following week, for the league match against Barrow, I decided to heed his advice and try and claim the track record outright.

Walking the track before the off, I noticed that the surface was wet but grippy, so conditions were ideal for a record attempt. In Heat 1, I lined up with Ian Cartwright against Tom Owen and Chris Roynon. Despite not making a perfect gate, I managed to hit the first bend just ahead of the pack. From then on I kept it screwed on for the whole four laps and when I crossed the line, I knew it was a fast time. It was. I had knocked a whole second off the previous record, but it wasn't until a few months later that I learnt my time of 68.0 seconds had been ratified by *The Guinness Book of Records* as being the fastest recorded average speed in speedway – a shade over 52 mph.

As the Crewe track was the biggest and fastest in Britain and, sadly, the place closed down at the end of 1975, my track record there would never be beaten.

There was more good news – or so I thought at the time – a few days later, when Len Silver informed Barry Thomas and myself that we had been selected for the senior England team for five of the seven Test matches against the USSR. But my pleasure was short-lived.

Len had been given a mandate to pick the England team by the BSPA but his policy of selecting youthful riders didn't meet with their approval, so we were both disappointed when told we hadn't been selected after all (although Thommo did appear in three of the Tests).

The Inter-League Four Team Tournament, which allowed the lower league teams to ride against Division One opposition, was introduced in 1974. For me, the draw could not have been better, with Belle Vue, Cradley and Hackney pulled out the hat as Crewe's opponents on August 19. For once there was a big crowd at Earle Street and I fancied we could cause a shock on the night. But when I trailed behind Arthur Price (Cradley) and Chris Pusey (Belle Vue) in Heat 1, I realised the gulf in class would be difficult to bridge. It was a great evening's racing, though, with Belle Vue the winners thanks mainly to double figure returns from Soren Sjosten and Pusey. I managed a solitary win, in Heat 14, beating my mate Thommo, Bruce Cribb and our Chris, but it was the Hackney riders who struggled on the night, finishing last behind the home side.

All speedway riders have tracks that they either love or loath and on September 13, Kings were riding at Coatbridge, a track built around the Albion Rovers football pitch. I made the long trek to Scotland after work. It rained for most of the journey and was still raining when the meeting was somehow allowed to start. The track was narrow and virtually impossible to pass on, and what made it worse was the concrete safety fence surrounding it. To put it mildly, I had a nightmare evening, falling in Heat 5, retiring in Heat 7 and falling again in the final race. Thankfully, I would never have to race there again.

Crewe were hammered 57-20 on that night at Cliftonhill, one of their worst ever defeats, but Hackney endured an even bigger thrashing (their worst ever in the BL) at Sheffield on September 19. I liked the Owlerton track but to this day I don't know why we were so poor that night. I do remember our Norwegian No.1 Dag Lovaas failing to make it after breaking down on the motorway.

The 1974 Crewe squad on press and practice day. Back row, left to right: Dave Parry (team manager), myself, Charlie Turner, John Jackson, Paul Wells, Colin Farquharson (who signed for Berwick), Jack Millen (on machine), Wayne Forrest, Keith White, Barry Meeks, Ian Cartwright and Len Silver (promoter). Kneeling: Mike Gardner, Cliff Anderson and Stuart Cope.

Had it not been for an exclusion suffered by Rod Haynes in Heat 2 and a fall by fellow Tigers reserve Craig Pendlebury in the eighth (while in second place), I am positive they would have racked up the maximum 65-13 win. In the end we did well to get 17 points. Hard to believe, just nine days later, we went to Coventry and won 42-36. Funny old game, speedway.

It was around this time of the season I had been toying with the idea of spending the winter months riding abroad. And it was again Jack Millen, after a chance conversation over a pint in The Kings Arms in Crewe after a meeting at Earle Street, who persuaded me to try my luck in New Zealand. The problem was getting time off work, because the trip was expected to last around three months. I approached my boss the next day but he couldn't sanction the prolonged absence as I was now out of my time, and had to adhere to the fairly strict holiday rules and regulations of the company. He gave me an ultimatum – work or New Zealand.

There was only ever going to be one winner, so I handed in my notice.

As the season drew to a close, so did my Crewe career. In all the time I had ridden at Earle Street, only Peterborough had won there in the league, but in my penultimate appearance during a double-header, Kings lost for the first time at Earle Street in 48 matches.

The first meeting against Canterbury went with the form book and we cruised home but the trouble with double-headers is that track conditions tend to change during the night (thus affecting gear ratios) and machines become unreliable. The fact that we were riding against bogey team Workington, who were fresh and up for it, didn't help matters. As mentioned previously, the Comets had several riders who relished riding at Crewe but halfway through the match, with Kings 23-13 up, very few in the stadium could have predicted the tremendous fightback by the Cumbrians. With three heats to go, we were still ahead by six, after I had beaten Tom Owen in the 10th race, but wins by Mitch Graham, Owen and Graham again in the last, saw them squeeze home by two points.

On October 21, I made my final appearance for Crewe, against Weymouth at Earle Street, just before my planned trip to New Zealand. In my last race I dead-heated with Cliff Anderson – my first shared race win.

It was quite a sad occasion saying goodbye to track staff and supporters at the end of the night but I wanted to further my career, and I couldn't do that in Division Two. If Crewe had been riding in the top flight I would have gladly stayed, as I loved that great big Earle Street bowl.

I shared the sadness of all the Crewe fans when the track folded at the end of the 1975 season due to financial difficulties, never to return.

Although I had gained an apprenticeship at Shell, my decision to head off to New Zealand for the winter of 1974-75 meant I'd lost a weekly wage and a 'job for life'. I was now a full-time professional speedway rider but confident I could earn enough money to pay the bills and be a real success in the sport. This was not in any way me being big-headed. I was just confident in my own abilities and with a few lucky breaks – well, who knew then how far the sport would take me?

With Chris and PC touring in Australia with the British Lions, I have to admit I was just a little bit jealous of their success, but in another way delighted in what they had so far achieved. Maybe this time next year we would all be riding together on the international stage? It was something to aim for and my goal for the 1975 season.

Showing my back wheel to Ole Olsen in one of my two race wins over the Great Dane.

Chapter 6

First class New Zealand

THE trip to New Zealand was organised in less than 24 hours following my final meeting with Crewe. Thanks to Len Silver and Jack Millen, everything was arranged for me. I was to stay with Jim and Paul Wells' parents (Jim was a former Sunderland rider) in Auckland, where I had a contract to race at Western Springs.

The next day was spent securing a sea freight passage for my bike and equipment and by 9.00pm the next night, it was packed in a wooden crate (courtesy of Jack) and on the quayside at Glasgow docks, booked in for the long journey the following morning. Fortunately I knew a guy, who knew a guy who worked for a shipping freight company, so I got a good deal.

As my dad worked for British Airways as a flight engineer, I managed to wangle a discounted ticket to Sydney, Australia on the first part of my journey to New Zealand, for the princely sum of £15. From there I took a connecting flight to Auckland, where I was met by Jim's father and his son Paul.

I soon settled in and found all the Kiwis I met warm and friendly. It was just like being at home in terms of being looked after. I paid my board and lodgings and as Paul was a similar age, I hung around with him, his mates and next door neighbour Terry Darwent, who all rode at Western Springs on a Saturday evening.

After a few days acclimatising to my new surroundings I went to claim my equipment from the dockside. Everything had arrived safely but I hadn't planned for the £120 import duty bill. Fortunately, the Western Springs promoters came to my rescue – but it was only a loan, so I would have to win a fair number of races just to pay off my debt.

I made my debut on November 16 in the Marlboro International meeting. Having obviously never ridden the Western Springs track before and not knowing how good the home riders would be, I felt a bit nervous beforehand. The format was also slightly different, with six riders – instead of the usual four – all on track racing at the same time, so to stay away from trouble, it was imperative to get ahead from the gate.

I lined up against Dave Allerton, Terry Darwent, Eric Grayson, Ian Ross and former world finalist Bob Andrews and managed to get that all-important start and then went flat out on track that was fairly big and wide, probably a similar size to Belle Vue. I hung on to record my first win on New Zealand soil, in a time just seven-tenths of a second outside Ivan Mauger's track record. I went through the meeting with a 12-point maximum.

I had enjoyed the night's racing, although track conditions had been a bit different to what I had been used to. Before our outing, midget and sprint cars had raced on the track, making the surface very slick. The composition of the track was completely different to British shale and was more hard-wearing to prevent the cars from completely ripping the circuit to pieces. I later learnt (from Colin Tucker) that the composition was 10 per cent clay combined with 90 per cent scoria tuff – the soft part of the outer edge of volcanic rock. Clay had only recently been added, which helped preserve the softer rear tyres used by the midget and sprint cars.

It had also been slightly surreal racing without a safety fence. There was a fence but this was on the outside of a banked cycle track which surrounded the speedway circuit.

It was an honour to skipper the British team in New Zealand in the winter of 1974-75. Standing behind me are (left to right) Craig Pendlebury, Colin Tucker (guest), Mike Hiftle, Alan Clark (team manager) and Ian Cartwright.

The following week should have been a Test match between New Zealand and Australia but due to a mix-up in the fixtures, the Aussies withdrew, so a three-match mini-series was hastily arranged between a British League Riders team and a Kiwi Select. I had the honour of skippering the British team, managed by *Speedway Star* writer Alan Clark, and also including my ex-Crewe team-mate Ian Cartwright, Mike Hiftle of Halifax, Sheffield's Craig Pendlebury and Oxford's John Davis, who had all made the same decision to ride in New Zealand for the winter. But as John wouldn't arrive until the following Monday after the first match, we drafted in Colin Tucker as reserve.

I had met Colin on several occasions while watching Chris at Belle Vue and knew of his involvement at Crewe and Hull and of the many other tracks he had constructed while over in Britain. He had returned to his native Auckland in 1973 but had resurrected his speedway career, so was an ample replacement for 'JD'.

I soon struck up a good friendship with Colin and his wife Diane. She was, in fact, a Crewe girl and not only kept me well-fed, but acted as a personal taxi driver, picking me up or taking me to anywhere I wanted to go, in a battered old Mini I nicknamed 'Grotty Bug' (because of the GB sticker on the boot).

Colin took over the maintenance and setting-up of my bike in his well-stocked workshop. He also found me some good Japanese tyres, similar to the Dunlops we used, which were perfectly suited to the slick Kiwi tracks. Depending where I was riding, he would often grind down the nobbles, so they wouldn't flex as much. He was a perfectionist when it came to the tuning aspect of my bike, so from the moment he took over, my machine was not only very quick, but reliable.

The former Nelson and Bradford star, Gary Peterson, who rode for Wolverhampton in the early 70s, was also a big help by passing on some useful tips about setting up properly.

It was at Colin's I earned a number of new nicknames. At Crewe I had picked up 'Buttons' from Jack Millen (haven't a clue about that one) but one day at Tuck's, he was pulling down an old fibrolite clad garage and a few of the speedway lads, including Paul Church, decided to lend a hand. I kept my distance by doing my bike in the workshop – there was dust everywhere and I was worried that the particles in the air were asbestos. When I told them that they could catch asbestosis, they all cracked up, saying I had made the word up and was taking the piss. So that was that and for the rest of my stay I was known to them as 'Asbestosis'.

Another one I was christened with was 'Diddy Dave', after the radio and TV personality 'Diddy' Dave Hamilton. At one of Tuck's barbeques, I wore a cowboy hat to protect me from the sun. He laughed out loud when he saw me and said I looked just like a Mexican drugs baron due to my long hair and 'el gringo' moustache.

The first match in the mini-series at Western Springs was rained off on the Saturday (November 23) but re-arranged on the following Monday night. This affected the attendance but it turned into a really competitive meeting. The Kiwis, represented by the legendary double World Champion Ronnie Moore, Graeme Stapleton, Gary Peterson, Ian Ross and Terry Darwent, started as slight underdogs but led 7-5 by the end of the second heat, despite my win in the first race. I won my next three rides and we held a slender 29-25 lead going into the final heat – the 10th.

In this series the last race featured the top two scoring riders from each team but, for once, I completely missed the gate and ended up at the back. Thankfully, I spotted a gap and found some extra drive and at the end of the first turn, had powered past Mike Hiftle and Gary Peterson, with only Ronnie Moore ahead of me. However, Ronnie's luck was out when suffering mechanical

Quick starts and taking an early lead was the way to go in the six-man races.

Close-up of me enjoying the wide, open spaces in New Zealand.
Although I knew I had left Crewe behind and was destined for
Hackney full-time on my return to Blighty, I still carried the
Kings' emblem on my rear mudguard.
Inset: How Speedway Star reported my NZ title win.

Dave takes Kiwi crown

HACKNEY WICK'S Dave Morton made it a happy weekend for the family by winning this year's New Zealand Championship. Even though the top Kiwi stars were absent from the meeting because of the World Champions series Morton was a convincing and deserved champion.

Scorers: D. Morton 15, J. Davis 14, C. Pendlebury 12, R. Adlington 11, I. Cartwright 11, G. Smith 8, B. Andrews 6, R. Trigg 6, P. Church 5, C. Farquharson 5, G. Wells 4, G. Darwent 4, D. Whittaker 4, B. Sparge 2, C. D. Cartnell 1, D. Ede 0.

troubles before the end of the first lap, leaving me to complete my 15-point maximum and help 'The Pommies' win the first 'Test' 33-27.

The next match, at Te Marua, Wellington, was not as exciting. We swept aside the hosts, 41-19, on a particularly bumpy track, despite the efforts of Robin Adlington. The scoreline did flatter us somewhat, because Ronnie Moore had a another night plagued by mechanical problems.

The final match, at Templeton, Christchurch a few days later, was against a New Zealand team made up entirely of Christchurch-based riders (Moore, Stapleton, Black and Ross) and they were in no mood to be part of a whitewash. At the half-way stage they led by two points but we stormed back to win thanks to maximums in heats 6 and 7.

With racing generally confined to the weekends, there was an awful lot of leisure time during the week. On the cloudier days I used to travel with Tuck when he was working on his building sites, as a building overseer for Universal Homes, inspecting all aspects from the foundations to the final paint job.

I also had a Yamaha trials bike (DT 360) – loaned to me by White's Yamaha shop in Auckland, kindly arranged by Alan Clark – on which to tour the lush, green countryside and scare the sheep. On the sunnier days I spent a considerable amount of time touring the local beaches on 'bikini patrol' and was accompanied by JD when he was in Auckland.

Because of the climate, there was always a barbeque or party to go to nearly every other night, although at the barbies I was banned from cooking due to incinerating countless sausages and steaks. Even Tuck's corgis, Monty and Mandy, turned their noses up at my burnt offerings.

Tuck even had a go at trying to teach me to cook. One day on the way home from work, he picked

Receiving the bumps after winning the New Zealand Championship at Palmerston North.

up a box of tomatoes from a market garden and proceeded to make a delicious tomato sauce from his mother's recipe. When the sauce was just about ready, he taught me how to sterilise the bottles in the oven, then whipped up a batch of scones, which I devoured after helping bottle the sauce.

It was one big holiday but a diet of hamburgers, milkshakes and home cooking did little for my waistline – looking at my Hackney photos from the early part of the 1975 season, I had put on at least a stone in weight.

During my time away in New Zealand, my prolonged stay had proved too much for Shirley and we decided to call it a day. This was also a bit of a blow for both families, as Dad often enjoyed a pint with Shirley's father, Albert, on a Saturday night.

I was just 21 years of age at the time, on the other side of the world and having the time of my life, although being quite a shy sort of person I didn't possess the big chat-up lines when confronted by the fairer sex. However, the local talent seemed friendly enough and they seemed fascinated by my Manchester accent – so who needed a chat-up line.

We were at one particular party one night and a girl called Raewyn chatted with me for most of the evening, then offered me a lift home, just as the party was winding down. We parked at the end of street where I was staying and I kissed her goodnight – but one thing led to another.

I also remember going to Christchurch for the third match in our mini-series with New Zealand. John Davis was based there, staying at Ronnie Moore's. I hadn't really had much to do with John while we were both racing in England but we soon became firm friends.

It was great meeting a legend like Ronnie at his motorcycle shop and his former Wimbledon team-mate, Graeme Stapleton, who helped him run it. After doing a few TV interviews to promote the meeting, John and I went for a bite to eat and met up with Ronnie's daughters, Kim and Lee, who were about the same age, who were with a girlfriend called Judith. I took a shine to Judith straight away and spent the whole week with her, apart from when tearing around the district with JD on loaned motorbikes, seeing who could do the best wheelie away from the traffic lights, much to the dismay of the local car drivers.

When I returned to Auckland I kept in touch with Judith and one week when there was a big car meeting on in Western Springs, I flew down to Christchurch and stayed at Ronnie's, even though I spent most of the week with Judith. When I went home, I still continued to write to her for a while. But, eventually, she met someone else and I got back with Shirley.

That was that . . . but then, completely out of the blue, in May 2010 I received a letter from Judith informing me about the terrible Christchurch earthquake and how her house had been badly damaged. Apparently, she had been clearing out her attic and found the letters I had written to her all those years ago, so decided to get in touch. Ronnie's daughter Kim had helped her find my address, and we are still in contact today.

Apart from speedway, one of my hobbies was listening to music, especially blues and rock, and I really enjoyed attending live concerts, so I jumped at the chance to see the Irish guitarist Rory Gallacher at the main theatre in town. I had heard some of his music before but was blown away by this guy's talents and stamina during the three-hour concert. After this, I became a huge fan, bought all of his records and went to see him every time he toured in the UK. It was a particularly sad day for me when Rory passed away in 1995, aged just 47.

I had now been away from home for about six weeks and it was quite strange celebrating Christmas in the sunshine, instead of freezing my whatnots off back home, and although I did feel a bit homesick around this time, I was treated like one of the family at the Wells', so contented myself with letters and phone calls home.

After the festivities, I geared myself up for the New Zealand Championship, which was to be held on January 11 at the Palmerston North Raceway, nicknamed 'The Boneyard' (a real bone-shaker of a track due to stock car racing) by the locals. The prestigious title, won the previous year by Ivan Mauger, was certainly there for the taking, with the line-up for this year minus the main British and Australian riders, due to the Test series, and the likes of Ole Olsen, Ivan, Barry Briggs and Ronnie Moore taking part in the World Series. This year's tournament was to be promoted by Ray New, a former winner of the title who had ridden in England for a time with Belle Vue, Coventry and Oxford.

Tuck generously sacrificed his place in the tournament to keep me "on the straight and narrow" and away from the distractions of the beach. He agreed to drive me to Palmerston after working all week on making sure my bike was in tip-top condition. He told me about the track being big but narrow but he was confident I could pull it off.

The local press had also bigged up my chances, making me the firm favourite, even though all the English riders would be there and John Davis was in red hot form having beaten me a few weeks previous in the South Island Championship.

But first I had to survive the journey. Tuck always drove fast and this day was no exception. He had this philosophy that the way to drive safely down long and windy roads was to drive at least 200 yards ahead of yourself, so you knew what was coming up, and what you had to do before you got to that point. He said that most people concentrated on what was 20 yards ahead of them, and this was wrong. Rightly or wrongly, it was still a hair-raising experience and I was mightily relieved when we finally reached our destination, still in one piece.

A total of 23 riders had been entered but only eight were seeded. Fortunately, I was one of the eight, along with John Davis, Colin Farquharson, Roy Trigg, Ian Cartwright, Craig Pendlebury, Robin Adlington and Mike Hiftle. The rest had to go through eliminating races and from these, Terry Darwent, Paul Church, Graeme Smith, Paul Wells, Dave Cartmell, Bob Andrews, Don Eade and Dave Whittaker made it through to the main event, with Bruce Spargo as reserve, in front of a good crowd.

JD began with a victory, so the pressure was on straight away when I lined up for my first outing in Heat 2, alongside Trigg, Darwent and Church. But Tuck had not let me down with my bike and I managed to win fairly comfortably in a time more than two seconds faster than JD's opening heat, even though Church had got a flyer. It gave me a massive boost knowing that my bike was quick and I managed to win my next three rides to stay unbeaten, although JD had kept up his form and maintained his 100 per cent record too.

The crunch came when we met in Heat 19, with former champion Bob Andrews and Robin Adlington making up the foursome. After two false starts which only added to the tension, I managed to make the gate, with JD breathing down my neck for all four laps. But despite him trying to pass on several occasions (he was on borrowed machinery after earlier wrecking his clutch), I just managed to hold on.

I was elated. Not only had I won the New Zealand Championship, but prize money of $500. In fact, the English took all the podium places, with JD runner-up and Craig Pendlebury third. After being tossed in the air and doused in water by my fellow riders, I was presented with the magnificent trophy and couldn't believe that my name was going to be on it, along with Ivan, Ronnie Moore and Barry Briggs – the three all-time greatest in New Zealand speedway history. I was allowed to take the trophy back to Auckland, but not home to Partington. I was on a high for the rest of the week. Now this was better than working at Shell!

I felt life couldn't get much better but a few days later I learnt that I had been awarded the Most Improved Rider trophy during the annual London Speedway Honours Ball, an award I shared with fellow Hawk, Steve Lomas. It meant a great deal to me knowing that my efforts for Hackney during the 1974 season had not gone unnoticed.

My trip had been an incredible experience and I managed to win another three titles before departure. I was awarded the Marlboro Solo Big Six and the Maury Dunn Memorial Invitation titles (after accumulating enough points in both competitions) and won the Auckland Senior Championship at Western Springs, when I again just managed to pip JD, with Colin Tucker third.

One incident I recall from this meeting was when Craig Pendlebury lost control and fell heavily. Despite Terry Darwent's best efforts to lay down his bike, he caught Craig full in the face, resulting in a bad laceration, with Darwent also carted off to hospital.

Just before my final meeting at Wellington at the end of February, I was approached to ride in the World Series meeting, promoted by Mauger and Briggs, in Auckland, but had to turn down the lucrative booking because my tickets had already been booked for my return, and I needed to get back to sort out my equipment for the forthcoming British League season. The Western Springs promoters, however, wanted me back the following season and promised to pay my airfare with improved prize money.

It was a genuinely sad day for me when I had to say my goodbyes to so many wonderful people and a country I had fallen in love with. I had forged life-long friendships and had enjoyed every single minute of my three month 'jolly'.

My trip home was also a pleasurable experience. I flew to Sydney but had to get off there, as the flight to the UK was fully booked. I had to wait for the next available flight along with 15 other hopefuls but when four seats became available on a VC10, three were taken up by pilots and the other, in first class, was allocated to me – thanks again to Dad's position at British Airways. As my ticket gave me priority over everyone else in the queue, even the hostesses, I spent the whole journey in a comfortable wide seat, where I was served free food and drinks. A first class ending to a first class trip.

On the long flight home I had time to map out my goals for the forthcoming 1975 season. Firstly, I wanted to establish myself in the Hackney team and compete for a heat leader berth. By doing this, I was hoping my performances would warrant a call-up into the England set-up. Anything else would be a bonus, especially a place in the British Final, and a chance to qualify for the World Final, which was to be held at Wembley. Ambitious, yes, but after my success in New Zealand, confidence was high and I couldn't wait to try my luck again against the best in the British League.

I arrived back in Blighty just three days before the start of the new season and had still not shaken off the effects of jet-lag for the Hawks' league opener at home to Newport.

Wheel to wheel with PC during the British semi-final at Sheffield, where we both finished on 11 points. Below: It was another struggle in front of a big crowd at the British Final, though. I'm on the inside at Coventry against Jim McMillan (7) and PC (8).

Chapter 7

Hot stuff in Sweden

IN New Zealand I had ridden the bike that had served me well at Crewe but it still hadn't arrived back in England when I landed at Heathrow. Fortunately, my other bike was ready for the start of the 1975 British League season, even if I wasn't. I had arranged to have my two-valve Jawa stripped and tuned just before I had gone to NZ.

There had been a number of personnel changes at Hackney and a lot of experience had been stripped from the squad. Our Norwegian No.1 Dag Lovaas, who had averaged over 10 points the previous season and reached his first World Final, had left for Oxford, the reliable Geoff Maloney decided to retire and join the Fire Brigade, while experienced Hugh Saunders dropped into the National League with Rye House, where Len Silver had switched his defunct Rayleigh team the previous year. Len also had an interest in the revival that year of Crayford, who loaned Laurie Etheridge from Hackney as their No.1, although he continued to double-up for Hackney as our No.8.

Len attempted to replace Dag with Swedish star and twice World Finalist Christer Lofqvist, who had been enormously popular in east London at West Ham before their closure and then at Poole. Steve Lomas (Weymouth), Ted Hubbard (Canterbury) and 40-year-old Mike Broadbank (Stoke), who had all ridden in Division Two the previous season, were brought in to fill the gaps.

I was pleased to be drawn at Belle Vue for one of my three British qualifying rounds of the World Championship in 1975.
Here I'm leading Aces' Geoff Pusey.

With the BSPA's year ban on commuting Swedes now lifted, Christer was signed to replace Dag at No.1 but due to the squad's lack of strength in depth, I was expected to fill one of the two other heat leaders spots with new skipper Thommo.

At this stage of my career, I wasn't expecting to be thrust into the role quite so soon. In what was my first full season of top flight racing, I thought I would hold down a second string position, fighting for the right to represent the club at heat leader level. Instead, I was riding at No.5, partnering Dave Kennett.

Len, however, told me that he had every confidence in me doing the job, and with his knowledge and experience as one of the top promoters in the business, this gave me a tremendous confidence boost.

A long, hard season had been predicted by the media but it started quite well, with three wins, including home and away victories over King's Lynn in the Spring Gold Cup. Cracks started to appear, though, with a home defeat to Ipswich in the same competition and a thrashing at Newport, where for the first time in my career I failed to show, after 'breaking down' *en route.*

Newport wasn't one of my favourite tracks. It was bumpy and square-shaped because it was constructed around the Newport County football pitch. It was my old Crewe team-mate Phil Crump's home track and he had no problems flying around the place but many riders considered it to be a dangerous circuit and would conveniently 'break down' on the way to South Wales. This was the best way of getting out of racing there and by using this excuse rather than refusing to attend the meeting, the Control Board couldn't fine or discipline you in any way. My absence from Somerton Park was also a cover-up, after Len gave me permission to miss the meeting to re-charge my batteries and regain full fitness following a few bumps and bruises.

The 1975 season saw the introduction of the Inter-League Knockout Cup competition, which featured the top eight teams of BL1 and BL2 (re-named the New National League, although the 'New' was dropped from 1976), with all round one ties held at the lower league tracks. Hackney drew Boston – a potential banana skin, as they were a formidable opponent, having won all of their home league matches the previous season. They also boasted a number of up-and-coming riders, including the hottest 16-year-old prospect in British speedway by the name of Michael Lee, who had been loaned out for the season by his parent club, King's Lynn, and was just starting his career.

I loved racing at New Hammond Beck Road, which reminded me a lot of the circuit at King's Lynn, so I really didn't contemplate an upset when I made the long trek to Lincolnshire for the meeting on April 13.

Conditions were not stacked in our favour. Torrential rain half way through the meeting not only made racing hazardous on the slippery surface, but extremely dangerous, especially when attempting to overtake.

Nothing went right for us that night, not helped by myself and Thommo each suffering a spill, tape exclusion and an engine failure in a 40-38 defeat. The media made quite a song-and-dance about our loss, as we had the unwanted record of becoming the only British League casualties of the '75 tournament.

I knew Michael Lee was already on the verge of the big time when he comprehensively beat Ted Hubbard and me in the penultimate heat. He was already too good for the NNL and long before the season's end, the future World Champion was a British League star thanks to his success when regularly doubling-up with King's Lynn.

About a month into the new season, Shirley came round to the house to find out about my trip to New Zealand and how I was coping with being a full-time speedway rider. I had seen her knocking about the area and it was great to see her again. One thing led to another and we decided to get back together. Within a few months we announced our engagement, much to the delight of both families.

In May, the World Championship qualifiers began and I did enough to progress to the British semi-final after my three rounds at Halifax, Hackney (where I tied for first place with England skipper Ray Wilson) and Belle Vue. Sandwiched between these, I secured my first full maximum of the season when winning all five at Halifax. It proved to be a good day for the Morton family when Chris won the coveted Peter Craven Memorial Trophy at Belle Vue, where he also remained unbeaten.

I managed to maintain my good form and top-scored in five of the Hawks' next seven matches, although in the majority of these we lost due to the lack of strength in the lower order.

I went into the World Championship British zone semi-final at Sheffield with high hopes. I really liked the set-up at Owlerton and despite the meeting being dominated by riders aboard the new Weslake powered machine, I won three heats, just missing out on a rostrum place. At least I claimed a spot in the British Final at Coventry –

With Thommo before the England v Sweden test at Hackney.

just one step away from appearing in my first World Final.

Things got even better for me a few weeks later when Len informed myself and Thommo that we had been selected to ride for England in the third Test match against Sweden at Hackney on July 11 – and this time, he wasn't forced to back-track by his BSPA colleagues.

As England team manager, Len picked his lower order riders on a horses for courses basis, so it was no real surprise that we had been selected. Even so, when he told me it was, without doubt, one of the proudest moments of my life.

But first I had to try and win the London Riders' Championship, one of the sport's oldest individual titles and which this year was being held at Hackney. Being a northerner, I was determined to take the trophy out of the capital but faced some stiff opposition despite being in top nick on my home track.

It turned out to be an ultra-competitive meeting, watched by a large Waterden Road crowd, with the majority hoping for a home favourite to carry off the title. It all boiled down to Heat 19, with Tommy Jansson (Wimbledon), Dave Jessup (Leicester – he had London connections as an ex-Wembley rider!) and myself yet to drop a point, and Thommo just one point behind.

I made a great start, bullying my way past Jessup and Jansson and into the first bend with a slender advantage. With my nose in front, I kept close to the boards and was getting tremendous drive as I increased my lead after lap three. All I had to do was hang on and the coveted trophy was mine.

Throughout the meeting my bike had performed immaculately and was also very fast. But with the chequered flag in sight, and just half a circuit to go, it ground to a halt. The pushrod arm had broken, so not only had I missed out on a major title, I had incurred a £200 repair bill. I could have stomached anything rather than this – finishing last, falling off, looping at the gate, anything but a bust engine. As I returned to the pits, no amount of consoling pats on the back or well-intended words such as "unlucky Mort" could bring me out of my foul mood. The only slight consolation was that Thommo, also on 12 points, sportingly allowed me to have third place overall in the meeting, rather than race me in a run-off on borrowed machinery. For the record, Jessup took the title ahead of Jansson. After a shower and a quick drink, I set off for home, cursing and swearing all the way back to Partington.

A week later, though, all was forgotten as I made my senior England bow, lining up alongside John Louis, Jessup, Ray Wilson, PC, Thommo, Terry Betts and Malcolm Simmons. Although England were 2-0 up in the series, the Swedes tracked a strong line up, with reigning World Champion Anders Michanek, Tommy Jansson and my Hackney team-mate Christer Lofqvist spearheading their assault.

I spent most of the week preparing my bike, fitting it with the engine I had used in New Zealand. I had no other choice. It was a good unit and I was sure it wouldn't let me down.

Len had partnered me with John Louis, who started like a house on fire when winning Heat 3, while I trailed in last, just behind Michanek and Jansson. It was not the greatest start to my top flight international career and things didn't get much better two heats later, when JL sped to his second race win, with myself again pointless.

Within just two heats, I realised that international speedway was a further step up in class from the British League, certainly when the opposition was this good. The easiest way of describing it was that it felt very similar to when I had first raced in Division One while still a second tier regular at Crewe. The top riders were using the best engines and parts and it was around this time the four-valve revolution was hitting the headlines. My old Crewe team-mate Phil Crump was going great guns for Newport aboard a Jawa-conversion built by his father-in-law Neil Street, while a handful of stars were finding more power on the British-made Weslake engine, notably factory-sponsored riders John Louis, PC and Ray Wilson.

Keeping one step ahead of your rivals was vital if you wanted to compete at the very summit of the sport. At this stage of my career, I was lagging slightly behind with my equipment – something I would rectify in 1976.

I managed to nick a point in my third ride of the Hackney Test against Sweden and finished the meeting following JL home in my final two rides. The Ipswich No.1 secured a brilliant 18-point maximum and, along with Ray Wilson, equalled the track record in a 16-point win for England – another clear indication of how the 'Wessie' was beginning to dominate the two-valvers. Although I had played my part, to be truthful, I was slightly disappointed with my score of just five, especially on my home track.

As expected, I was left out of the final two Tests, as England went on to secure a 5-0 series whitewash against a speedway nation in decline. All I could do now was score as many points in the league as possible to force my way back into the Test squad for the return series in August.

Hackney's season had gone from bad to worse and was typified by our efforts at Exeter a few days after the third Test. Everybody connected with the Hawks thought Christer Lofqvist would be a good signing who would score big points but for some reason, he just didn't settle and missed several meetings for unexplained reasons.

His bikes – the new Swedish four-valve ERM (Endford Racing Motor) – didn't seem overly quick either and Len criticised him for experimenting too much with his machinery in important matches. Christer's problem was inconsistency – he'd win a couple of races and then follow it with a third or a last. He would often tinker with his bike between races too.

There was no doubt he had class and his own style of riding, although nothing like the fence-scraping tactics employed by myself and Thommo. His lack of points put pressure on the other riders in the team, as we struggled to keep away from the foot of the table.

Christer failed to show for our match at Exeter and when three others turned up just before the start, it wasn't ideal preparation and we inevitably suffered yet another heavy away defeat.

A rare picture of Christer Lofqvist (far right) in Hackney colours. Next in line after me are (left to right) Mike Broadbank, Cradley's John Boulger, Steve Lomas, Kelvin Mullarkey and Dave Kennett.

Len was furious about Christer's no-show and a few days later things came to a head when he cancelled the Swede's contract, although I've since read that Christer was no longer interested in riding in the British League anyway and, in fact, never did so again. It seems that he and Len never hit it off from the start, although from the riders' perspective Christer was a popular member of the team, who got on with everyone. He'd talk to us, and certainly wasn't a loner.

But the bottom line was that he didn't do the job he was brought in to do. Averaging just 7.61 from 12 official league and cup matches in Hawks' colours, his performances fell way short of what was expected from a No.1 with his obvious ability.

Christer returned to ride in the Swedish league in 1976 season but was diagnosed with a brain tumour and died in 1978, aged just 33. Who knows when his health began to deteriorate – perhaps it may have had something to do with his erratic form and was part of the reason why he missed meetings for no apparent reason? I certainly never saw him display any physical signs of ill health in 1975 and it's sad that his life ended at such a young age.

One defeat followed another in July as we endured a wretched month. On the 18th we lost at home to Poole and then the next day at Coventry, where I blew another engine. It always sounded quite dramatic when this happened but it usually meant either a valve had broken or a con-rod had snapped. The average cost of a re-build was usually between £150-£300 depending on what was broken. The engines had to be stripped and parts replaced every six-to-eight meetings anyway, so it was never a financial disaster, especially if you were earning enough points to pay for the damage or maintenance.

I used to maintain my own engines, having learned the basics from Dad whose engineering background stood me in good stead. I would only go to an established engine tuner, such as Guy Allott and later Dave Nourish and Keith Stephenson, for any major rebuilding work or tuning.

During my Hackney days, former Hawk Gerry Jackson also did a couple of motors for me.

We suffered another home defeat at the hands of Wimbledon on the 25th, when I rode a Weslake (borrowed from Chris) for the first time. The miserable month was completed with a heavy loss at King's Lynn – our eighth league defeat on the bounce. At the end of July I was glad to put thoughts of our league struggle aside and focus on the British Final at Coventry, as I was starting to grow tired of being on the losing side.

I had scored a dozen points (five rides) for Hackney at Coventry 11 days earlier but this would be a completely different calibre of opposition. Brandon was a hard track to pass on, so it was ultra-important to gate well.

British Final night was always a special occasion, when fans turned out in force – we're talking around the 10,000 mark – to cheer on their particular favourite. In 1975, the first year in which the Australian and New Zealand riders weren't part of the British qualifying route, there were four places up for grabs at the World Final, which was to be held at Wembley. I was just five rides away from appearing in front of nearly 100,000 at the national stadium, on the biggest night of the speedway year . . . and I felt slightly overawed by it all.

John Louis, PC, our Chris, Malcolm Simmons, Martin Ashby and my old hero Chris Pusey were just a few of the big names on show, so I had a monumental task of qualifying, never mind winning it.

I wasn't only competing against the best in Britain, the 16-man line-up at Coventry featured some of the best riders in the world. England were at the peak of their powers, just a few weeks away from winning the World Team Cup for a third consecutive year (despite riding as Great Britain in 1973, the five who triumphed at Wembley that year were all Englishmen).

Martin Ashby won the first heat and I lined up in the next alongside PC, Louis and Jim McMillan. Everything I had told myself about the gate came true as I came out of the first bend at the back. Nothing changed, as Louis scorched home on his Weslake, ahead of PC.

In my next outing I tried to pass coming out of the bend, overcooked it and fell off. My night was as good as over before it had hardly begun. Chris faired a little better but neither of us troubled the leaders. Louis continued his hot streak with another faultless performance, while PC pipped Malcolm Simmons to the runners-up spot after a run-off. A second decider saw Ray Wilson beat Ashby to complete the qualifiers for Wembley. The *Speedway Star* summed up the night perfectly: 'The others, frankly, never looked in the same class: they were merely the cannon fodder'.

I couldn't have put it better. I still had a long way to go if I wanted to compete consistently with this class of '75.

Gating was still a strong point of my game but rules had been tightened compared to the old Division Two days, when you could do virtually anything at the tapes and get away with it. Referees and starting marshals clamped down on any misdemeanours and on July 31, during a rain-affected four-team tournament at Wimbledon, I found this out to my cost.

The controversy came in Heat 12, when I was aiming to complete a maximum after three wins. As we took up our starting positions, I initially refused to move over when asked by the starting marshal. Reluctantly, I edged over about an inch from where I wanted to be, and another one when he asked me again. Enough was enough for the referee, who then excluded me for 'ungentlemanly conduct'.

Hackney ended their appalling run with home victories against Sheffield and Halifax, where I dropped only one point. These were the sort of performances I needed to reclaim a place in the Lions squad, and my chances received a further boost when I was the surprise winner of King's Lynn's Supporters' Trophy after beating Malcolm Simmons in a run-off. A maximum in a narrow home victory over Hull continued my good form and after the meeting Len took me to one side and informed me that I was definitely in the squad for the forthcoming Sweden tour.

Before I knew it, we were at Heathrow Airport, flying out for the punishing schedule of five Tests in six days. The boyhood dream of representing England – three Partington boys racing for their country – was about to come true, because Chris and PC had also been selected, along with Chris Pusey, Terry Betts, Doug Wyer, John Davis and Martin Ashby, a good blend of youth and experience and a mixture that would ensure some fun and games.

But before all that, the speedway side of the tour began on August 26, with the first Test at Kumla, and to say my first appearance for England on foreign soil was quite eventful would be an understatement. I was selected as reserve and had to view the action from the pits until Heat 13, when I was sent out with PC – the match finely poised, with the hosts holding a slender two-point advantage, the first time they had led in a pulsating encounter.

PC had already won twice and had a couple of second places, so he'd adapted to the track well and took an early lead from the gate, as I tucked in just behind. Not really being a team rider, I blocked and guarded PCs lead and we recorded an important 5-1. But it was in my next race when the trouble started.

Still on a high after my previous ride, I was paired with Chris Pusey and keen to record my first international win – too keen in fact. Before the tapes went up and with the clutch dragging, I bent the tapes so much, both wheels crossed the starting line. Incredibly, the tapes didn't break. But new regulations stated that a rider *could* be excluded for such an offence, whether breaking the tapes or not. It was all down to the referee's interpretation –and he excluded me. Len went ballistic and it was a good 10 minutes before the heat was re-started, with him still ranting and raving at the official. Fortunately, Chris won the re-run but a home 5-1 and 4-2, with just two heats to go, left us trailing by four and on the brink of defeat.

Talk about pressure. I realised that one slip in the penultimate heat and it would be curtains but I kept my nerve and followed home skipper Martin Ashby to tie up the scores, with one to go.

I was to ride in this one as well, lining up with PC for the grand finale. Tommy Jansson split us

Looks like I've got to Broady's favoured inside line just ahead of him.

SPEEDWAY STAR, September 6, 1975

SWEDEN 0
ENGLAND 5

ENGLAND CRUSH SWEDES

How *Speedway Star* splashed the news of our whitewash of the Swedes.

after the first bend and the order remained the same. PC was never going to be caught and while his three-pointer ensured the draw, my point won us the Test. We had pipped them by two, 55-53, in one of the best speedway matches I had ever ridden in.

We celebrated in the pits – young and old, management and pit crew, plus a few supporters – as though we had won the football pools. What a start to the tour.

Next night the series moved on to Eskilstuna, the home track of Tommy Jansson who had top-scored for the hosts the previous evening. Len promoted me into the main body of the side, with our Chris this time filling the reserve slot (John Davis was the other reserve for the tour). I was paired with PC and we again contributed valuable points when I followed him home in the fifth, and he ensured my first senior win in an England race jacket when I held off Tommy Johansson and Karl-Erik Claesson six heats later. This maximum came at a crucial time as the teams were locked together, having shared the points in four successive heats.

The second Test was every bit as exciting as the first. My second victory, in Heat 13, gave us a two-point advantage, although this was cancelled out in the next. Chris won the 15th and then ensured we couldn't get beaten when he and Martin Ashby won Heat 17. PC wrapped up our 57-51 victory with another three-pointer.

I was pleased with my night's work – two wins, a second and two third places for 10 paid 12 from my six rides. This victory really made me feel part of the whole set-up and I finally believed I was in the team on merit, not because I rode for the team manager's club side.

England wrapped up the series in Stockholm (Gubbangen) the following night with a comfortable 20-point victory, thanks mainly to a maximum 18 from Ashby and double-figure returns from PC and Dave Jessup. Chris replaced me in this one but I returned at Vetlanda. And although the series was already won, Len drilled into us that this one was as important as the first and not to drop our standards. It resulted in my best return to date, 12 paid 15 points from six rides, with myself and PC winning two each. We won 68-40 and then completed the 5-0 whitewash at Mariestad on August 31, despite an 18-point maximum from Anders Michanek, who was making his first appearance in the series.

SWEDEN v ENGLAND 1975 TEST SERIES – HOW ENGLAND RIDERS SCORED						
Matches	**1st Test**	**2nd Test**	**3rd Test**	**4th Test**	**5th Test**	
Venues	**Kumla**	**Eskilstuna**	**Stockholm**	**Vetlanda**	**Mariestad**	**Totals**
Results	**53-55**	**51-57**	**44-64**	**40-68**	**50-58**	**Points**
Martin Ashby	13	14	18	14	–	59
Peter Collins	16	14	15	11	–	56
DAVE MORTON	**5**	**10**	**–**	**12**	**10**	**37**
Dave Jessup	–	–	12	9	10	31
Chris Pusey	8	5	7	8	–	28
John Davis	5	6	2	3	11	27
Malcolm Simmons	–	–	–	11	10	21
Chris Morton	3	7	6	–	–	16
Gordon Kennett	–	–	–	–	11	11
Terry Betts	5	1	4	–	–	10
Eric Broadbelt	–	–	–	–	6	6
Doug Wyer	0	0	–	–	–	0

Sweden is a beautiful country, not that we had much time to explore the scenery or fineries on offer. But our hectic racing schedule didn't stop us having a good laugh, usually at the expense of the older riders. I shared a room with PC, having had enough fall-outs with Chris throughout our childhood to last a lifetime.

Chris Pusey was the joker of the pack and after being on the receiving end of more than one of his jokes, PC decided to get his own back. I think it was at the end of the third Test in Stockholm. Myself, Chris and PC were getting changed in the dressing room while the rest were still in the pits messing around with their bikes, or conducting interviews. On one of the pegs was Pusey's clothes and PC borrowed some of my Radian B cream, an alcohol-based liniment used to treat muscular pain, bumps and bruises. Very much like Fiery Jack but a lot hotter when rubbed into the skin. PC smeared a large amount in the crotch area of Pusey's underpants and then hung them back on his peg as we waited for the Halifax skipper to have his shower and get changed. We could hardly contain ourselves when 'Puse' walked towards his clothes.

Unfortunately, though, PC had messed up big time . . . instead of sabotaging Pusey's underpants, he'd made a mistake and put the hot stuff in Martin Ashby's instead – they were both wearing the same style trousers!

Within a few seconds of 'Crash' slipping on his pants the cream had the desired effect. Well, I don't think Swindon's normally mild mannered captain could have been in more pain if we had blow-torched his bollocks!

Martin was a great, laid-back type of guy but he didn't see the funny side of what we had done.

I was convinced it was about to kick off but, fortunately, Martin calmed down before blows were exchanged, much to PC's relief.

One night we had been drinking at our hotel, having eaten our "small gas board" (smorgasbord), as we called it. We were all a bit worse for wear having been drinking all night, so when we retired, about four or five of us got in the lift instead of taking the stairs to our rooms. Between the third and fourth floors, Terry Betts decided to press the emergency button and the lift stopped with a sudden jolt. Being pissed, we thought this was hilarious, so we re-set the button and did it again . . . and again . . . and again. By this time, some of the older riders had had enough and decided to get out but we continued the fun for another 20 minutes, before the novelty finally wore off and we went to bed. Such a childish prank but it seemed really funny at the time.

Swedish people have a very open and liberal view about sex and nudity, as we discovered, first hand, after the final match at Mariestad, the home town of one-time Sheffield rider Bengt Larsson, who had been helping out the Swedes in the pits.

He was a lovely fella and invited us all to his house for a bite to eat, where he made us most welcome before taking us out for the night. We were just sitting around chatting and having a laugh when his gorgeous wife walked in, wearing a see-through blouse and no bra. She greeted us with a great, big friendly smile but most of us just sat, open-mouthed, and weren't looking at her face. We continued chatting for about 10 minutes before the minibus arrived to take us out.

We thought we were just going on a tour of local bars but Bengt had arranged a trip to a local sex show. The audience was mixed and anybody could partake if they wished, not that any of the team had the balls to perform. It was certainly a bit different to going out for a few pints of Boddingtons around rainy Manchester!

Talking of my home city, on September 5, we entertained Belle Vue in a British League match, which was on the eve of the World Final. I thought PC would take it easy but I couldn't have been more wrong as he recorded a faultless maximum – perfect preparation for Wembley. Hackney's

Happy to narrowly avoid the wooden spoon, the Hackney team that ended a troubled '75 season. Standing, left to right: Dave Erskine (team manager), Dave Kennett, Barry Thomas, Mike Broadbank, Zenon Plech, myself and Len Silver. Front: Laurie Etheridge, Ted Hubbard and Steve Lomas.

problems were summed up in the 43-35 defeat, where all but five of our points were scored by Thommo, Laurie Etheridge and myself.

I stayed over at Thommo's place on the Isle of Sheppey in Kent and the next day joined 85,000 other fans at Wembley, where the vast majority were hoping for an English winner.

Back in 1975, Wembley was still a magnificent stadium but, sadly, the track didn't match its famous historic surroundings. There was in fact a bomb scare half-way through the meeting but nobody left the stadium or seemed overly concerned. One man in front of me, however, did quip: "If they blew the track up, you wouldn't notice any bloody difference."

Ole Olsen won his second world title at a canter but PC, one of the favourites, struggled to tame the shit-heap of a track, which was a dust-bowl at the start and a mud-bath (after a severe watering) before the interval.

Chris and I after winning the British Grass-track Pairs title.

Alarmed at Hackney's slump, Len decided to strengthen the squad and somehow managed to persuade the highly-rated Polish star Zenon Plech to sign for the last month or so of the season. He was the current Polish Champion and had appeared in the last two World Championships (finishing third in 1973) and had also qualified for Wembley, so this was a real coup.

Apparently, after the World Team Cup Final in Germany in September, Len drove Zenon – who didn't have a visa – to England and smuggled him into the country in the boot of his car.

I got on with Zenon from the moment he arrived. He was very friendly, likeable and keen to share useful tips and tricks. And when I had the pleasure of riding with him, he gave me choice of gates.

One tip of his that I'll always remember was when he told me how to gain more grip on tracks that were hard and slick. He suggested adding about a quarter-of-a-cup of water in the fuel tank. He explained that mixing water with methanol, which is alcohol-based, meant the water was absorbed, so the fuel wouldn't burn as efficiently when ignited. This would take the edge off the engine revs, which meant the back wheel didn't spin as much and, consequently, you would get more drive and grip.

Throughout my speedway career I continued with my grass-tracking and had a number of notable successes in Britain and Europe, so towards the end of the season I entered the inaugural 500cc British Pairs Championship with Chris. This was one meeting we both really wanted to win and despite our growing speedway commitments, we managed to keep the date free at Lydham in Shropshire on September 14.

We identified the Baybutt brothers (coincidentally, Chris and Dave) as one our biggest rivals but we both rode well and a mixture of team-riding and basically just going flat out secured us the title from Mike Garrard and Julian Wigg. We did attempt to defend our title the following year at Church Stretton but had to be content with the runners-up spot when pipped by PC and Steve Hartley.

After the Swedish tour, the rest of the season was somewhat of an anti-climax and fizzled out with no improvement in Hackney's league results. In the end we did well to avoid the wooden spoon, finishing 17th, three points clear of Swindon. Eight home defeats had not helped, as well as an appalling away record (one win in 17).

On the positive side, I managed to finish top of the Hawks' averages but it was as plain as the nose on your face that the team needed major surgery, and Len promised there were to be a number of major signings in the close season.

At the start of the 1975 campaign I had set out my goals for the season. Apart from not appearing at Wembley, I had achieved all I had set out to do, maybe a little bit more. Now it was time to take it to the next level.

Towards the end of October I was all set to book flight tickets to New Zealand to defend my national championship, when an unexpected phone call changed my plans. I had already been offered a contract by the Western Springs promoters, who were also offering to pay my air fare, so it was going to have to be a really tempting offer to change my initial plans.

It was Len who would disrupt those plans: "Dave, good news – you've been selected for the British Lions tour to Australia and New Zealand."

Although no longer tour manager due to other commitments, the Hackney boss was on the tour selection panel and no doubt had fought for my inclusion, in a squad packed with big-track riders who knew the Australian circuits and conditions. There were many fantastic British riders around at the time but not all could commit to a long tour, especially those who had families to consider. Due to the length of the tour, we also had three team managers. Reg Fearman was to take charge of the first three Tests, ex-Rayleigh manager Charlie Mugford the fourth and Ipswich promoter John Berry the final two, plus the three in New Zealand.

Despite doing well on my first overseas tour in Sweden, to be involved in an Ashes series was quite another step up for me and, to be honest, I was quite surprised at my inclusion.

Another feature which made the trip so exciting was that the team was a very northern affair, with our Chris, PC, Chris Pusey and Doug Wyer also selected, so I knew we were going to have a lot of laughs during our four months away.

Chapter 8

Money issues

ONE positive the other Hackney riders could take from Christer Lofqvist's absences was the opportunity for extra rides – and earnings – if we used the Rider Replacement facility. Don't ask me where they got it from after 40 years but my publisher Retro Speedway have somehow came up with a copy of the Hackney riders' pay-sheet (reproduced here) from our BL match at Oxford on July 3, 1975.

This is the paperwork the home promoter – Danny Dunton in this case – sent Hackney, along with a cheque for £262.73 for our night's work. Len Silver would, in turn, have paid us at our next home meeting.

As you can see, Christer rode and scored five points at Cowley, where Dave 'Crockett' Kennett and I top-scored with seven each (plus a bonus point in my case) from our four rides in yet another (44-34) away defeat.

It's interesting to examine the basic figures and compare the sums involved. Back in the day, we were all paid the same standard British League rates of £2.40 per start and £3.60 per point.

If you analyse my payment column, you'll see it confirms that I earned £9.40 for four starts in the league match and £25.50 for scoring seven points, plus £3.60 for the odd bonus point.

In the second-half, for which we were on the same basic money, I scored four-and-a-half points from two rides, including a rare dead-heat with my race partner Dave Kennett.

So my second-half income, when adding the points and start money together, was £21.00. Add this to the £38.40 I earned from the earlier match and it left me with gross earnings (after £1.35 deducted for insurance) of £58.05.

Now on the face of it, that might seem a low figure today, especially when you consider the risks undertaken by riders. But according to an online financial comparison website, the £58.05 I was paid for that one night's work would be the equivalent of roughly £550 today – not bad considering it wasn't a great night for me, having dropped four points to the home team's riders.

The same website confirms that the UK's average working weekly wage in 1975 was £54 (compared to the 2014 average of £519), so I'd earnt a little more than that from just one meeting.

I should also point out that the figures you see here on the Hackney pay-sheet relate only to our BASIC earnings from this meeting. Some riders, especially the top boys, had private agreements with their promoters which boosted their earning capacity. In my case, Len Silver paid me an extra £2 per point, over and above the standard BSPA rate, so I was effectively on £5.60 per point at Oxford. The following year, I received other bonuses, which I'll come to later.

I wouldn't say Len was difficult to negotiate with and neither was he unfair. You would typically ask for a bit more than you thought he would pay you, he would tell you what he was offering and you'd hope that he'd meet you somewhere in between, which is basically how it worked out. Looking back, I was probably a bit soft when it came to discussing a deal at the start of each season and, as you now, Len was a very experienced and skilled negotiator.

Back then, when crowds were still measured in their thousands and not hundreds and an adults were paying £1 to see 13 heats and a full second-half, there were so many more opportunities for top riders to earn decent money. With 18 BL teams contesting league, cup and challenge matches, plus a

RIDERS' PAY SHEET No. 7.7.75 DATE	**OXFORD SPEEDWAY** VAT NO 1952711 50 Telephone Brighton (0273) 732286	Denmark Works Denmark Villas Hove Sussex					
Team/Rider's Name	HACKNEY	This sheet must be returned with any query		All enquiries to Speedway Office			
Date of Meeting	3.7.75						
Rider Track	B THOMAS	M BROADBANKS	C LOFGUIST	D KENNETT	D MORTON	T HUBBARD	S LOMAS	
Starts 1st Half	4 9·60	4 9·60	4 9·60	4 9·60	4 9·60	3/1 7·20	4 9·60	·
Match Points	6 21·60	5 18·00	5 18·00	7 25·20	7 25·20	–	4 14·40	
Bonus Points		1 3·60	3 10·80	·	1 3·60	·	1 3·60	
Starts 2nd Half	1 2·40	1 2·40	1 2·40	2 4·80	2 4·80	1 2·40	–	
Points 2nd Half	1 3·60	2 7·20	2 7·20	4½ 16·20	4½ 16·20	–	·	·
Guarantees					·	·	·	·
Sub-Total	37·20	40·80	48·00	55·80	59·40	9·60	27·60	·
% Added	·	·	·	·	·	·	·	·
Total for V.A.T.		·	·	·	·	·	·	·
Addition of V.A.T.		·	·	·	·	·	·	·
Total with V.A.T.		·	·	·	·	·	·	·
Travelling Expenses	·	·	·	·	·	·	·	·
GROSS TOTAL	37·20	40·80	48·00	55·80	59·40	9·60	27·60	·
Fuel & Oil	19 ·70 1P	19 1·10	19 2·90 3P	19 2·30 2P	·	·		·
Insurance	5 ·13	5 1·13	5 1·13	6 1·35	6 1·35	3 ·68	4 ·90	·
Refunds	·	·	·	·	·	·	·	·
V.A.T. Retained	·	·	·	·	·	·	·	·
TOTAL DEDUCTIONS	2·83	2·23	4·03	3·65	1·35	·68	·90	
NETT TOTAL	34·37	38·57	43·97	52·15	58·05	8·92	26·70	·
PLEASE FIND ENCLOSED CHEQUE No.			£ 262 73					

One of my 1975 pay-sheets, showing the Hackney riders' basic earnings from our visit to Oxford.

Another shot from the 1975 World Championship qualifier at Hyde Road, looking for the outside grip to pass John Louis.

multitude of individual events, World Championship rounds, occasional guest appearances and Test matches, it kept us busy from March 'till October, so we were well rewarded for our efforts.

Here is the finishing order of the 1975 British League, boosted by a new national sponsorship from Gulf Oil, with regular race nights shown in brackets. It illustrates perfectly how much variety was on offer to supporters and riders alike.

1. IPSWICH (Thursday)	10. HALIFAX (Saturday)
2. BELLE VUE (Saturday)	11. CRADLEY UNITED (Saturday)
3. NEWPORT (Friday)	12. KING'S LYNN (Saturday)
4. EXETER (Monday)	13. WOLVERHAMPTON (Friday)
5. SHEFFIELD (Thursday)	14. HULL (Wednesday)
6. READING (Monday)	15. POOLE (Wednesday)
7. OXFORD (Thursday)	16. COVENTRY (Saturday)
8. LEICESTER (Tuesday)	17. HACKNEY (Friday)
9. WIMBLEDON (Thursday)	18. SWINDON (Saturday)

It was possible, in the most hectic periods, to be riding six nights a week (this was before Eastbourne joined the senior league in 1979 and were given permission to stage Sunday meetings). Amazing to think now that there were SIX Saturday tracks in operation. Sadly, though, NINE tracks have closed and only SEVEN – Belle Vue, Leicester, King's Lynn, Wolves, Poole, Coventry and Swindon – were still running in the top flight Elite League in 2015. Ipswich and Sheffield are now established in the Premier League (second tier).

But let's get back to 1975. If you rode, on average, three or four nights a week and scored double figures each time, you would have been looking at picking up somewhere between £200, £300 or maybe £400 . . . or the comparative equivalent of £2,000-4,000 today. Thinking about it, that was probably in line or not far short of what many professional footballers, including my Manchester United heroes, were getting in 1975 – even big-name first division stars.

You certainly can't equate what speedway riders earn today, no matter how well some of them are paid, with that of any Premier League footballer. Due to the astronomical TV deals that basically fund the Premier League and, to a lesser extent, The Football League too, players' earnings have not just gone through the roof, they have burst the stratosphere. I bet double World Champion Tai Woffinden wouldn't mind receiving the 'small change' from Wayne Rooney's reported weekly wage of £300,000!

Even allowing for the fact that we had to buy and maintain our bikes and equipment, paying for any engine blow-ups or bent machinery out of earnings, I do remember thinking at the time how fortunate I was that speedway had given me such a a good standard of living. When I quit working as a fitter at Shell at the end of 1974 to become a full-time professional speedway rider, I was taking home about £25 per week.

I've given this glimpse into the financial state of speedway in '75. not to boast about my personal income at that stage of my racing career (it didn't last forever and, like most of you reading this, I'm now working full-time again, getting up at 3.00am for a 12-hour shift of 'four on, four off'), but because I believe readers will find it interesting.

It's funny how we all tend to be secretive about our personal financial affairs and earnings and speedway riders were no different in my day either. We'd happily chat in the dressing room and on tours about different women and the things you got up to but the sensitive subject of money and what we were paid for riding was always a no-no. I suppose you wouldn't bring it up for fear of embarrassing yourself, or a team-mate or rival. Knowing a rider, who you may consider to be less capable than yourself, is being paid more could easily cause resentment in the ranks and damage team morale.

Malcolm Simmons told the story in his book about how England's World Team Cup squad sat around chatting on a ferry to some overseas destination and they decided to each reveal what they were paid by their British clubs. Apparently, Martin Ashby was shocked and dismayed to find that his earnings at Swindon were way short of what the others were paid, and you can imagine how hurt 'Crash' must have felt given all the many years loyal service he gave the Robins.

I didn't have a clue what deals my Hackney team-mates, or the riders in any of the other teams I represented, had with our respective promoters – it was none of my business and the subject never came up in conversation.

To be honest, and this may surprise you, I never even knew what my brother was paid by Belle Vue. Chris and I never discussed our deals.

The point I would like to make here, though, is that for the vast majority of former riders, including myself, money wasn't the issue. We didn't take up the sport because we thought it was an exciting job that paid well.

When I was a kid tearing around PC's dad's farm on my pushbike, dreaming of becoming World Champion, it didn't enter my little head how much I might be paid if I ever fulfilled my dreams. Okay, as you get older and settle down, marry, have kids, take on a mortgage and other responsibilities, circumstances inevitably change.

But it's true to say that most of us would have ridden for nothing. We were just very lucky that that we got paid for something we loved doing.

The British Lions certainly weren't thinking about money when we waved goodbye to chilly England in November 1975 and set off on our tour of Australia and New Zealand.

Chapter 9

Laughs with the Lions

WE flew from Heathrow to Perth in Western Australia, the venue for the first two Tests. The long flight gave us time to have a few beers and gel with the southern boys, John 'Mavis' Davis and Gordon Kennett.

The opening test on November 14 saw us line up against a number of my former Crewe teammates, Phil Crump, Glyn Taylor and Pete Thompson, and the series started with a bang when Crumpie smashed the track record in the first heat. This was going to be no easy opener – or so we thought, before we won the next three races with maximum points.

Foot up and flying . . . I loved the big, wide open spaces of the tracks in Australia and New Zealand.

I was again partnered with PC and in our six outings, the only pair to beat us were Crumpie and Pete Thompson in Heat 6. JD and Dougie Wyer lowered the track record further, as we recorded a 67-41 victory.

Only Crump, who dropped just one point, and to some degree Glyn Taylor, performed for the hosts, who had underestimated the strength and determination of the England squad by fielding a somewhat weak and inexperienced team, in the hope that home advantage would see them through. They had been humiliated in their own backyard.

We were obviously delighted but, at the same time, slightly shocked at how easy it had been. The Aussie selectors reacted immediately for the second Test, scheduled for a fortnight later, and called up their big guns in the form of Billy Sanders, Phil Herne and the wily old veteran John Langfield, who was to skipper the team.

We were warned of a backlash and an even bigger crowd turned up to see Australian national pride restored. But once again, only Crumpie turned up for the Kangaroos, scoring half of their total. The rest were yards slower and completely outclassed after a masterclass from PC on the huge Claremont track, with the victory margin even greater than the first.

The Lions were two up in the series and had not broken sweat. Already the local newspapers were predicting a humiliating whitewash and the pattern continued at Jerilderie Park, Newcastle on December 5, when we slaughtered them 76-32. Despite the result, I really struggled to adapt to the smaller Newcastle track, mustering only three points from my four outings. PC had no such problem and led the way with a brilliant six-ride maximum.

Next night it was all over following another one-sided affair, this time in Sydney. At the notorious Showground, Dougie Wyer took the plaudits on his turbo-charged ERM, which eclipsed even the Weslakes and Neil Street four-valvers on show. Mission accomplished, the Ashes had been regained.

Nobody could work out just how bad the Aussies had become, for virtually the same riders had won the series 5-2 just 12 months previously. Had they lost their fighting spirit? Well, you wouldn't have thought that halfway through the tour, in one of the pre-Test warm-up matches at Rockhampton.

John Langfield and our Chris had a real ding-dong in one particular heat, with Langfield attempting to bring Chris down from the start! Whether it was sheer frustration on John's part, I don't know, but he was determined to teach this young Pommie upstart a lesson.

Lions ready to roar . . . Team manager John Berry, Chris Pusey, John Davis, Doug Wyer, Chris, PC, myself and Gordon Kennett.

Tucking in on the outside of John Davis at Sydney Showground. The big fence a few feet from us was made of solid concrete.

As the tapes went up Langfield went almost sideways into Chris's machine, trying to put him on the infield, but somehow Chris managed to stay upright. Although the other three riders hit the first turn with Chris a considerable distance behind, he regained his composure and did what he did throughout his speedway career, by attempting to win the race from the back. It turned out to be a tremendous scrap between the pair, with the Aussie veteran using every trick in the book to stay ahead, until Chris feigned to take him on the outside, before nipping inside to do him like a kipper to take third place.

As Chris returned to the pits it all kicked off.

Langfield dragged him off his still moving machine and started to lay into him, with fists flying in all directions. I jumped in to lend our kid a hand and Aussie Bob Valentine decided to make it a four-man scrap. Bob was ready to ride in the next heat, so had his helmet on. I grabbed him in a headlock and we toppled into a bike on its stand, which sent another three or four down like dominoes. Before we knew it, there were about 15 involved – riders, pit crew and staff.

Eventually it all calmed down and my one abiding memory of this 'handbags at 10 paces' altercation was seeing Chris standing with Phil Crump watching us all make fools of ourselves, after Crumpie had pulled Chris out of the melee and told him not to get involved!

Whether it had been staged to add some spice to the Test series, I'm not sure, but a week later we were all friends again when John invited all the Lions round to his house for a barbeque. 'Langy' was a showman and reminded me a lot of the things Jack Millen would do to stir up a crowd.

We spent Christmas Day in the sunshine on the beach, which took some getting used to, before John Berry took us all to a restaurant for dinner. The next two days over the festive period were spent preparing for Test matches at Liverpool and Sydney. The first, on Boxing Day, resulted in a hard-fought 14-point victory, but it was to be the following day's penultimate Test that stole the headlines. Five-nil down in the series and facing the prospect of a 7-0 drubbing, the Aussies decided to ensure that they would win at least once.

The sixth Test was back at Sydney but when we arrived and walked the circuit, we noticed that the

Two views of PC and me team-riding, taking it in turns to use the inside and outside lines.

surface was completely different compared to our previous visit. It was rough and ready, with extra loose dirt strewn all over the place, four inches deep in some places, which was not properly bedded down. Sydney was a massive, banked track, although narrow, with a concrete 'safety fence' which made it a fast exciting venue. But in this condition, someone could be seriously injured.

A downpour of rain on a heavily watered track just before the off made racing conditions even worse, and the inevitable happened in the fourth heat when Chris Pusey clipped Langfield's back wheel, hit the fence and was then speared by Billy Sanders, resulting in him being rushed to hospital with a bad leg injury.

The crash prompted us to stage a walk-out. We packed up our equipment and were ready to return to the hotel after the referee insisted the conditions were "fit for racing".

Protests and threats to send us home did little to change our decision but after a long delay, reluctantly, we decided to give it a go for the sake of the Aussie public and our own national pride, although John Berry told us to take no risks, or attempt any overtaking. "I am not prepared to have a death on my conscience," were the words John later used in interviews with the press.

We went through the motions and even though I scored nine points, the whole affair was one to forget in terms of a speedway match. The Aussies achieved their victory but the crowd had been cheated out of a proper contest.

Fortunately, Pusey's injuries were not as bad as first feared (ligament damage and a chipped bone in his right knee),and even though he would miss the final Test against Australia, he would be available for the New Zealand matches.

The seventh Test, in Brisbane a fortnight later, was again staged on a wet and greasy surface, although this time the track had been prepared well. Heavy rainfall proved a great leveller but it was the hosts, all mounted on Street four-valvers, who adapted better to the conditions and led comfortably until the track dried out and we stormed back to take the match 57-50, courtesy of two fine wins from Malcolm Simmons, deputising for the injured skipper. It proved to be the best match of the series.

Despite the hostilities of an Ashes series, the Aussie riders and public could not have been any more friendly or accommodating. On one occasion the riders took us out for the day, water-skiing on a river in Sydney. Former Australia and Sheffield No.1 Jim Airey and Ipswich's Billy Sanders had boats and we were all keen to have a go. For some it was a first time experience. All the Aussies were experts and showed us how it was done, on one ski, or even with no skis at all.

I was in Jim's boat with PC, Pusey, Gordon and our Chris. We all took it turns but when it was Gordon's go, he seemed quite nervous. Jim set off slowly taking the slack up on the rope, and for the first few yards Gordon seemed to be doing okay, before overbalancing and hitting the water with a mighty splash. Now the norm was to wait for the boat to turn and then have another go but Gordon's life jacket had come loose and instead of treading water, he was flapping about and struggling to keep his head above the surface. What he hadn't told us was that he couldn't swim – not a stroke!

We quickly turned the boat around to pick him up but by this stage he was in a right panic, so Jim Airey jumped in to help him alongside the boat. In his panic, Gordon just lashed out in the hope of grabbing anything to help him keep afloat, so Jim had to keep his distance and did his best to push him towards the boat. After several attempts, Gordon, like a cat clawing at the side, managed to get hold of the edge of the boat, where PC and Pusey pulled him aboard. He lay on the deck choking and spluttering but mighty relieved he had survived the ordeal.

Were we sympathetic to Gordon's plight? Not a bit of it. After realising that the Oxford star couldn't swim, we seized upon any opportunity to test him in the hotel pool, where we enjoyed playing water-polo. He was fine in the shallow end but when we chucked the ball in the deep part of the pool, he refused to go after it. *Cruel* but very amusing.

Pits debate with John Davis, Billy Sanders and Doug Wyer.

We did have a lot of fun on the Australia part of the tour and also had some 'fun' with the opposite sex. We came across some stunning ladies and one in particular took my eye after the first Test at Perth. We were on the victory parade when we all clapped eyes on a stunning girl standing on the centre green, who was there to present the prizes. Not only was she very good looking, she had a very large chest.

Later in the clubhouse, this model was surrounded by men trying their best to impress her, so we basically ignored her, until we were all invited to a downtown nightclub ('The Godfather') belonging to a local businessman who had been at the meeting. We all sat around a table and watched this gorgeous girl as she gyrated away on the dance floor. Before we knew it, Pusey was on the dance floor with her, even though he was old enough to be her grandfather. After a few dances he sat down by me and we learnt her name was Kym, and she was actually English.

"Hey Mort, she fancies you," Puse whispered in my ear.

"Don't take the piss," I replied, knowing how good he was at winding people up.

"No, really Mort, I'm not kidding this time, she really does."

So I decided to take the bull by the horns and fuelled with a few Aussie lagers, I beckoned her over. She didn't need a second invitation and was there like a shot – and for once Puse had been telling the truth. I spent the rest of the night chatting her up, the envy of every male in the place – she was 18 years of age and had a body to die for.

After the club, she returned with me to the hotel and fortunately for us, the place I was sharing with PC had two rooms, so we locked ourselves in the dining room/kitchen which housed a convertible bed settee.

For the rest of the Perth part of the tour I stayed with Kym in her flat. We had motorbikes and cars for getting around the city, so I would arrive on my bike, stay until the morning, and return to the riders' hotel tired but content!

I don't know why but she was besotted with me, and even came to the airport to see me off. We

I met up with a few people with Crewe connections on the 1975-76 tour. Above: Colin Tucker, Nicky Allott and Barry Smity and his daughter wait to see what I've cooked up on the barbie. Below: In the pits with Paul O'Neal, who rode for Crewe in their first two seasons.

Captain Chris Pusey after we had clinched our 6-1 series victory over the Aussies. 'Bert' wasn't smiling, though, when he encountered a spider!

wrote to each other a few times but I never saw her again, even though some of the guys who later returned to Perth had seen her and said she was asking about me.

We had some laughs in Sydney. While there we used a workshop which belonged to a guy called Cess who dealt in Porche cars. It was underground and dark and dingy, and a young lad there used to help us a bit with the cleaning and building up of our bikes. Here we used to boil our chains in a stove in a mixture called 'LinkLife' which coated the chains in a solution. We would hang them up to drip-dry but one day we asked him to get the chains which were hanging up after being in the boiling solution.

We thought he would get himself a cloth to handle them but he just grabbed them with both hands. Well, he screamed out in pain and dropped them back into the solution, which spilt all over the floor. He held up his hands, which were still smouldering, but nobody cared about his injuries – we were too busy pissing ourselves laughing. From that moment on, he was known as 'LinkLife'.

We lived on a diet of milkshakes and burgers and close to our hotel, The Glen Synd, there was a burger bar called The Colonial Diner, in the middle of a park, where we usually ate. Nearly always in there was this tramp who was the spitting image of John Louis, so that's the name we christened him with, even though he hadn't a clue who we were referring to. There was also a jukebox and we would always put on the same record – Led Zeppelin's *Black Dog*. Whenever I hear that song, I always think of The Colonial Diner and our tramp friend, 'John Louis'.

While at the hotel, we had to do our own washing in the laundry room at the top of the building. We were in there one day and the top window was open – the only one which wasn't frosted glass. I took a peek out to see what was on the roof, only to discover the manageress sunbathing topless. We all took it in turns to have a good look at her. After that, we couldn't help but snigger behind her back whenever she was dealing with us in the hotel – she was totally unaware she had been ogled by a bunch of horny speedway riders.

It was also in Sydney where we nearly had a set-to with a group of Italians. One night we decided to go ten-pin bowling. Unlike in this country, you paid for the games and were given your bowling shoes, but didn't have to hand your own in (very trusting those Aussies).

Anyway, we were having trouble with our lane, so we decided to swap, and we brought our shoes with us. Next to us were some Italian lads who were a right bunch of tossers and clearly out for trouble. All of a sudden, a couple of them came over ranting and raving and one of them said: "You pincha da shoooes, you pincha da shoooes."

Someone had picked up a pair of their expensive leather shoes by mistake but we managed to calm them down. Another giggle at someone else's expense.

I can't finish recalling our time in Sydney without a couple of stories about Chris Pusey. On this tour he acquired a couple of nicknames – one being 'Bushfire'. This came about during one stage of the tour when he grew a really bushy beard. We were having a few beers one night when someone commented that if his growth ever caught fire, it would cause one hell of a bushfire, which we all found very amusing.

That nickname stuck, as did 'Bert'. At Hackney, there was a resident mechanic Len employed, who helped many a rider over the years. His name was Terry 'Bert' Busch ('Bushfire' – Busch, get it?), so one day I started to call Puse Bert. Soon all the other riders were calling him by this name and even today, if you ask PC or our Chris about the Aussie tour of 1975-76, they will talk fondly about old Bert.

One night he got off with this bird and took her back to his room. And when we returned from our night out a bit later, we decided to see what he was up to. Myself and PC climbed over our balcony on to Puse's next door, where we stood on a chair to see through the top of the window, as the curtains didn't go all the way to the top.

We couldn't believe he wasn't 'at it' but, instead, was just sitting on the bed fully-clothed and chatting away, so we went to the other lads in the corridor and decided to bang on his door and tell him to get on with it. But for once he didn't see the funny side and came to the door in a furious rage.

We ran down the corridor, just as Puse came out of his room and launched an aerosol can at us. It caught PC on the thigh and he went down as though he had been shot. A New York Yankees pitcher could not have hurled it any harder or more accurately. Puse was effin and blinding as he slammed his door shut while we headed back to our room in fits of laughter.

After his leg injury at the Sydney Showground, he couldn't get around very well and was totally dependent on his crutches. One day he was resting on his bed when John Langfield, his brother and a couple of the other Aussie riders came to visit him to see how he was going on. We were all there but what we didn't know, was that they had brought with them a get-well present – a giant spider in a big glass jar. While we were chatting away, John produced the jar, took off the top and threw the spider on the bed. We all shot out of the room but Puse, without his crutches, couldn't move, and he literally shit himself as the spider climbed all over him. All the colour drained from his face and he let out a scream so high-pitched, it nearly cracked the windows.

His screams turned to curses as we fell about in hysterics outside in the corridor. The spider was in fact harmless but we didn't tell him, which made it even funnier when, next day, he informed us he could have died if the spider had bitten him.

After bidding farewell to Australia, we still had three matches to ride in New Zealand, with two of them at Western Springs. It was great to be back in Auckland, where I knew my way around the place and so acted as tour guide for the rest of the lads. I also met up with many old acquaintances, including Tuck, Paul Church and Terry Darwent, as well as a few old girlfriends.

Without Ivan Mauger and Barry Briggs, the Kiwis didn't have any riders to really trouble us and we slaughtered them 85-23 in the opening Test, when the track record was lowered on seven occasions.

I felt sorry for the hosts, who really tried their hardest, and all the home supporters who had paid good money to witness a competitive meeting. But we had arrived in red hot form, with myself and John Davis more than familiar with the Western Springs track. PC won all six rides and I followed him home for a paid maximum.

Then it was on to Christchurch, where I met up with Ronnie Moore and Graeme Stapleton, but Judith was nowhere to be seen, much to my disappointment. I later learnt she had got engaged, so it was probably best that we hadn't bumped into each other.

A different venue didn't change the one-sided nature of the match, as the Kiwis again capitulated by a margin of 60 points. However, the meeting ended on a sour note when PC overcooked it coming out of the bend, breaking his wrist and dislocating his collarbone, when chasing his second successive maximum.

Finally, we returned to Auckland to complete the series with another emphatic victory. Ten Test matches, nine victories and a contentious defeat. I would have settled for that on the outward flight.

Before we knew it we were back in England preparing for the 1976 season – and I couldn't wait for it to start. Although I had ridden well throughout the previous campaign, I had yet to reach the very pinnacle of the sport. Ivan Mauger was still the man, in my eyes, to try and emulate – the ultimate professional – but I also aspired to equal and even better PC's tremendous consistency and success.

While away, I had realised that I had to join the four-valve revolution to progress. My Jawa machine was quick but not as fast as the Weslake and Street conversions, so I bit the bullet, drew out £1,000 and joined the Weslake club. Now I had no excuses.

Chapter 10

Four-valve revolution

IT was the perfect marriage for me – and I'm not talking about my wedding to Shirley Atherton that was planned for August. No, what got me most excited at the start of the 1976 season was obtaining a new Weslake long-track engine mounted in a Jawa frame. It was time I joined the four-valve revolution.

But why a long-track engine for speedway? The long-track motor was fitted with a longer con rod and a smaller piston – we're only talking a matter of millimeters here but it gave the engine better characteristics, more of a power band. The standard Weslake speedway engine was more about top-end revving.

Even when I invested in a second Weslake, an ordinary speedway engine, I still continued to use the LT version for the bigger northern tracks like Belle Vue, Halifax and Sheffield, where I found the long-track motor had a better power band at the bottom end it, was particularly good when conditions were grippy and went quicker at top speed. Even on mid-size tracks, it offered more flexibility with the throttle.

Why a Jawa frame? Simple. I much preferred the Czech-built rolling chassis. Due to the inferior quality of the mild steel, it would bend and flex and was easier to handle when throwing it into the bends compared to the more rigid English frames.

I now had a machine that was as fast as anything on the circuit and I was confident that, barring injury, I could compete at the very top.

The Hackney team that started the 1976 season. Standing, left to right: Myself, Trevor Hedge, Dave Erskine, Keith White, Zenon Plech and Len Silver. Kneeling: Dave Kennett and Steve Lomas, with Barry Thomas on machine.

TV personality Freddie Starr brought some fun to pre-meeting proceedings at Leicester, where the Lions beat England. Left to right: Chris, PC, Gordon Kennett, John Davis, Doug Wyer and myself, with Chris Pusey in front of the comedian.
PC and me were on our way to a 5-1 ahead of Martin Ashby (3) and Reg Wilson in the all-England clash at Leicester until my bike reared and I crashed.

Len had kept his promise over the close season to improve the strength and depth of the squad and somehow persuaded the Polish authorities (bribed them with speedway equipment, I believe!) to allow Zenon Plech to return to east London for his first full British League season.

Our showman promoter wasn't afraid to give young, hungry riders a chance and had swooped for Keith 'Chalky' White, whose potential he had spotted when promoting at Crewe. Len was positive Keith could challenge for a heat leader berth.

The third main signing raised a few eyebrows, bringing the highly experienced Trevor Hedge back to Waterden Road, where he had ridden for the Hawks in the 1963 Provincial League, before spending over a decade starring for Wimbledon. He became the 'grandad' of a team of ambitious twenty-somethings.

Determined to erase the memory of a disastrous '75 season, Len informed us that there were incentive bonuses to be earned, which worked out at around £2,000 each if we were successful.

My personal deal at Hackney improved in '76 when Len paid me a £300 'retainer' and supplied a new engine, which probably cost about the same again. He also helped by topping up my hefty travel expenses, above the basic rate of whatever it was per mile.

Despite the league campaign opening with a narrow home 42-36 victory over Newport, things didn't go that well for me. Tormod Langli's throttle stuck open in Heat 7, leaving me no room to manoeuvre and I ended up in the second bend fence. Battered and bruised, I returned to the pits to learn that referee Peter Downs had excluded the rider who he thought had caused the incident – me!

With us already down in the match, Len went absolutely berserk but, thankfully, Newport team manager Maurice Morley stepped in to calm the situation by sportingly admitting that it was his own rider that was at fault. His gesture almost certainly cost his team the points, because we won the re-run with a maximum.

One of the most attractive fixtures of the season took place on April 6, when the English Lions team that had toured Down Under took on England's World Team Cup winners in a one-off match at Leicester. PC, who had a wheel in both camps, decided to ride with the tourists, which I felt just gave us the edge.

To be honest, I was not 100 per cent fit after falling at King's Lynn three days earlier, which earned me five stitches in a lacerated ankle, but I started well by winning Heat 2 with my partner Gordon Kennett. It certainly was competitive but after a fall in Heat 4, my race was run.

The medical men had their hands full in an eventful match with saw Ray Wilson, John Davis and Reg Wilson all end up in hospital during the meeting. PC's maximum decided the result in our favour but the anticipated clash of the season didn't live up to the pre-match hype due to the falls, stoppages and withdrawals.

About a week after the Leicester meeting I had a visit from a Manchester-based photographer, Gail Crowther, who was working for the *Daily Mirror*, who were big into speedway sponsorship in those days. They were running a feature called 'Daily Male', where each day female readers voted for a 'beefcake'-type picture of their sporting favourites to be published in the national paper – the male equivalent of the Page 3 model, I guess.

Gail came up to my parent's place on Warburton Road but for the photo shoot we went across the road, to a car park by some flats, so that she could take pictures of me posing in various positions in my leathers sat on my bike and clutching my crash helmet. It was quite embarrassing having to unzip my leathers down to my waist with Joe Public walking past. It just wasn't me at all and I was glad when she eventually put her camera away.

A few days later I went to Shirley's parent's house, where in the front room was a batch of A4-size prints of me posing. After my initial shock at seeing the results of my very short-lived modelling career, we all burst out laughing. They got the prints from a friend of theirs who was a cousin of the

Searching for the grip on the outside of Keith White and Poole's Pete Smith.

photographer. I think the *Mirror* also ran similar posey pics of Mavis (of course!) and Simmo, and possibly Tommy Jansson too. Admittedly, it was good publicity for speedway in a paper that was still selling a few million copies a day at that time but I never saw myself as a pin-up.

The Hawks continued their good start to the season with a win at Cradley, one of our happier hunting grounds, where I secured my first maximum of the season. My early form convinced Zenon and Keith to also purchase Weslake engines, while Barry Thomas tried a Jawa-Street conversion, as more and more riders jumped on the four-valve bandwagon.

However, our early season confidence would be dented during our traditional Easter Bank Holiday home and away clash with Ipswich in the Spring Gold Cup on April 16. The Good Friday meeting at Foxhall proved to be an expensive afternoon's work, despite scoring a dozen points in the match itself. During the second-half, my Weslake engine was damaged after a rocker arm broke – an early teething problem of the unit manufactured down in the East Sussex coastal town of Rye.

So it was a race against time to get it stripped and fixed for the return clash with the Witches at Hackney that evening. I phoned the Leicester-based Weslake dealer Dave Nourish, who picked up the parts, and with the help of Bert Busch, who looked after Zenon's bikes, they proceeded to try and get the job done before the scheduled 8.00pm start.

As pre-meeting parade time approached, the work still wasn't completed, so Len pulled a fast one to give us a few more precious minutes. He persuaded the referee and Ipswich manager John Berry to delay the start for 30 minutes on the pretext of allowing the remainder of the large holiday crowd time to get into the stadium. His little white lie didn't matter – we still hadn't got the engine ready for the off, so I borrowed Thommo's bike for my first ride (in which I pulled up). And then with my own equipment finally sorted, I fell when trying to pass Billy Sanders in the seventh. Ipswich riders won every heat and we were hammered 55-23 in what was possibly Hackney's biggest ever home drubbing.

I again failed to show for our league meeting at Newport but contributed to another away win at Wolverhampton, which kept us among the early pacemakers.

Being an ex-rider himself, Len understood why I – and many others, including world class stars such as PC and Malcolm Simmons, who also failed to turn up for meetings at Newport – hated the South Wales track. It wasn't just the awkward square shape that bothered visiting riders, the solid fence was also poorly maintained. Eric Boocock smashed his arm badly on a metal pole protruding from the Newport fence in 1973 and it was the main reason why Booey – who still bears the scars of that crash – retired the following year even though he was still the Halifax No.1 and reigning British Champion.

A lot of riders who did go down to Newport simply went through the motions and were just relieved to get away from the place in one piece for another year. That's no good for them or the public who pay to see two teams RACE. You want to go to every meeting to race 100 per cent and put in a good performance but it wasn't possible at Newport because it was too dangerous.

I rode there once in my early Hackney days but not in 1975 or '76 and it's fair to say I wasn't heartbroken when the Wasps pulled out of the British League at the end of '76 and dropped into the National League for what turned out to be their final season at that stadium in '77.

While Len wasn't exactly happy about me giving Somerton Park a miss, he never put pressure on me to ride there either. "It's up to you," he'd say. I suppose the way he looked at it, it wouldn't have done Hackney or him any good if I'd ridden there and got injured.

Throughout May I continued to pile up the points – especially on the away tracks, including a 17-point haul at Halifax. As I mentioned before, I loved riding at The Shay and on this particular night the track was fast, with deep shale in just the right places. Many of the Hackney boys preferred the smaller tracks but with the banking and plenty of room to pass on the big bowl, I could have ridden there all night.

I was grabbing the headlines but so was Len. Following an explosive meeting at Swindon, he had an altercation with ref Martin Palmer following Zenon's exclusion from the decisive final race for 'foul and dangerous riding'. Our team manager was furious about the decision and decided to pay Mr Palmer a visit in the Blunsdon officials' box, where he threw a punch and the ref went tumbling off his stool. Len's actions cost him a £100 fine and a month's ban.

On May 20, I guested for Wimbledon at Sheffield as a favour to Dons manager Cyril Maidment. I was standing in for their No.1 Tommy Jansson, who was back in his native Sweden riding in a World Championship qualifier. Sheffield was another favourite track of mine but my 15-point maximum and Dons' well-earned 39-39 draw was totally overshadowed when the tragic news broke that Tommy had crashed and been killed at Stockholm that night. The fatal incident happened at the same Gubbangen track, with its solid

Posing for a Daily Mirror photo shoot in a car park just wasn't me!

In the pits with Chris at Sheffield, one of my favourite tracks. The night I scored a maximum there for Wimbledon was marred by tragic events in Sweden.

Popular Pole Zenon Plech was hard but fair. That's Hackney machine examiner and pit marshal Ken Archer behind.

wooden board fence, where I'd ridden for England against Sweden the previous summer.

Many had predicted that the young pin-up was destined to be one of the best riders of all time. Sadly, we would never find out. Tommy's death shook me for a while – it brought home the risks riders take every time they go out to race – but it was something I had to put to the back of my mind.

Tommy was due to ride at Hackney in the Southern Riders' Championship round the following day and as a mark of respect, his rides at No.3 were left unfilled while his fellow countrymen, Bengt Jansson and Christer Sjosten, withdrew from the meeting.

I qualified for my second successive World Championship British Final after doing enough in the qualifiers at Poole and White City. The problem for me, however, was that the final was at Coventry again. Halifax, Sheffield, Belle Vue or Hackney would have suited me fine! Unsurprisingly, I didn't make the podium and finished well down the score chart after taking a first bend tumble in my opening ride.

Spectator involvement is a major part of any sport, some bend over backwards to support their team, but on occasions these passions can overstep the line. One such incident took place at Hackney in the league encounter with Wolves. Nothing untoward happened until the penultimate heat, when Zenon rode hard under Wolves skipper George Hunter as they headed into the third bend of the final lap. Hunter lost control, smashed into the safety fence and was excluded.

Zenon was a tough, but fair, rider and did allow his opponent some room for manoeuvre. But George, who was an old school rider and spent his time riding on the inside, had to move off his racing line and got into a bit of bother in the dirt. So when the bike picked up, he lost control.

Suddenly, from absolutely nowhere, an irate Wolves fan jumped the safety fence and confronted Zenon, before throwing a few haymakers. Fortunately, the supporter was frog-marched from the stadium before any harm was done and we all saw the funny side of what could have been a nasty incident.

In Denmark for one of the big international matches of the '76 season. On parade at Vojens are (left to right): Martin Ashby, myself, Malcolm Simmons, Dave Jessup, PC, John Davis, Gordon Kennett and team manager John Berry.

Victory over Wolves meant we remained unbeaten at home, although their No.1 Finn Thomsen caught the eye with an impressive 12 points. The significance of this would not become apparent for another 18 months or so.

We continued to punch above our weight in the league, with Chalky and Zenon improving match-by-match as the season went on. On July 23, the home record was to be well and truly tested when Belle Vue were the visitors. It was the night before our Chris was due to be wed and with me as best man, we were both warned to be careful and not take any undue risks by our parents and bride-to-be Jackie. Of course, we ignored their advice and gave everything in what turned out to be one of the matches of the season at Waterden Road.

We travelled down to the meeting together with both bikes on one trailer, along with Chris's mechanic Gary Miller, who agreed (he was bribed) to chauffeur us home after a good drink following the meeting.

Thommo won the first and gave us a 4-2 lead but we wouldn't be ahead again until the 12th, when Zenon secured his first ever British League

With PC in the pits at Vojens, the purpose-built track Ole Olsen had opened the previous year.

I should have been taking it easy the night before Chris' wedding day but that was never going to be the case with PC and Belle Vue in town.

Before my Golden Helmet match-race against Simmo at Hackney. Below: Despite leading in this one, I couldn't stop the super stylist from beating me twice to retain the title.

maximum by defeating PC for the second time in four heats.

Two points up with one to go, I was partnered with Chalky and faced Chris and Alan Wilkinson. The gate would be key to the outcome but for a change, my starts had not been the best on the night. Even so, I still didn't expect to be at the back as we approached the first bend. Chris and Wilkie blasted to the front and an exemplary spot of team-riding secured the 5-1 and a 40-38 away win. Our proud home record had gone but it had been a fantastic contest and a great advert for the British League.

After a quick shower, Chris and I headed into 'The Smoke' for a good session, which eventually ended at around 2.00am. Halfway home, Gary stopped for a quick kip and we eventually arrived back, still much the worse for wear, at around 6.30am. As Chris wasn't tying the knot until two o'clock that afternoon, we both slept off our hangovers and had a good six hours.

It didn't take long for Chris to be suited and booted but I was having trouble with my shirt and tie, and the fit of my monkey suit. Before we knew it, it was 1.45pm – and the church was 12 miles away!

As the main obligation of the best man is to get the groom to the church on time, I basically floored it, ignoring red lights, police cars or anyone approaching the zebra crossings, overtaking anything that was doing less than 60mph and covered the distance in 15 minutes. We arrived just as the bride was on her third trip around the block. Unfortunately, I couldn't stay for the reception. I was riding for England in Denmark the next day, so I bid my farewells and headed to the airport.

The match at Vojens was against a Rest of the World team, in front of a 20,000-plus crowd, and it turned out to be a classic. The England team, shorn of three main riders (Doug Wyer and John Louis were injured and Chris had other things on his mind) came within a whisker of upsetting Ole Olsen's side in his own backyard. But we just fell short, despite our best efforts.

It was great to be involved in important international matches as good as that one but the bread and butter meetings at home were the way you made a living, and I continued to rack up the points on the domestic front.

In a league as competitive as the BL, you had to earn your points but on rare occasions they were handed to you on a plate, like on the night we faced Reading on August 6, where I earned six points without having to beat an opposing rider. The match was heading for an exciting conclusion, with the scores tied with three heats to go.

Trouble started in Heat 11, when Dave Jessup and I were involved in a terrific tussle, which ended on the third lap when Dave attempted to pass me on the inside, clipped my back wheel and I hit the deck. Referee Terry Golledge took his time in making his decision but with Len chewing his ear off, there was only ever going to be one conclusion, and Mr. Jessup was excluded for unfair riding.

And that was that as far as the match was concerned. The Reading management and riders disputed the decision and withdrew from the rest of the meeting, also refusing to compete in the second-half, after stating that they had no machines left that were fit to race. It was an unbelievable decision and we raced the final three heats unopposed.

It was sour end to a night that began disappointingly for me when I lost the second leg of the Golden Helmet, 2-0, to Poole's Malcolm Simmons. Simmo had also won both races in the first leg at Wimborne Road but I didn't disgrace myself at either venue and, to be honest, it was an honour just being nominated to challenge the holder of the Golden Helmet in the days when the famous, old match-race title was staged on a monthly basis.

Defending champions Ipswich were romping away with the league by the time they came to Hackney in mid-August but, before the off, Len reminded us of our humiliating home defeat earlier in the season – and demanded revenge. Ipswich were something special, head and shoulders above everyone else, and they hammered us once again, this time by a 20-point margin.

Shirley and me on our wedding day . . . but I was off to Germany to race the next day.

AFTER appearing in the London Riders' Championship at Hackney on August 27, I enjoyed my last night as a single man with a few drinks in the capital. Next day I married childhood sweetheart Shirley at Our Lady of Lourdes catholic church in Partington, with the reception at Shirley's parents' house just down the road.

It was in the middle of the glorious summer of 1976 and the house was packed with neighbours, family and friends, as well as all the Hackney lads, who arrived in a minibus, courtesy of Len, who no doubt charged them for the privilege.

Chris did a much better job as best man than I did, and everything went to plan. We spent the wedding night in our new house, just a stone's throw away, but I had my priorities right – the honeymoon in Windermere would have to wait a few weeks. The day after the wedding I headed off to Germany for a grass-track meeting!

I bought our three-bedroom semi-detached house in Partington for £6,500 – ironically, it was built on land I'd ridden on as a kid on my pushbike before the houses were finished. It had a fair sized garden and I had a large double garage built, where I'd work on my bikes.

In chapter 8 I touched on speedway finances and this is perhaps a good time to revisit the subject. Being Hackney's established No.1 gained me an increasing number of open meeting bookings, which further enhanced my earning capacity. For example, I remember shopping in the Habitat store for home furnishings and paying something like £100 cash for a three-piece suite. I wouldn't say money was no object but I felt we were comfortably well off.

I treated myself to a Jaguar Mk10 – I'll tell you a funny story about this car and Barry Thoma later – and, after that, bought a Mercedes 220 from Taffy Owen, who was doing a bit of car trading at the time.

BUT money doesn't always buy happiness – and how much would I have given to have been one of the 16 riders lining up for the 1976 World Final in Katowice, Poland. I had a hectic schedule of six meetings in five days, so didn't travel out there to shout on PC, Chris and team-mate Zenon, but all the schoolboy pipedreams came true that day when PC beat Malcolm Simmons to win the coveted title in front of a reported crowd of 120,000.

For me, PC was always destined to win it. He was a proper racer, had great track-craft, was very aggressive and had a fantastic racer's brain. His hunger for the ultimate goal never diminished throughout his illustrious career. It was ironic and very fitting that PC became the first Englishman to win it since Peter Craven, his schoolboy idol, in 1962.

It had been a final packed with riders I knew, raced with, or against. Phil Crump finished third, Zenon fifth and Chris just failed to get into the top 10 in his first World Final. These were all riders I had ridden against and beaten, so I knew I had it in me to get to a World Final too.

Earlier in the '76 season I had been called up by Exeter to ride for them at Belle Vue as a guest replacement for their missing American Scott Autrey. My maximum included a win against Chris and two victories over PC and afterwards Falcons' skipper Ivan Mauger was full of praise for my match-winning performance. So as a relative youngster at 23, I still had a few good years to realise my own pipedream.

When writing the book, certain events or incidents always stick in the memory bank and one such incident happened in the home match with King's Lynn on September 17. I was very fortunate

PC, Chris, former Ellesmere Port rider Steve Hartley (far left) and myself were not auditioning for a part in The High Chaparral. This was a publicity shoot to promote the British Grass-track Grand Prix at Hereford Racecourse in August '76, where Ivan Mauger was billed as the 'Wanted Man'.

On parade before the '76 BLRC with Dave Jessup. Our previous close encounter led to me crashing and a Reading walkout.

during my career to be liked by the fans of all the clubs I rode for, and the Hackney supporters were among the best.

In this meeting the home support seemed in good voice and when I was pushed out from the pits approaching the tapes for my first outing, they seemed overly excited to say the least, pointing and shouting as I passed. Then I realised what they were getting so excited about. Just as I stopped to do a practice start, I felt a warm sensation between my legs, prompting me to look down at my engine . . . which was on fire!

The cause was a leaking fuel line – the spark from the electric box, which was right under the carb between the engine plates, ignited the fuel. Methanol burns with a light blue flame, so is very hard to see, but the supporters had spotted it and, thankfully, due to their prompting, I soon extinguished the flame and replaced the fuel line. Those supporters really did have eyes like hawks!

Another strange incident that I remember from the season came during the home match with Leicester towards the end of the campaign. I was on for a maximum in the 13th but to my astonishment, when Steve Koppe fell after only half a lap, the referee somehow allowed the race to continue, with rider, machine and three track officials still on the track up by the fence. This hindered any chance I had of catching (guest) Martin Ashby, as they were on my preferred racing line.

For once, at the end of the race, I stormed into the pits, grabbed the phone and gave the ref, M Bower, a severe tongue-lashing, using swear words that I didn't even realise I knew.

But I would have got more sense talking to the floodlight pylon, as he stated that his decision to allow the race to continue was justified. What would he have thought if one of us had ploughed into man or machine? It would be one of the worst refereeing decisions I experienced in my 16 years of racing.

After narrowly losing to Halifax in the quarter-final of the KO Cup, our last chance for silverware saw us at Monmore Green for the semi-final of the Inter-League Cup, with Hull awaiting the victors. Now if we had chosen to face anybody, it would have been Wolves, because our record against them in the past three seasons was exemplary.

It didn't start well, though, when Chalky and Thommo were comprehensively beaten, although we stayed in contention right up to the death. I was on for a five-time, but when Jim McMillan spoiled my chance of a maximum in Heat 12, it was effectively all over, and the trophy cabinet would remain empty for another season.

After the meeting I agreed terms for the following season to end speculation that I was after joining a club closer to home. I had been tempted to leave after an exhausting period during the season which saw me travel the length and breadth of the country but with no concrete offers on the table, I was more than happy to continue my career at Hackney.

Overall, the 1976 season had been a good one for me. I was pleased to finish eighth in the final British League averages (see chart), with figures of just over 10 points a match, despite an indifferent time with machinery. It was only recently pointed out to me that all seven above me that year finished in the top three on World Final night at least once in their careers, so I was there or thereabouts in

At Hackney's dinner-dance. I had plenty to be happy about at the end of my best ever season.

terms of what was required at domestic level.

In his end-of-season programme notes, Len Silver wrote: "It is mathematically impossible for Dave Morton to continue improving at the rate he has done so this past two seasons but he appears destined for a long run at the top." Alas, the Hackney safety fence would have something to say about that . . .

Hawks finished seventh out of 19 in the BL table but with a little more luck could have challenged for a top four spot – half of our league matches were won or lost by eight points or less, which proved great entertainment for our supporters.

Happy times off the track too. To complete the trio of weddings, PC tied the knot on November 20.

Always the professional, he organised their big day for after the season had finished. He had announced to the world that he was getting married to fiancé Angela immediately after his triumph in Katowice but when he became concerned that the ceremony could be spoilt by over-zealous fans and the media, he had the wrong church printed on the invitations, only informing the official guests a few days before the big day.

All three Partington boys were now married, responsible and doting husbands – and if you believe that, you'll believe anything.

1976 BRITISH LEAGUE 10-POINT MEN

	Matches	Rides	Points	Bonus	Total	Average
John Louis (Ipswich)	28	116	315	7	322	11.10
Ivan Mauger (Exeter)	32	136	368	6	374	11.00
Ole Olsen (Coventry)	31	136	360	14	374	11.00
Peter Collins (Belle Vue)	34	141	379	8	387	10.98
Phil Crump (Newport)	35	164	434	4	438	10.69
Dave Jessup (Reading)	36	152	385	11	396	10.42
Malcolm Simmons (Poole)	34	158	399	8	407	10.30
DAVE MORTON (HACKNEY)	**32**	**137**	**346**	**6**	**352**	**10.28**

IT'S A COLOURFUL LIFE . . .

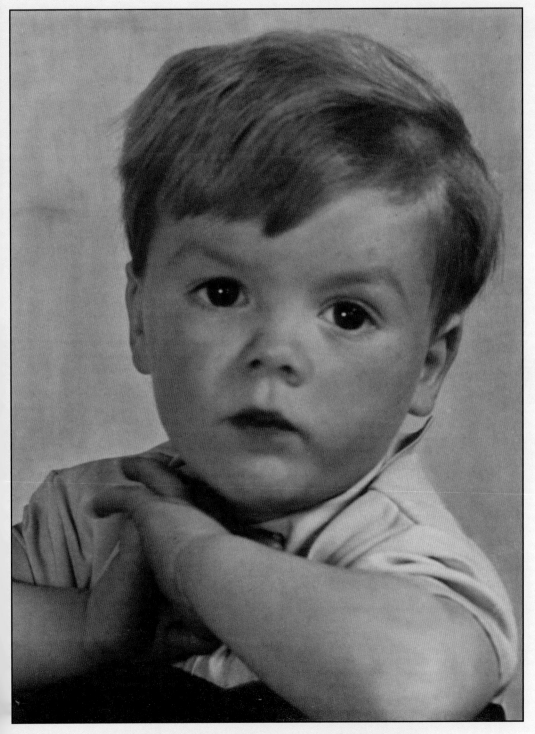

Where dreams of speedway stardom began for a young boy from Partington.

CREWE

Before our 40-34 league victory at Bradford in June, 1972, on our way to the double. Left to right: 'Myself, John Jackson, Dave Parry, Gary Moore, Dai Evans (on bike), Les Moore (team manager), Phil Crump and Garry Flood.

Right: Doing my best to keep up with fellow 'Hairy Bikers' Chris Pusey and Tom Leadbitter with the bushy sideburns.

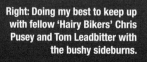

This was taken at Crewe in 1973. Left to right: Len Silver (promoter), Dave Parry, Keith White, Tudor Blake (team manager), Gary Moore and Garry Flood. Kneeling: Geoff Ambrose and myself, with John Jackson on the bike.

Even after I'd left Crewe to go full-time British League with Hackney in 1975, I still made an appearance on the front cover of the programme in the Kings' final season.

HACKNEY

The Hawks of 1976, my best season in the sport and a much improved one for the team, who leapt 10 places up the British League table to seventh. Left to right: Trevor Hedge, Zenon Plech, Keith White, Barry Thomas, Steve Lomas, myself and Dave Kennett.

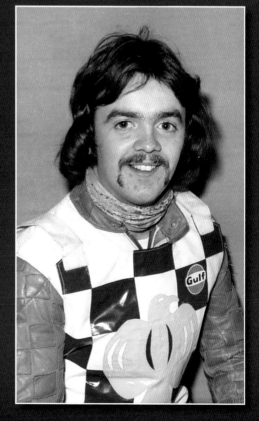

Waiting at the pit gate with Keith White in 1976.

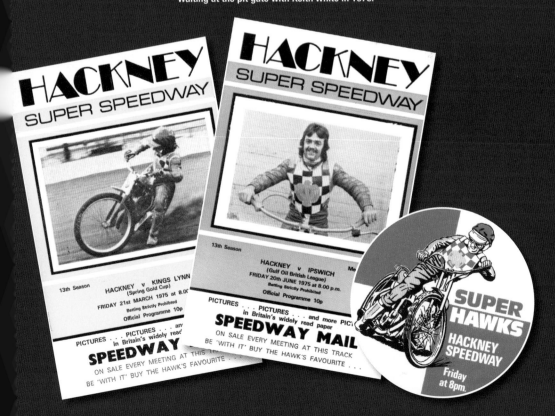

WOLVERHAMPTON

Wolverhampton in 1980, my last season at Monmore Green, when the traditional black in the club colours was replaced by blue at the request of our new team sponsor. Left to right: Myself, Hans Nielsen, Hans Christensen, Bruce Cribb, Ivan Blacka and Dave Trownson, with Jim McMillan on the bike.

SHEFFIELD

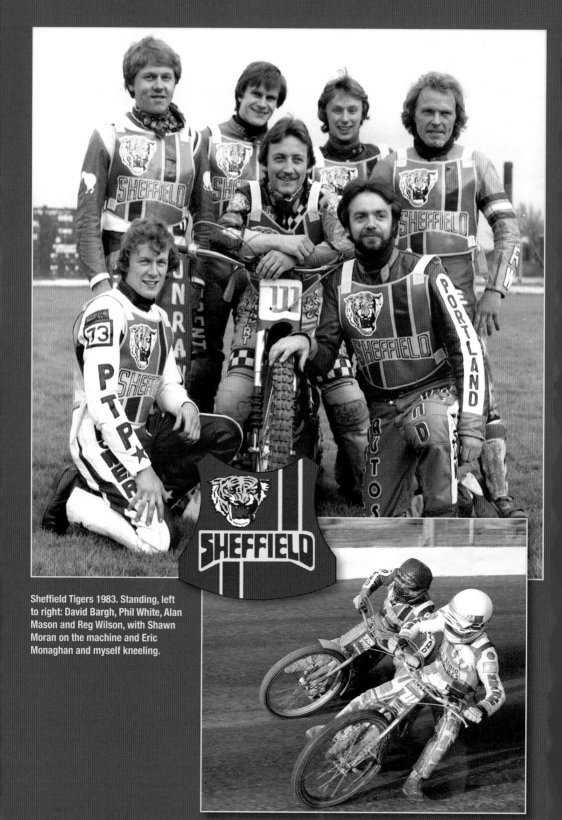

Sheffield Tigers 1983. Standing, left to right: David Bargh, Phil White, Alan Mason and Reg Wilson, with Shawn Moran on the machine and Eric Monaghan and myself kneeling.

Looking for the dirt on the outside of Halifax's Kenny Carter during a Yorkshire derby clash at Owlerton in 1983.

With my good pal Reg Wilson in 1984.

Keeping two of Cradley's World Champions, Erik Gundersen and Jan O Pedersen, at bay.

We were presented with the National League trophy at Poole in 1985. Standing, left to right: Phil Alderman, Stan Ward, Chris Bond (joint-team managers), Paul Heyes, Mervyn Porter (promoter) and myself. Front: Gary O'Hare, Miles Evans, Louis Carr and David Walsh.

The Diamonds were back in 1987, albeit with the red 'Ace' added! Left to right: Bernie Collier, Mark Courtney, Tom Owen, Gary O'Hare, David Blackburn, myself and Shane Bowes.

BROTHER CHRIS

In front of dad's garage at our parent's house with my KSS grass-track bike in 1974.

Another gating lesson for Our Chris, as I beat him and his Belle Vue team-mate Andy Smith to the
first turn at Hyde Road in 1983.

Before a Sheffield-Belle Vue clash in 1981.

Chris pulled on the Gunners racejacket again on Boxing Day,1985, when we rode vintage machines at Joe Owen's benefit meeting. It was the last speedway meeting staged at Thornton Road.

FAMILY

With Jamie, my first born son who we lost so tragically at the age of just three.

My second son, Rory, ready for his lunch.

Right: With daughter Kara, who made me a grandad and gave me two beautiful granddaughters, Isla and Kendall (above).

GRASS-TRACKING

Charging round the outside during the European Grass-track Championship semi-final in May 1979. But before the final, the injury jinx struck again and a broken ankle ruled me out.

PC and me taking a break between races at Altrip, Germany in 1976.

Out in front during the European Grass-track Grand Prix at Bad Waldsee, Germany.

Chapter 11

... Get me out of here!

ALTHOUGH I knew I had ability, during a self-critical analysis of my career so far I knew I had to address the mental side of my racing, so I could eek out that extra few percent required to take me to the highest level. I still needed to be more ruthless and aggressive. I had to develop a 'killer instinct'.

It was a great start to 1977. Towards the end of January I received news that I had been named Top London Rider of 1976 but due to the impending birth of our first child, Thommo picked it up on my behalf at the London Speedway Honours Ball, held annually at the Picketts Lock Sports Centre in Edmonton.

Jamie Morton was born on February 15 after Shirley went into labour the day before. But instead of pacing up and down the hospital corridor for hours on end awaiting the imminent birth, I pitched in with words of encouragement, telling her when to breathe, when to push and so on, which as you can imagine, were well-received by the mum-to-be!

With a new baby in the house, sleepless nights, endless nappy changes and a complete change in the way you live and operate, I couldn't wait for the new season to begin, so I could earn some extra money to pay for all the niceties that are needed for a new-born.

Watching captains Thommo and Edward Jancarz exchange pleasantries before our match against Stal Gorzow.

Tense moments before the pre-meeting parade at Hackney in April 1977, with Edward Jancarz (Wimbledon), Gordon Kennett (White City), myself and Chris leading the four teams in the 4TT.

Plans for the new campaign had been disrupted somewhat when Len failed to secure Zenon's signature for another season after his Polish club Stal Gorzow and the PZM blocked the deal. This, as it turned out, would have been pointless anyway, because in May he received his army call-up papers. Tony Featherstone, Vic Harding and Bent Rasmussen were brought in for what was predicted to be a long, hard season.

The season opener was against King's Lynn at The Wick. Rain had fallen throughout the day and was still coming down when the Spring Gold Cup match began but conditions only helped produce a great speedway contest. My 16 points – we were using R/R for Zenon at that stage – contributed to a narrow 41-37 victory and some welcome extra cash for the newly-extended Morton household.

Another home maximum, against Polish visitors Stal Gorzow the following Friday, was another tonic after failing to score on a heavy Wimbledon track in the Daily Express Spring Classic the previous night. I blamed all those sleepless nights at home for my rollercoaster start to the season and my bike not being set up properly (many of us were struggling to adapt to the new Roe silencer) – nothing, of course, to do with my riding!

April proved a hectic period as I mixed speedway with grass-tracking. At the start of the month, PC and I missed a big long-track meeting at Plattling, Germany due to a British Airways strike but I did make it to Amsterdam to win a speedway individual meeting at the massive Olympic Stadium.

I also represented Great Britain against Rest of the World in a unique international sand-track challenge match at Chasewater in the West Midlands, where we competed at high speeds on a trotting track more than 800m in length. All the top speedway and long-track riders were there, including six past and present world champions . . . PC, Barry Briggs, Ivan Mauger, Egon Müller, Ole Olsen (riding the new Jawa four-valve) and Anders Michanek. The two Scandinavian superstars dominated the meeting but PC and myself, having won my first ride, had bike troubles and we were well beaten by The Rest, 171-136, in front of a large crowd.

It was a pity that it turned out to be a one-off event at the Staffordshire venue. There were complaints over noise, so the bikes never appeared there again and the site eventually closed. Ironically, the M6 toll road, with its continuous drone of traffic, now goes right by where the track used to be.

By the end of April I was already feeling jaded by all the travelling and a lack of shut-eye at home. Long road trips to Ipswich, White City and Wimbledon, combined with three home fixtures, made me realise that even though this was all part and parcel of being a professional rider, a switch to a northern club could help my career. By spending much less time on the road, I would be more refreshed before racing and have more time to spend at home on bike preparation. But for now, I put the thought to the back of my head and concentrated on winning as many points as possible for my club.

On May 4, I set off for the trip down to Wood Lane in west London to take on champions-elect White City and for the first time in my career, I genuinely failed to make it in time. Having set off from home later than usual, I then suffered a puncture. By the time I got the car running again, I ran into heavy traffic. I crawled along for ages and arrived at the stadium around Heat 10, only to witness the final stages of a 61-17 massacre. We were already operating R/R for Zenon but had lost Thommo mid-meeting following a fall.

Of course, I felt partly responsible and sorry for the large band of Hackney fans that had paid good money to endure such an embarrassing one-sided affair, so for the home match against Poole two nights later, I was in the mood to put things right.

After edging out Malcolm Simmons to win the opening race, I passed Bruce Cribb to follow Thommo home for a 5-1 in my second (R/R) outing, Heat 3. But in Heat 6 my season came crashing to a spectacular halt.

Partnering Steve Lomas against Eric Broadbelt and Colin Gooddy, I missed the gate but had battled back and was challenging for the lead when the bike hit a grippy patch coming out of the second corner and started to lift. I struggled to gain control and with the safety fence looming large, I managed to get off the bike. Unfortunately, it was far too late to prevent me and my machine from smashing into it.

Just hitting the wire mesh fence at that speed would have been bad enough but just beyond where I hit it there was a concrete slab, about six-to-eight inches long, probably something to do with the dog track, and that's what did the damage to my right leg.

I knew I'd badly injured my leg and knee but not to quite what extent until I tried to stand, only to collapse in a heap because my leg wouldn't support my weight. Then, as the adrenalin wore off, I was hit with an excruciating pain at the top of the leg.

I was stretchered off by the St. John's people and taken to the first aid room at the back of the pits, where the track doctor was quickly on the scene. I refused to let them cut my new multi-coloured leathers made by Sportac, so they somehow managed to take them off in one piece to reveal the full extent of my injuries.

It was a bad break and my season was over.

Looking at this picture, I must have missed a few starts on Good Friday at Ipswich, where a snowstorm before the first race made conditions wet and tricky.

There was a big crowd at Chasewater to see the one-off sand-track meeting. In this shot I'm going wide to try and pass Kristian Praestbro.

Little did I realise at the time, this would be my final appearance for the Hawks.

The femur had been broken and I was taken straight to Hackney Hospital, or more like the local asylum.

I knew I was in trouble in the A&E department when the nurse had four attempts to insert a needle into a vein in the back of my hand, to set up the drip.

Now A&E, least of all one on the edge of the city of London, is not the place to be on a Friday night. Typically, this one was full to capacity with drunks who had simply had too much booze, or their over-indulgence had resulted in physical harm that required treatment. The overworked staff didn't have a clue and to make it worse, a guy in the side room opposite the bed I was eventually put in was screaming and shouting all night. Apparently, he had jumped out of a third floor window high on drugs and bounced off the pavement.

Although still in a lot of pain, very little was done to ease my situation, apart from a few painkillers, and they decided to wait until the morning before treatment could begin.

When Len arrived first thing to see how I was, I told him I wasn't staying there for another second, broken leg or not. Fortunately, he had already spoken to Carlo Biagi, a speedway injury specialist at Peel Hospital in Galashiels, Scotland and later that morning Colin Pratt – Len's co-promoter at Rye House and a former Hawks No.1 – arrived to take me all the way up there. The hospital staff in Hackney were none too pleased when I announced that I was leaving but we left anyway, for what would be one of the worst road trips of my life.

Just getting into Pratty's car was an ordeal but with pillows and cushions lodged around the injured limb, a fistful of pain killers and a bottle for me to wee in, we set off for the Scottish Borders. Every jolt of the car and bump on the road made me yelp out in pain until I managed to doze off for a few hours.

Three hundred and seventy miles later we arrived and I was sent straight to the ward and into a bed. Carlo, who had fixed up many an injured speedway rider over the years, was there to greet me and he soon assessed the damage and set about putting it right.

Minutes from disaster . . . I managed to get ahead of Bruce Cribb and Pete Smith to join Thommo at the front for a 5-1 in Heat 3 of our home match against Poole on May 6 but it all came crashing down for me in my next ride.

He decided to set up a weight on a pin through my knee to pull the femur bone into line but after a few days, with heavier weights used every few hours, the bone stuck to the muscle. The only way to remove it was with an operation, where the bone was then plated together using a stainless steel plate. This was a permanent fitting which would be in place for life.

Another option was discussed involving the insertion of a pin up the centre of the bone to help it knit together but this would have had to be removed at a later date, because another bad crash would have resulted in the bending of the pin and splintering of the bone, which would never heal properly again.

Carlo told me I would be out of action for around six months. I had been due to ride at reserve for England in the first Test against Rest of the World at White City five days after the crash. I was gutted to miss out on representing my country on such a big occasion but at least Chris, my replacement, kept the family flag flying by scoring a few points.

It was a massive body blow to miss the rest of the season – not only my speedway commitments but also a number of lucrative German grass-track meetings which I had lined up with PC.

It's easy to feel sorry for yourself when you're injured for a period of weeks or months, lying there bored stiff and counting the days and weeks until you are back on your feet and can ride again. But as hard as this may seem at the time, you also have to be thankful to still be in one piece and able to walk again. Others have not been so fortunate.

The Hackney track, with its safety fence lined by metal lamp standards, as many other tracks with greyhound circuits outside them were back in the day, was more dangerous than some simply because of the speed it generated. For an average-size track of 345 yards (approx 315m), it was very quick, probably a little too fast, for its long straights and relatively tight bends that provided more drive and speed off the banking.

Not that I can or would complain about the shape of the track or the way it was usually prepared, either by Len or his track curator Ivan 'Jack' Jackson. Me and Thommo always wanted plenty of dirt down to enable us to ride right out wide, within a few inches of the fence, and gain maximum grip and it was set up perfectly for us most of the time.

Another factor in my accident is that the bike wouldn't have lifted, I wouldn't have got the same extra drive, had we all still be on the two-valve Jawas or JAPS we were using a few years earlier, instead of Weslake, the Street conversion or the new DOHC Jawa that came out in '77.

The laydown GM and JRM engines they use today for the GPs and domestic Elite League and Premier League racing are too fast for most modern tracks, but can you imagine them around places like the Hackney track I rode without an air-fence. They would be lethal.

Once I got over the initial shock and realised that it could have been a career-ending injury, or worse, I started to think positively about regaining fitness and looking forward to getting back on a bike.

For two weeks I lay in that hospital bed and would have given anything to have been able to get up and go to the toilet. Using the bed pan to wee in was easy enough but trying to do a 'number two' lying down doesn't come naturally!

The first time I tried to stand up to use my crutches, I went all dizzy and nearly hit the deck. Using the crutches was another ordeal. As I'd also badly injured my knee, I couldn't bend my right leg at all.

I was discharged after spending three weeks in hospital and one of my immediate concerns was how I was going to make ends meet. Fortunately, I had taken out some speedway insurance, which all riders did, but I had also wisely invested in a few policies from the Combined Insurance Company of America. Their company representatives were always visiting the tracks touting for business and, because they did pay out, even in a high-risk sport such as speedway, most of the riders did buy policies off them.

Shirley was also working as a hairdresser, which brought in a few quid, and those marvellous supporters at Hackney had a whip-round which helped pay a few bills and bought some nappies and other essentials. Len also chipped in too, as well as family, and it's at times like this that you find out who your real friends are.

Boredom was another factor in the rehabilitation process but during the early days I rested as much as possible – even attempting to stand, or put any pressure on my leg, was very painful.

I always remember that the year of my accident was The Queen's Silver Jubilee year and the cul-de-sac where we lived staged a big street party. Not that I could join in the fun. I spent most of this red-hot sunny day resting on the couch feeling very sorry for myself.

I went back to Galashiels about once a month for a check-up and X-rays and, thankfully, the leg was healing well. Shirley took me a few times but after I was off the crutches and had the stitches out, I drove myself.

Now able to hobble about, I spent my spare time mucking about in the garage, sorting out my bike and other equipment.

Carlo had given me a series of exercises to ensure my knee would not seize up and I pushed myself through the pain barrier, determined to be

Hackney
SPEEDWAY
77

MEETING No. FRIDAY, MAY 6th, 1977 at 8.00 p.m.   15th Season
        Gulf Oil British League
8   v.   Magazine
        POOLE   Programme
                                              20p

fit and raring to go for the start of the 1978 season.

I did venture to Hackney a few times to meet and thank everyone who had supported me but it was hard work watching when you were desperate to be out there yourself. It was a long and rather uncomfortable journey to and from Manchester, even though the leg was much improved, and it was during one of those drives back up the M1 and M6 that I decided I wanted a move to a track much nearer home. Apart from saving myself thousands of miles a season, I wanted a home track that was more to my liking. Even though I had a good record at Waterden Road, I have to admit that it was never one of my favourites.

Eventually I plucked up the courage to inform Len that I was looking to move on. As you can imagine, he wasn't too happy but did try to persuade me to stay for another season with a really good deal – and that's when our relationship broke down. He was adamant I had to stay; I was adamant I had to go. Stalemate.

To be fair, Len had always treated me well. He even helped me once when I was caught speeding and got another three points on my driving licence. On the totting up system this took me to 12 points and with a ban imminent, Len hired a barrister to fight my case in a London court, at his expense. The barrister put forward a great case for why I should be spared a ban. He stated that as I was a professional speedway rider, my senses were much sharper and I was more aware than a normal driver. That I drove on average thousands of more miles than a conventional driver. And lastly, it would threaten my livelihood if I was banned.

The majority was bullshit, of course, but I played my part by looking suitably sad at the woman magistrate throughout his plea. Anyway, she must have felt sorry for me because she let me off a ban. Instead, she hit me with a hefty fine, which Len kindly paid on my behalf.

Although he did eventually accept the fact that I wanted to leave, he stipulated I could only go if I was replaced by a fellow No.1 from another club. Back in those days you signed a 12-month contract but were still tied to the club even when it expired, so I couldn't leave without my promoter's approval and a top rider coming the other way.

Len wanted a big name replacement to appease the fans and insisted on a rider swap, stating that no way would I be sold. It was a stressful situation   I could have ended up sitting on the fence with no club to ride for at all, which I couldn't afford to do.

I was hoping that Sheffield would come in for me but Tigers' No.1 Dougie Wyer lived in the steel city, so why would he want to travel all the way down to London every week?

There were rumours that Cradley and Halifax (not for the first time) were showing interest but the stumbling block was again the rider swap.

Then I heard that Finn Thomsen was looking to leave Wolverhampton after a fall-out with the management and Len was interested in his signature. He probably recalled how well Finn had ridden for Wolves at Hackney the previous season.

Wolverhampton was another track where I didn't really enjoy racing but I had been thrown a lifeline. So, reluctantly, I decided that this was my best option at the time.

It is always a sad moment leaving a club behind, especially the supporters and track staff. The people at Hackney were always behind me throughout the few years I spent there, even when I was having a bad time. I think they knew I always tried my hardest, and I know how they appreciated my efforts.

One of my biggest fans at Hackney was Tony McDonald, whose Retro Speedway company published this book. Tony Mac tells me he was only 13 when I first joined the Hawks in 1973 and that he used to wear a rosette with my picture on it. In more recent years we've met up socially for a few real ales on his occasional visits to Manchester and I know how much he treasures the couple of old Hackney racejackets that I gave him.

Whenever I meet up with other familiar faces at reunions, they still remind me of those fence-scraping days at The Wick. And when I see Barry Thomas it always brings to mind a hair-raising experience I had with him following a home meeting.

As we were due to ride down south the next day, Thommo offered me a bed for the night at the home his shared with his wife Barbara on the Isle of Sheppey. I followed him and Babs for a number of miles but then my Jag started to cough and splutter and eventually gave up the ghost.

"No problem, Mort, I'll tow you the rest of the way," Thommo said reassuringly, as he produced a piece of rope from his boot about four feet in length. By the time we had tied knots in it to connect both cars, the rope was even shorter but we set off after I advised him to 'take his time'.

We eventually reached the island where he lived in Kent and this is where the fun started. There were no road lights and I noticed that the speedo was climbing. So much so, we were soon doing 70mph. As I didn't know the roads and there were a number of unexpected bends, I was virtually standing on my brakes (the servo wasn't working due to the engine not running) in an effort to slow him down. I flashed my lights at him and shouted out of the window but all to no avail. I just prayed that he didn't brake suddenly.

But he was on a mission to get us home as fast as possible and after a terrifying journey we finally arrived at his place, with Thommo none the wiser about my ordeal. I crawled out of my car in one piece but with my arms and legs aching as though I had just ridden six successive meetings. I didn't know what was more knackered, me or the Jag. After a few beers we both saw the funny side but at the time I could have killed him!

Apart from that one painful night in May 1977 when I crashed badly, I have nothing but happy memories of my time with the Hawks and the people like Thommo who made it a special time in my career.

Dr Carlo Biagi was well known for treating many injured speedway riders and he got me back on track a few times.

Chapter 12

'Mister Comeback'

I MET Wolverhampton promoter Mike Parker and his front man Bill Bridgett at the White City stadium in Manchester to sort out my Wolverhampton contract for 1978. White City used to stage stock car meetings as well as dog racing and though the stadium has been pulled down, the facade at the front is still there. Whenever I drive past it, it reminds me of the time I went there to meet Mike and Bill for the first time.

As well as his interests in speedway (previously at Stoke and Newcastle, as well as Wolves and National League Edinburgh in '78), Mike was also prominent in stock cars and had a little, dingy office just off to the right after you went through the main entrance at White City stadium.

An outspoken former BSPA chairman and one of the main men, along with Reg Fearman, behind the formation of the Provincial League in 1960, Mike was the businessman of the Wolves operation, although he didn't look very businesslike when sat the other side of the desk in his donkey jacket.

Although a hard man to deal with, he was fair and we got there in the end. If memory serves me well, I managed to negotiate an improvement on my Hackney deal. I was a bit wiser by now. I agreed a three-year contract with Mike, who paid me £1,500 at the start of each season, plus an extra £4 or £5 per point above the basic rate.

I never had a problem with Mike over money he always stuck to the deal we'd agreed and paid up on time.

Bill Bridgett was the speedway man in the partnership and from then on it was him I went to if I

Moving to Wolverhampton in 1978 was really a case of taking my best available option.

On the outside of Steve Gresham, with my team-mate Knud Ellegaard and Tony Garard behind, during Wolves' match at Bristol.

had any issues. We saw very little of Mike.

Dave Parry, who I knew well from our days at Crewe, was Wolves' team manager and also prepared the track at Monmore Green at the time, so it was great to meet up with him and his wife Gail once again.

By winter time I was ready to get back on my bike and try out the injury. I'd been getting myself fit with regular trips to the gym with a neighbour who was an amateur wrestler, and the main part of my fitness regime was to rebuild the muscle strength in the right leg .

It was early January before I tried a few laps at Belle Vue, where I started cautiously but by the end of the session was going flat out without any real pain or problems. It felt fantastic to be back riding again, although next day I did suffer the consequences of my long lay-off. But that was a small price to pay, I couldn't wait for the new season to begin.

The pressure was on from day one at Wolverhampton, where I had replaced a crowd favourite in Finn Thomsen, but I was still battling back to full fitness. At each of my previous clubs, I had been the hungry rookie, a bit wet behind the ears, although willing to learn. Here I was not only expected to fill Finn's role as a heat leader, but do even better, especially if I was going to win over the home crowd. Time was not on my side, I had to impress from the off.

Carlo Biagi officially gave me the thumbs-up to resume in February and my leg had healed sufficiently for me to ride relatively untroubled, even though I could not bend my knee properly. I knew I would never regain full movement – just walking down the stairs was a problem – but it could have been worse, especially if I'd broken my left leg. I found by raising the seat a fraction, it took the strain off the knee when cornering.

After a few more practice laps, I soon forgot about the injury, although it continued to be sore, especially when riding rougher tracks, or taking extra rides. Other parts of my body also ached for a while, which was obviously down to the fact that I'd been out of the sport for 10 months.

Monmore Green was a place where I had encountered few problems. The track had been well prepared by Dave Parry, with plenty of dirt on it. It was definitely a racer's track, with slight banking on the bends, and was similar though slightly smaller than Hackney. I found it best to ride mid-track and follow the dirt out towards the fence – but not too far out, because there was an adverse camber right near the fence where you would lose ground.

In terms of riders, Wolves were very similar to Hackney, in having a strong heat leader trio but relied heavily on the lower order coming up trumps. The West Midlands club hadn't finished in the top half of the table for five seasons and in 1976 were just one place above Hackney, 15th in a league of 19.

Scottish No.1 Jim McMillan, a Glasgow Tigers legend, became a firm friend almost straight away. He was an experienced and dependable rider to race with and always on hand to offer advice or help with my machinery. He reminded me a lot of Dai Evans at Crewe.

The other heat leader was up-and-coming Danish star Hans Nielsen, who possessed bags of ability, an immaculate riding style and a steely determination which would see him win multiple World Championships and countless other major titles.

But it would be the contribution of the second strings that would decide whether we had a chance of competing for honours. Other team members included Steve Lomas, who had also left Waterden Road (possibly as part of the Finn Thomsen deal but I can't be sure on that), and a so-called superstar Polish rider Jerzy Kowalski, who at 24-years of age had supposedly finished fourth in the Polish averages.

The club shelled out a considerable amount of money to secure his services and thought they had made a real steal. Trouble is, he wasn't the rider they thought they had signed – he turned out to be 10 years older and 20 places further down the averages! He would fail to score in his first three matches and despite blaming his equipment, was sent packing.

The management acted quickly to fill the gap by signing young Swede Hasse Danielsson. Personally, I was disappointed that Soren Sjosten had left the club at the end of the 1977 season. Even though he was past his best by then, it would have been fantastic to ride alongside my old Belle Vue hero. When he retired in 1979 after the tragic death of his younger brother Christer, he sadly became an alcoholic and ended up on the streets of Manchester.

The 1978 British semi-final at Sheffield, where our Chris finished second overall to PC and I also qualified in sixth place.

The season started with the obligatory regional trophy and challenge matches but the signs were not good from the off when we lost at home to Birmingham and Belle Vue and away at Cradley. I recorded double figure scores on each occasion, so had settled in well, but after another home defeat to Swindon in our opening league match, the management were poised, with itchy fingers, to pull the trigger on Dave Parry's reign.

Things went from bad to worse with a poor performance at Halifax and Dave's job was hanging by a thread when we faced Coventry at Monmore on April 14. The management and fans demanded a vast improvement but they didn't get it and we were thrashed 51-27 by the side led by former Wolves hero Ole Olsen. This proved to be the club's worst home defeat to date since the formation of the British League in 1965.

The following week it was Wimbledon's turn to inflict yet another massive, 50-28, home defeat on us. Hans was out injured, leaving Jim and I to score all bar one of the points. That was enough for the management and Dave was relieved of his duties.

Whether he resigned before he was pushed, I don't know, but he was extremely successful at running his coach company, so probably didn't need the hassle of running a struggling speedway team anyway. Personally, I was very unhappy about Dave leaving. I had known him for a long time and he was one of the reasons I had decided to go to Wolves in the first place. The day he left the club, the track was never as good and became too slick.

Chris Harrison came in to steady the ship but apart from a narrow home victory over my old side Hackney, where Finn returned to a hero's welcome and secured a maximum, we continued to rack up the defeats, although admittedly the margins were narrow.

However, the long-suffering fans remained upbeat and were there in large numbers for the first

Although Monmore Green was a good track, I still wanted the wide, open spaces of a northern venue.

league derby at Cradley Heath. I had heard all about the bitter rivalry between the Black Country clubs and was told to expect fireworks. The supporters really did hate each other – it was more like a football match atmosphere on the night – so it was important that we put on a show for the Wolves faithful.

But despite providing seven heat winners, we were never quite in contention to take home the points and went down 44-34. It was a really hard-fought meeting, with all the riders putting in that little bit extra. I had a terrific tussle with Alan Grahame in one race, which I just edged. He was a difficult rider who could sometimes be 'over-competitive' but I gave as good as I got, and all the needle only added to the tension of the occasion.

Our lower order did show some improvement but it was one of the Heathens' reserves who caught my eye, a young blond-haired American newcomer by the name of Bruce Penhall, and it wasn't long before he would become a big star. It was on the recommendations of PC and Ivan Mauger that Bruce came over after they had seen him racing in the States. He was the typical handsome Californian rich kid but deadly serious about making it to the top in speedway, and Cradley proved to be the ideal place for him to further his career. The Dudley Wood track was fast, yet not too big, and gave you plenty of opportunities to pass. His success would herald the beginning of a whole host of Americans coming over to try their luck in the British League.

Jimmy Mac and myself ended a disappointing '78 season with victory in the Strongbow Best Pairs at Poole, where we finished just ahead of PC and his brother Les.

After 17 league matches we had just two points – yes, two, thanks to a 41-37 home win over my previous club Hackney, in which I scored 11 out of 12 – but things did get better during the second half of the season, when we started to turn narrow defeats into wins as our second-strings and reserves improved.

My own form was good enough to qualify for a third British Final in a row, after doing enough at Hull, Wolves and Cradley in the qualifiers, while nine points at Sheffield in the semi also earned me an unexpected England recall for the second Test against Australasia at Birmingham, where I won two races to help the Lions to a 10-point victory.

The British Final was again at Coventry and that meant Groundhog Day for me all over again. I struggled from the gate and with Brandon being a difficult track to pass on, I didn't threaten the podium. The main talking point of the meeting centred on PC, who had not completed any of his races due to engine failures. It was alleged that his bike had been sabotaged, so his fuel was drained and sent away for analysis, where traces of sugar were found to be present.

Looking back on my British Final failures, I should have been a lot fitter and far more aggressive at that level of speedway. But for this 1978 meeting, my desire to get to the very top had waned slightly due to the broken leg, which I realised meant I could never be 100 per cent fit again.

Of all the away fixtures, I was really looking forward to returning to Waterden Road. The Hawks were enduring another very poor season and, like us, were struggling near the foot of the table. But it was no fairytale return for me.

The last time I had ridden there was the night of my accident, so I was a little apprehensive when I

With the fast-rising Hans Nielsen and Hasse Danielsson in 1979.

lined up for my first ride. But as soon as the tapes went up, everything from that night was forgotten, as I held off Keith White and Ted Hubbard to win Heat 3. The home fans cheered the victory as though I was still one of their own, which made it a special moment for me.

I only scored two more points but Hans was flying and went through the card unbeaten. Despite his efforts, though, we lost the bottom-of-the-table clash by eight points. While in the pits I bumped into Len and we exchanged a quick "hello" but that was all. Everyone else there was friendly, though, and seemed happy to see me back.

At the start of September we won three league matches in a row, including a shock away victory at high-flying Wimbledon, so we approached the return derby with Cradley in a more confident mood than when we had faced them a few months previous. The crowd was massive that night, boosted by a few thousand visiting fans who added to a terrific atmosphere, and the vast majority would not be disappointed, in what turned out to be the match of the season at Monmore Green.

While signing a few autographs before the start a number of Wolves supporters reminded me just how important it was to end the season with Black Country bragging rights. Our '78 campaign had been very poor but the fans would forgive all for a victory here against their bitter rivals.

After finishing at the back in my opening outing, I redeemed myself by leading from the gate to win my next to put us two points up. The second string, so often criticised during the season, came up trumps in the next, with Edgar Strangeland and Brian Woodward riding a brilliant race to put us on course for victory. Cradley then fought back to within two points going into yet another last heat decider.

I lined up with Jimmy Mac against Steve Bastable and Kristian Praestbro. After an indifferent night at the gate, I timed this one to perfection and hit the first bend ahead. But as we started lap two, Jim, in his efforts to split the Cradley pair from the back, fell and was excluded.

So I faced the re-run alone with the hopes of around 5,000 Wolves fans resting on my shoulders. Fortunately, I made another good start and took the inside line to open up a commanding lead. And apart from a wobble on the final lap, when I slightly overcooked the bend, I held my nerve to secure victory. From the fans' reaction, you would have thought we had just won the league title. It was good, for once, to get the better of our near neighbours.

Having a laugh with Sheffield's Henny Kroeze and Neil Collins. I couldn't wait to join the Tigers.

As heat leaders we all had our moments throughout the season but all three of us wanted to be the top rider in the team. I had been No.1 at Hackney and was determined to end the campaign as No.1 at Wolves. We all managed an eight plus average, although Hans just shaded it in the end, with Jim and I half-a-point behind. This healthy competition was good for the team and was part-responsible for the improvement in results during the second half of the season. We finished third from bottom in the league table, ahead of Hackney and Birmingham, after winning our last three home matches.

I had defied the doctors and critics by completing the season and my efforts were recognised in the *Speedway Star's* New Year Honours List when columnist Eric Linden awarded me the title of 'Mister Comeback'.

Although reasonably happy with my overall fitness, I still visited Carlo Biagi at the end of the season to see if I could improve the movement in my knee joint while under anaesthetic. But, hard as he tried to bend it, it just wouldn't budge.

I was happy to ride another season at Wolves but didn't quite feel at home there. I had learnt my trade on a big track at Crewe and still had hopes that a big track northern club would come calling. Obviously, Belle Vue would have been my dream move but this was never really an option for as long as I retained heat leader status, what with the new maximum points limit that was about to come into effect and the fact that the Aces already boasted one of the most powerful twin spearheads in the country in PC and our Chris, so for now I was happy to stay in the Midlands.

Things, however, had not been happy at home with Shirley, and we had split mid-season. As well as my speedway commitments, I was also doing quite a lot of grass-track events in France and Germany, which took me away from home for most weekends. It put quite a strain on our relationship and we had slowly drifted apart.

She hadn't been happy with the marriage for a while and, to be honest, I was no angel. But I found out she had been seeing speedway photographer Mike Patrick behind my back and she decided to leave me to live with him in Oxford.

As a couple, we had got quite friendly with Mike during my time at Hackney, and I knew that he mainly covered the southern tracks for *Speedway Star*. But then he started turning up at places where he didn't normally go, especially when I was racing, knowing full well that Shirley would be with me.

Looking back, it was pretty obvious something was going on. Mike would often take a few pics at the start of the meeting and then, after a few races, retire to the bar, where the riders' wives and girlfriends would congregate, and that's where they became close.

He also knew when I would be away racing and would come up to Manchester on occasions when Shirley didn't accompany me. It got to the point where nearly everybody else in speedway knew what was going on, so eventually I confronted Shirley over the "so-called affair." She confessed straight away and told me it had been going on for about 10 months.

After waking out to live with Mike, she decided that our 18-month-old son Jamie could stay with me, saying that she didn't want to take him away from both sets of grandparents, especially as her mum and dad only lived four doors away.

But after a few months, she changed her mind and decided, instead, that she wanted custody – and that's where things turned ugly. There was no way I was giving up my son and have him living down south, so I hired a solicitor to fight my case.

After a few weeks of arguing and falling out, the final decision rested with a judge at the Manchester family court. It was quite a traumatic experience being grilled by the barrister, especially when he made me out to be unfit to look after Jamie due to my racing commitments.

When I knew that the judge was a woman, I thought there was no way she would see my side of the argument – but to the surprise of everybody in the room, she did.

It was a hollow victory, though. It not only caused a great rift between me and Shirley's parents, but both our families, who naturally took sides. In the end, I sold the house and moved to Wincham, near Northwich, just to get away from her parents. This meant that not only did Shirley not get proper access to Jamie, but neither did they. It was a very sad time, because Betty and Albert, her mum and dad, had been great friends and did a lot for us.

Shirley had a daughter with Mike Patrick around the same time and I lost contact with her altogether – until a tragic event brought us back together a few years later.

Mike never came near me again at speedway meetings – well, he rarely came up north anyway, only to see Shirley, so you won't find any pictures of me taken by him in old issues of *Speedway Star* from 1978 onwards! – but life goes on. He and Shirley weren't together for very long and when I was in Bydgoszcz to watch the Polish GP with Chris the other year, we had a friendly chat with Mike and agreed that what happened is now water under the bridge.

AS a rider competing in the top league of British speedway, still the biggest and best in the world at that stage, a certain amount of perks and trips abroad were part and parcel of the job. Even so, the phone call I received from promoter Reg Fearman in September was greeted with great surprise and pleasure.

"Hi Dave, how do you fancy a week in the Middle East?"

Reg and Terry Chandler, who was his general manager at Poole, were organising the trip, which would be sponsored by Rothmans who were keen to promote the sport in other parts of the world.

I didn't need asking twice and after arranging with my parents to babysit Jamie, I accepted the one-off retainer deal offered to all the riders involved and confirmed that I would be going.

Other riders to receive an invite were: our Chris, PC, Les Collins, John Louis, Dave Jessup, Reg Wilson, Thommo, John Davis, Tom Owen, Jim McMillan, Bernie Leigh, Craig Pendlebury, Ian Cartwright, Richard Greer and Neil Middleditch.

Due to transportation costs, only 12 bikes – mine included – were to be shipped out, so machinery had to be shared. We were paid before the trip, as a retainer so to speak, and were promised expenses and some pocket money.

It was mid-November when we flew out to Kuwait City for the two-day competition, which was to be held at the national football stadium.

At the airport, we were picked up by minibus and taken to the Messilah Beach Hotel – a top class, five star establishment, where a room cost a hundred quid a night. We were made to feel at home straight away with a welcoming meal of roast beef and Yorkshire pudding and treated like royalty. But the one thing that was missing, something we all craved for when we arrived, was alcohol, which was strictly forbidden in the country.

We arrived at the stadium in good time for the first day's racing and had our first look at the track. It was narrow but the surface, which was sand-based and laid on top of the running track, was nice and flat, having been baked rock-hard by the sun.

However, I wasn't really looking forward to riding. I'd travelled with what I thought was a heavy cold and by the time of the first race, I was as weak as a kitten. I felt so terrible that if I'd been back in England, I wouldn't have ridden. I basically went through the motions and scored a measly three points.

The next day was no better, although the track was much improved, having been re-laid in six hours by Terry and Eric Boothroyd. I finished with just five points overall.

Racing had been competitive but we took no chances. The only casualty was Jim McMillan, who clouted the fence on the home straight and bruised his ankle.

The team spirit over both days was fantastic. We all doped and oiled for each other, and acted as emergency pushers-off. Poor old Reg Wilson typified the spirit by continuing to loan his bike to whoever wanted it, even though it probably cost him the chance of winning, as it finally gave up on him halfway through the second day.

The undoubted idol among the crowd was PC, who had a narrow escape via the pits after being swamped by excited youngsters at the end of the first day's racing. Although the crowds had certainly been enthusiastic, they had been poor, with only a few thousand there on the first day and even less the next.

It was not as though the sponsors hadn't advertised the event. They had plastered Kuwait with posters, spent a considerable amount of money in newspaper adverts and had thousands of leaflets and programmes printed. One thing we did comment on as we lined up for the introductions before the start of racing was the lack of females in the crowd. There were none to be seen.

My condition continued to worsen, so a doctor was called and glandular fever diagnosed. I could do nothing but stay in bed and try to sleep it off. On one occasion the lads did their best to cheer me up by organising a darts tournament in my room but they all turned up absolutely arse-holed. Earlier in the day they had been invited to an American Air Force base and, not wishing to be rude, accepted the invitation to partake in the home-made moonshine. The darts flew around the room, with very few actually hitting the board, and it was a miracle nobody lost an eye, or even worse.

After a few days, I felt a lot better and managed to do a bit of sightseeing and shopping. Many of the shops sold just gold jewellery and it was all 22-carat – no nine carat rubbish here. There were also gold ingots on sale, which would have been a good investment if I'd taken enough money with me.

On our travels, the one thing that struck me was the amount of abandoned cars left by the roadside. Some had been bumped, while others had simply run out of petrol – Mercs, Rollers and BMWs were just left there to bleach in the sun, even though petrol was only about 8p a gallon.

We spent our leisure time swimming in one of the two pools at the hotel, or fishing off the rocks, and a number of the lads visited a camel farm. We also managed to get a side together and had a knockabout with the Kuwait national football team.

Despite the disappointing attendances, it was announced, before we stepped onto the plane for the journey home, that Rothmans were keen to run the event again the following year, with the possibility of further stints in Egypt and Saudi.

It had been an amazing experience and in spite of my poor showing, I was hopeful of an invite for the next trip, barring injury or another bout of glandular fever.

THE 1979 season was to be a big one for me personally and the club. Credit must be given to the management, who tried to strengthen the squad with a number of high profile signings but it brought little success.

They did improve things in the second string positions, with the arrival of Kiwi Bruce Cribb, who was welcomed with open arms by the Wolves faithful despite being an ex-Cradley rider, and later coaxing former favourite George Hunter back to Monmore from National League Oxford. However, their best piece of business was to persuade Hans Nielsen to sign-on for another season after he'd originally requested a transfer.

Another plus for the team was that I was feeling fit, fresh and eager to regain my status among the elite of the sport and wanted to get back to the level I was at before my broken leg. If I could stay injury-free and avoid a spate of mechanical problems, I was positive that I could give Hans a run for his money for the No.1 jacket, force my way back into the international set-up and maybe even reach my first World Final.

I was also keen to continue grass-tracking and by February had organised at least a dozen meetings abroad. I usually bought my speedway spares from Taffy Owen's shop, which was opposite the old Belle Vue track in Hyde Road, so I was delighted when he offered to help me out with spares for my KSS Weslake grass-bike, when I mentioned I was competing in the European Championship.

As most of these meetings were on a Sunday, they could easily be fitted around my speedway commitments, and I worked out that I could drive to them straight after our Friday home matches. The only ones that clashed were the actual championship meetings when you had to be there for Saturday practice but this only occurred once or twice throughout the season and, being FIM events, they took preference over speedway.

In April, I received a surprise phone call from John Berry to learn that I had been chosen to appear for England as one of the reserves against the England Lions at Leicester. Eight points from four rides, which included a win against Alan Grahame, Gordon Kennett and Dave Jessup, justified my inclusion and did wonders for restoring my self-belief and confidence. This was further boosted when I sailed through the World Final qualifiers at Poole, Wolverhampton and Ipswich and I knew I had a real chance of another British Final appearance when I was drawn in the semi at Poole – one of my favourite tracks and where I had top-scored in the qualifiers a few weeks previous.

It couldn't have started any better when I beat home favourite Malcolm Simmons and our Chris in my first ride. What pleased me most, though, was my third consecutive win, in Heat 10, when I battled from last to pip Ian Turner. Who said it was only Chris that could battle from the back!

I then came in second behind Dave Jessup who beat me from the gate, which meant I needed to win the penultimate heat to claim the gold medal and £200 prize money, although second place would still guarantee me a run-off with Jessup. I blasted away from the tapes and had victory in sight when the race was stopped after Craig Pendlebury fell. In the re-run I took full advantage of a mistake from Kevin Jolly to take the chequered flag and my place on top of the podium. This was another positive step forwards.

But another bad injury was just around the corner, another reminder of just how quickly fortunes can change in speedway.

On June 14, I made the journey down to Ipswich to ride in a new individual meeting called the Daily Mirror-Weslake Classic, with the joint sponsors putting up a new Wessie engine to the winner. I was confident of making it through the qualifying stages to the 16-lap final but the night ended on the second lap of my first race after Danny Kennedy and I collided and crashed out.

During the impact, my right ankle was squashed between the two engines and as I hit the deck, I knew straight away that I had broken it. So much for an injury-free season.

A broken ankle was not the worst injury in the world, it wouldn't cause me to miss the rest of the season, but I realised that there would be no British Final, no international comeback and the loss of some highly lucrative continental grass-track meetings, including the European final.

The next day I made the long trip back to Galashiels, where Mr Biagi was again on hand to greet me upon my arrival.

"Hi Dave, long time no see!" he quipped, rather sarcastically, as I hobbled my way to the

Jimmy Mac and Cribby gave us plenty of experience.

X-ray room, where it was confirmed that the ankle was indeed broken and would have to be pinned and plated, meaning that I would be out for a few months.

But after hearing how keen I was to ride in the European final, which was only a few weeks away, he came up with a plan for me to compete, with the aid of a light cast made from material similar to fibreglass. We painted it black and cut an old boot up to fit over the bottom of it, which covered my toes.

I travelled to Holland with every intention of riding. The ankle felt fine in the cast and to be honest, it felt quite strong. But one of the officials had noticed the cast and informed the track doctor, who told me that I would not be allowed to race.

Looking back now, it was the correct call – I could have caused more damage to the ankle if I had fallen but it was incredibly frustrating at the time, having brought my bike and all my other equipment over at considerable cost.

I was then left to twiddle my thumbs until mid-August and my return at Exeter, where I failed to score in three outings and was well off the pace. My ankle was quite sore at the end after taking a bit of a battering due to the track being bumpy.

Wolves had done quite well during my absence, maintaining a comfortable mid-table position, as well as knocking title chasers King's Lynn out of the KO Cup. Although there had been definite improvement, we were still a long way behind the teams battling for league honours. This was obvious when firstly Coventry came to Monmore and thrashed us by 22 points and then Hull did an even better job on us, inflicting a club record 26-52 home league defeat a week later. Ironically, in-between these two batterings, we had gone to Wimbledon and won by a record score, their biggest ever home league reversal. Hans had continued his rise to the top, boasting another 10-plus average for the season and there was a more solid look to the Wolves' score charts as we climbed from the previous season's 17th place to a more respectable 11th.

The 1980 season seemed a long way off as I set off on another Middle East adventure.

Ready for the Middle East tour at the end of 1979. Left to right: Les Collins, Terry Chandler, Joe Owen, myself, John Davis, Reg Wilson, Chris, Neil Middleditch, Jim McMillan, Craig Pendlebury, Bernie Leigh, John Louis, PC, Phil Collins, Eric Boothroyd and Reg Fearman.

On parade before our first meeting in Cairo, with Middlo at the front and me next in line.

Chapter 13

Sun, sea and sand

A T the end of the 1979 British League season, I flew out for the Middle East Masters series that was held in Cairo, Kuwait City and Abu Dhabi. Having ridden in the region a year earlier, I thought I knew what to expect. But nothing could have prepared me for Egypt, one of the most surreal, exciting, but frightening, experiences of my speedway career.

As we touched down in Cairo in 90 degrees heat, I spared a moment's thought for family and friends shivering back at home.

The 16 riders on this trip were virtually the same as those who travelled out there the previous year, apart from John Louis and Tom Owen who were replaced with Phil Collins and Tom's brother Joe. For this trip, we all brought over our own bikes and equipment, as sharing on a three-week, three-venue tournament was simply out of the question.

We soon settled in to our new home for the week, a luxurious five star hotel on the banks of the River Nile. I again roomed with PC and we soon got used to the room service with complimentary food and drink.

After a few days acclimatising, we were due to ride in a warm-up event (Cairo Championship) at the Zamalek Sporting Club, and next day in the first round of the Craven "A" Middle East Masters. There was, however, one drawback. Just three hours before the first heat was due to start, our bikes and all our equipment were still impounded at Cairo Airport, and it was only through Reg Fearman's negotiations, and help from the British Embassy, that they were released just in time for the start.

The track was narrow, more than 400m long and had been laid on the old running track. The shale surface seemed okay, although a bit rough and ready. What stunned us, though, was the size of the crowd – around 20,000, who soon got to grips with the racing format and went wild with delight at every passing move, or even any attempt to overtake. I had never seen anything like it and as the meeting progressed, they became more and more excitable. At times, the roar from the terraces was deafening. During the meeting they showed their approval by showering the track with various items, so they had to be told by the stadium announcer to refrain, as it was dangerous for the riders.

As for the result, Chris became the King of Cairo with a faultless five-ride maximum, which included a from-the-back victory over PC, who finished in the runners-up berth, although I didn't do too badly with a joint-fourth finish and a string of fast times.

It was at the presentation that things took a turn for the worse. Just as Chris, PC and Jim McMillan stepped onto the makeshift rostrum to collect their trophies, hundreds of excited fans spilled onto the centre green and attempted to carry off the prize winners.

We, too, were caught up in the melee. To be honest, it was quite scary, especially when grown men with beards and bushy moustaches tried to kiss you!

Somehow, we managed to fight our way through the crazed mob and back to to the pits, where the security guards slammed the gates shut, to keep them at bay. Nobody could believe what had just happened but it was only when the crowds dispersed that we laughed about the incident.

We were assured by the organisers that the next day would be different and stadium security would be beefed up. When we arrived the following afternoon, the car park was full of black security vans, with the windows protected by wire meshing. In the stadium, upwards of 2,000 riot guards, armed to the teeth with batons, tear-gas and shields, ensured that the crowd invasion would not be repeated. They sat on the centre green throughout proceedings and were an intimidating sight.

As word had spread about the previous night's racing, an even bigger crowd turned out (believed to be 30,000, with around 10,000 locked out), with many clambering onto the nearby roofs of office and apartment blocks in the hope of catching a glimpse of the action.

The track, which had cut-up quite badly the previous day, had been vastly improved, thanks to the hard work in sweltering temperatures by Eric Boothroyd and Pete Jarman, and their efforts were rewarded with a great night's racing.

It proved to be an exciting first leg of the Middle East Masters and it was Chris who again topped the score chart, with four wins and a second. I ended up in a run-off for the runners-up spot but Phil Collins beat me at the gate and kept his lead to the chequered flag. We were presented with our trophies, again on the centre green, and were relieved that the crowd stayed behind the barriers and behaved themselves. Our 2,000 'bodyguards' had done their job.

With racing concluded, we had a few days to see the sights of Cairo and the surrounding area before the next leg of the tour. One of the most unforgettable excursions was our trip to the pyramids, which were basically only a short taxi-ride away from the hotel. It was only when we walked up to them that we realised how big they were, and the effort which must have gone into the construction. For the more adventurous, we were allowed to go inside one to inspect a burial tomb but to get there you had to negotiate a narrow flight of stairs. It was impossible to stand up, so you crouched down all the way up to the chamber. Every so often there were little lay-bys so people descending the stairs could get past, as there was only enough room for one person at a time. It was well worth the climb and the chamber was beautifully decorated with drawings and inscriptions. But on the way back down the dark and claustrophobic conditions even got to me. With very little air to breathe, I was glad to get out and back into the sunshine. Some of the lads didn't fancy it at all, so stayed outside, but I'm glad I experienced it.

Riot police were called in to protect the riders from over-exuberant Egyptian fans in Cairo.

A view of the home straight and the vast crowd that came to watch us in Cairo.

Victory parade in Cairo with Chris and Phil Collins.

We also went over to the Sphinx and, unlike today, where it is fenced off, we were allowed to climb on it.

Chris and I then tried riding a camel. It was nothing like riding a horse, as someone had mentioned, because it was very uncomfortable and you were a lot higher off the ground. The worst part was getting off and it doesn't matter who you are, jockey Frankie Dettori or whoever, it was virtually impossible to make a dignified dismount. When the camel went down on its front knees, you needed all your strength to hang on, or basically you went arse over tit!

Another memorable outing was a river cruise on the Nile, fuelled with plenty of food and beer. It was fascinating seeing the small villages and townships lining the banks and crocodiles basking in the sunshine. Every now and again you would spot a dead hippo or buffalo float by.

During the river trip, a few of the lads wanted to throw John Davis in as part of his birthday celebrations but we were a bit worried that he would be eaten by a croc, or contract a deadly disease, so we waited until we were back at the hotel, where we chucked him, head-first, into the swimming pool at a party thrown by some of the British Embassy officials, who seemed quite shocked at our antics. But Mavis being Mavis, he'd been posing around the pool all night, so deserved his soaking.

As for Cairo itself, it was busy and hectic, a city where motorists drove around without any thought for their fellow drivers. No Highway Code here and you should have seen them at the roundabouts.

On a sightseeing visit to the pyramids. Next in line after me are (left to right): Reg Fearman, Terry Chandler, Barry Thomas, John Davis, Joe Owen, Neil Middleditch, PC and Harry Louis.

From Partington to the pyramids, Chris and me get ready to explore ancient history.

There were also a lot of beggars around, many of them filthy, who tried to sell you everything from trinkets to pieces of fly-infested meat. It was a pitiful sight and we were warned not to buy anything from them.

Another thing you didn't do was drink the tap water. Even though we all adhered to the rules by drinking only the bottled stuff, at some stage we all got 'the shits'. Fortunately, you only got them once. Within a few days you recovered and your stomach got used to the different food and drink.

We certainly made an impression in Egypt and there were rumours that an Egyptian league was being planned, staffed by British riders. Craven "A" officials were also delighted in the Egyptian experience and were looking into setting up future tours and branching out in Morocco and Tunisia. After an enjoyable week we packed up our belongings, said our goodbyes to the hotel staff and management and headed to the airport for our next port of call – Kuwait.

We had stayed in some plush hotels but nothing had prepared us for our week in the Kuwait Marriott. This certainly was luxurious accommodation but it wasn't a traditional five star hotel, but a beached former Caribbean liner. Quite literally, it had been plucked out of the sea and plonked on dry land. Everything had been retained bar the lifeboats. The swimming pool became our playground, where everybody – riders and officials, clothed or not – were pushed or chucked in, with Phil Collins, Bernie Leigh and Thommo the main culprits. Very childish, but great fun.

For this year's racing we had switched tracks and the organisers did us proud. The Qadisiya Stadium sand-based circuit was around the football pitch, so typically big and fairly wide. Dave Lanning in The *Speedway Star* summed it up perfectly when he described the track as 'a beautiful 50-foot-wide, sand surfaced track rather like a more sweeping Sheffield...' I loved the track at Owlerton, so knew I would enjoy riding this.

Around 5,000 turned up for the Premier Award meeting, which was well up on the previous year's attendance, and the track *was* fabulous to ride. You could really open up the throttle on the long straights. It was PC who again took the spoils when he beat me in a run-off (leading from the gate), after we'd both scored 13 points.

The next day, more than 10,000 fans turned out for the second stage of the Masters – apparently, the biggest crowd for any motor sport event in Kuwait – and they were treated to some thrilling cut-and-thrust racing. Chris reaffirmed his top position after a classic Heat 19, which saw him emerge victorious after a titanic struggle with PC, Dave Jessup and Joe Owen. For the majority of the race there was less than a bike's length between them before Chris dived inside Joe on the last lap to send the crowd wild, in what was later described as a possible contender for 'best heat of 1979'.

I finished just one point behind but faced Dave Jessup in a run-off for the runners-up spot. As hard as I tried to pass him, he blocked my every move until the final lap, when I found extra grip and drive and went past him on the outside to snatch a dramatic win. With two rounds completed, Chris led the tournament with 28 points but I was only two points behind in second, with Phil Collins third.

Another week flashed by and before we knew it, we were at the airport preparing for our flight to Abu Dhabi. Fog, however, delayed take-off for 16 hours and, being in Kuwait, we couldn't even console ourselves with a few beers.

After settling into another luxury hotel, Le Meridien, we spent a few hours practising on the track which had been laid around the football pitch at the Emirates Sporting Club stadium. The track in Cairo had been a bit ropey but more than adequate, while the one in Kuwait was an absolute joy to race on. But this was far from satisfactory – it consisted of a tarmac surface.

We were all a bit taken aback when we first saw it but riding on the thing was another story. None of us could get the back end of the bike to break away. Because there was too much grip, the bike simply wouldn't turn, so we asked the organisers to sprinkle about half-an-inch of sand on the corners, as well as the track leading up to the bends. Although this made things better, it was still too

The tracks provided a much smoother ride than the camels did, with Chris looking particularly uncomfortable.

dangerous when attempting to pass, so on the first night we put on a no-risk show.

On the next night, the final leg of the Masters tournament, we decided that the current standings would be the finishing order, which meant that Chris had won and I was runner-up. As it was, a few riders still fell off. It was like riding on ball-bearings going into the corners and several of the lads suffered with 'Abu Dhabi finger' – a painful injury when your finger was caught between the handlebars and the surface when falling.

Even though we had 'fixed' the final leg, Chris nearly scuppered the standings when he fell off in his penultimate race, before managing to win the last and nobody suspected a thing.

Abu Dhabi itself was a wonderful place but incredibly expensive. Among the guests staying in the hotel was Don Revie, the former England football manager who at the time was managing the United Arab Emirates team, who were in action on the same day as our first outing. On one occasion, I did bump into him in the lounge but being a Man United fan myself and him being the ex-manager of Leeds United, one of United's biggest and most hated rivals, I totally ignored him.

As for football rivalries, nothing in Abu Dhabi compared with the North v South speedway cup final, which was hastily arranged one morning, when the temperature was still at a reasonable level. We were determined to show them southern softies that us northern lads were top dogs and although we lost a keenly contested match by the odd goal in nine, some thunderous challenges resulted in a number of injured players, including myself. I suffered a sore shoulder when bouncing off the post while trying to tackle John Davis, much to the amusement of all participants.

As usual there were plenty of fun and games but, again, it was on the water where we had the biggest laughs. We all had a go at wind surfing and water skiing but a trip on a show boat proved to be an unforgettable experience. Dolphins swam alongside and we persuaded the skipper of the vessel to stop for a while when we were a few miles out, so we could swim with them, but the problem was a lack of swimwear. So there was no alternative but to jump in bollock-naked. Even the old ACU rep Harry Louis stripped off and dived in, to great cheers from all on board.

On one of the last nights before leaving the Middle East region we celebrated the success of the

Chris claimed first prize in Kuwait ahead of myself and Dave Jessup.

tour with a party. Among the party pieces was a hilarious ventriloquist act featuring Reg Fearman and our Chris. How it come about, I haven't a clue, but Chris, sporting rouge cheeks and playing the dummy, sat on Reg's knee, and they somehow pulled it off. Another funny moment was Phil Collins doing an impersonation of Briggo, who was a regular co-commentator for meetings covered by ITV. Phil got his accent and catchphrases to a tee.

Three weeks had flashed by and before we knew it, we were on our way back to Blighty, where sun, sea and sand were replaced by freezing fog, ice and snow. It really had been a stunning success. Six meetings, with over 70,000 fans witnessing the action, and as for Cairo – well, I will never forget that experience!

Chris and me are joined on the rostrum in Kuwait by promoter Reg Fearman.

The 1980 season brought a new team sponsor for Wolves but promoter Mike Parker's attitude or the club's fortunes didn't improve. Standing, left to right: Dave Trownson (one of the original Partington gang), Alan Morrison, Bruce Cribb, Mick Blackburn, George Hunter, Steve Crockett, Hans Nielsen and myself, with Jimmy McMillan and the Goodyear sponsor's rep on the bike.

The heat leader trio of Hans, Jimmy Mac and me all put in for transfers at the end of a miserable season.

Chapter 14

Jamie

OF all of the chapters in the book, this one was the hardest to write. One tragic incident towards the end of the 1980 season changed my life forever and still haunts me even to this day.

A few months after returning from the Middle East, rumours circulated that I could be part of a rider exchange deal involving Coventry's Alan Molyneux. In reality, though, Alan was never going to leave super-smooth Brandon to ride at a track where the surface was getting worse and worse since the departure of Dave Parry. Monmore Green was slick, bumpy and would cut up badly, because the shale they used was of very poor quality.

Whether I'd have agreed to the deal, I don't know, as Coventry wasn't the big, fast home track that I really craved. Although you needed a fast engine to compete at Brandon, it did tend to be a bit slick at times.

So I decided to concentrate on doing my best for Wolverhampton in the third, and final, year of my contract. For the '80 campaign Wolves had a new general manager in Mick Blackburn, who had left his role at Reading as stadium manager at the end of the '79 season and had previously been associated with Coventry for nearly a quarter of a century. Wolves also had the backing of a major tyre company and would be known as the Goodyear Wolves. But there were no real major signings, so we basically went with what we had from the previous season, although journeyman Reidar Eide did sign halfway through from Reading and performed well.

A badly bruised arm, sustained while grass-tracking in France, didn't stop me hitting three double-figure scores in the opening four Midland Cup matches, including a 15-point maximum at Leicester. Soon after, I racked up another 15 full house at Sheffield in a narrow KO Cup defeat. The track at Owlerton really was a belter.

By mid-June Wolves were struggling for league points and had suffered a series of home defeats against teams we should really have been beating. I didn't help matters when I received another injury when grass-tracking in France which would keep me out of action until the start of September. It happened during a club meeting near Bordeaux.

The event was meant to be decided on a points basis. Mike Beaumont and I finished equal first but because I'd beaten him during the meeting, I should have been declared the winner. However, the club president wanted us to have a race-off, so we both agreed as it meant extra money.

The track was only small, more like a speedway track, so I definitely had the advantage and was confident of taking top spot. Although Mike led from the start, I caught him down the back straight but instead of waiting until we got to the corner to pass him, I tried to go around him on the outside. As we went into the corner, I was travelling far too fast and as I was 'powering out', the bike picked up some extra grip, lifted and threw me off the back.

The first thing that hit the floor was my left arm, which snapped like a twig at the top.

I went to hospital but the cast they put on was completely useless, so when I got home I went up to see Carlo Biagi, who laughed his head off when he saw the French 'repair' job. He operated on me straight away, plated the break and then put on a proper cast.

Understandably, my Wolves boss Mike Parker was furious when he heard I'd been badly injured while grass-tracking and he made his feelings known in an interview with *Speedway Star*. But as a professional motorcyclist, I was free to earn my living from any form of racing I wanted to compete in. If he had paid me a large retainer to race speedway exclusively, then there wouldn't have been a problem. But he hadn't, so I told Parker that he could like it or lump it!

The only consolation of another long spell on the sidelines was that I could spend some quality time with my son Jamie, who was now three-years-old and developing quite a character.

When I was away racing there were always a number of babysitters I could rely on, although for the majority of time my parents did the job. And for a spell Shirley's mum Betty, until things got so bad between me and her daughter that she stopped calling round. Shirley herself saw Jamie only a couple of times up to this point – and always around at her parent's house.

The arm continued to get better and on August 25, I was due to visit Carlo to get the all-clear to resume racing again. Tom Owen, who was also recovering from injury, picked me up at around 6.30am, and I left a close neighbour to look after Jamie. The long journey to Galashiels passed by quite quickly as Tom and I chatted away about speedway and our trips abroad.

We arrived about four hours later and went for our X-rays. We were in Carlo's waiting room when he confirmed that my arm had healed well . . . but in the same breath told me that I had to go home straight away because he'd received a phone call informing him that Jamie had had an accident and was rushed to Leighton Hospital in Crewe.

We left straight away and the return journey was a nightmare, with all sorts of things going through my head. Poor old Tom didn't know what to say, so the journey was spent virtually in silence. He dropped me off at home and I rushed straight to the hospital, where I was told that Jamie was in intensive care on a life support machine, after falling down the stairs at home.

My parents were already there in a small waiting room, just off the ward. The doctors took me in to see him and he was lying there with his head heavily bandaged and his eyes closed. He was hooked up to various machines, with tubes helping him to breath.

Grass-tracking at Bad Waldsee in Germany in July.

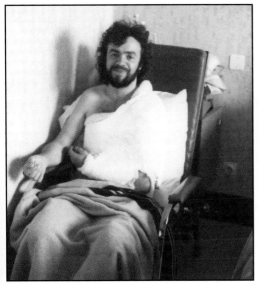

Sitting it out with a broken arm after crashing in France.

My first son Jamie, who died when he was just three-years-old.

I sat down at his bedside, took hold of his hand and just burst into tears. I prayed like I had never prayed before that he would pull through.

The doctors informed me that the next 24 hours would be critical and the tests they were going to perform would determine the extent of the brain damage.

I stayed for a few more hours, then returned home, although sleep was impossible. I went through all sorts of 'what ifs'. What if my hospital appointment had been the day before or the day after, or what if the club president in France had not asked Mike Beaumont and me to have an extra run-off? There would have been no arm break, no trip to Galashiels. I would have been at home, probably playing football with Jamie in the back garden, instead of him being upstairs.

I returned to the hospital early the next morning but there had been no change in his condition. I sat with Jamie most of the day, talking to him and reassuring him that everything was going to be okay. Occasionally, I would go for a walk down the lanes around the hospital to grab some fresh air, remembering the time when I had spent a few weeks in the very same hospital, in 1972, when I broke my arm riding for Crewe. How ironic that my son was in the same hospital – but in a far worse condition than I ever was.

Little changed over the next few days, which I mostly spent sitting with him, hoping and urging him to wake from his coma. It was now a waiting game – the doctors and nurses had done all they could.

On the odd occasion that I grabbed a few moments of sleep, I would awake, and for a split second think that the whole nightmare episode was just a dream and that everything would turn out all right.

On the fourth day the doctors came into the waiting room to speak to me. I could tell by their demeanour that the news was not good. They informed me that all the tests had been completed, there was no brain activity and all that was keeping Jamie alive was the ventilator machine.

They asked for my permission to switch off the machine and let him drift away. I nodded, unable to believe what I had just heard.

I went in to Jamie to say my goodbyes. It was heartbreaking to see him lying there, totally helpless and showing no sign of life.

I would never experience him growing up, never see him in his school uniform, or tease him over his first girlfriend.

The nurses were very good and just left me alone.

And then, after about half-an-hour, I kissed him on his cheek and left the room. I went outside for another walk, to gather my thoughts and fathom out how on earth I was going to cope without him.

The one thing that I regret over the whole tragic affair was that I had not informed Shirley that Jamie had been taken to hospital.

Things had not been good between us at the time, there was still a lot of resentment on my part about how we'd broken up, and we hadn't spoken for months.

But as I had custody of him, I was responsible for his welfare.

I rang her up to give her the bad news. As you can imagine, she was very upset – and with me for not informing her.

She visited Jamie at the funeral directors but we never spoke at the funeral, which was a very private affair. Apart from both families, the only other person that came was PC.

Thankfully, years later I got back in touch with Shirley and we met and sorted things out between us. Since splitting with Mike Patrick, she re-married and had a couple more children with her second husband.

I know how much Jamie's death really upset all my family, especially Chris who was due to ride in the World Final in Sweden. It couldn't have helped his preparation and, unfortunately, he didn't threaten the podium.

A week after the funeral, and probably too soon, I returned to ride for Wolves, where everybody was very sympathetic towards me. I needed something to take my mind off the tragic events off the track, although Jamie was never far from my thoughts.

I made my return at Sheffield on September 4, in a British League match, and won my first heat back, beating Eric Broadbelt in a tight encounter. But in the next two heats I was badly off the pace and finished pointless in both races.

I continued to ride until the end of the season but hardly scored a point. My slump in form wasn't just about what happened to Jamie. Without making any excuses, my arm was playing up again and giving me a lot of grief.

Wolves somehow avoided the wooden spoon (despite losing seven times at home), due mainly to Hans Nielsen's heroics. He tied with PC at the top of the BL averages and also won the Golden Helmet.

Things, however, were not quite right at Monmore Green. The team spirit had gone and the management didn't seem interested, so before the conclusion of the '80 season I slapped in a transfer request, along with Hans and Jimmy Mac. At the time we had no idea that Wolves were about to drop into the National League, although Mike Parker must have known what was happening.

He was a business man through and through and didn't seem to be interested in Wolverhampton Speedway at all. In fact, during the three years I was there, I don't think I saw him once – it was Bill Bridgett we always dealt with. No wonder they didn't spend any money on improving the track. Surely those loyal Wolves supporters deserved better.

A fresh start and a new challenge was what was required for the 1981 season. My experience at Wolverhampton had been a somewhat frustrating one and in that final season, through injury, loss of form and the tragic circumstances of Jamie's death, I had recorded a poor 5.36 average from 17 official meetings and not scored in nearly half of my competitive rides. The 1975-76 Ashes series when I was on the brink of breaking into the big-time, seemed a million miles away. I felt I was losing confidence and belief in what I could really do.

It had been an awful season. And the worst year of my life.

Chapter 15

New club, new wife

THE Christmas period is a particularly difficult time when you have lost a loved one but with the help of family, friends and neighbours, I managed to get through it, although there were moments when I had to find a quiet corner to compose myself.

Wolverhampton's decision to withdraw from the British League and enter the National League meant I had to find a new club for the 1981 season. Jimmy McMillan joined Belle Vue and Hans Nielsen was snapped up by Birmingham, whose promoter Dan McCormick had made a surprise takeover of Wolves.

Leicester made a tentative enquiry but, thankfully, I didn't have to wait too long for a proper offer. Again, though, it wasn't the one I had been hoping for. I received a phone call from the Poole management, who made me a more than attractive offer, including a house to stay in for the season.

I'd always gone well at Poole, it was one of my favourite tracks, but the travelling was the big downer on the deal and this time I was determined to hang on for a move I actually wanted. Fortunately, I didn't have long to wait – and it was an offer I wasn't going to turn down.

Ray Glover at Sheffield got in touch and I agreed to meet him at The Gun Inn, near Glossop, on the

With Halifax duo Craig Pendlebury (left) and Ian Cartwright, two pals from a previous New Zealand tour, just before my Sheffield debut in the Yorkshire derby at Owlerton, where I scored 17 in a 50-46 League Cup victory.

road to the steel city. A real speedway man, Ray's sons Carl and Les had both ridden and he was as enthusiastic about the sport as Len Silver. Ray was keen to build a youthful, competitive team with a family spirit, and one which would perform much better than the Tigers team who had finished rock bottom the previous season. Six riders had been shown the door, including long-serving Sheffield legend Doug Wyer, who was transferred to Yorkshire rivals Halifax.

To be honest, I was really excited about the prospects of riding at Owlerton and hoped that the terms of the contract would be acceptable. They were! Ray offered me £15 a point and a £2,000 signing-on fee. I wasn't going to turn that down and told him that if he could agree a fee with Wolves, I would be delighted to sign on the dotted line.

Within days Wolves accepted a bid of £10,000, which broke the club record fee paid to Hull the previous September for American star Shawn Moran.

For the first time since my early days at Crewe, I was at a track where I really wanted to be and felt at home. No disrespect to any of my previous clubs, but I had signed for Hackney after intense pressure from Allied Presentations. And I joined Wolves simply to get away from Hackney.

I had fallen in love with the Owlerton track ever since I attended a training day there one Saturday morning just after acquiring my first speedway bike in 1971. It was always well-prepared, even after the stock cars had battered and bruised the surface, with a good top layer of dirt on it. Like Crewe, you could ride it virtually flat out.

Sometimes when riding there in previous seasons, I would swap my Weslake for a Godden. The GR500 engine I had was really quick but difficult to ride on the smaller tracks when it came to cornering, as the weight balance was a bit top-heavy. Once you had leaned over, it was harder to get the bike upright again for the straight, but it was a good engine for Sheffield and the other bigger circuits.

I was now fully fit again thanks to our Chris who helped me through a punishing fitness regime, which included swimming sessions and squash. I felt at home at Sheffield straight away and following a few pre-season practice laps, soon felt part of the squad which included my old England team-mate Reg Wilson and the up-and-coming Californian Shawn Moran.

It also helped that Ray Glover and his wife owned a bakery and sandwich shop across from the stadium in Penistone Road. The sarnies we were fed after practice (and future home meetings) in the changing rooms were fantastic. No curled up, stale cheese or ham sandwiches here, but roast beef, salmon and chicken. They were bloody lovely!

I finally made my debut in a League Cup match against local rivals Halifax. Being the first home meeting of the '81 season, there was a bigger than average crowd and I was teamed up with Sheffield stalwart Reg Wilson for the first heat. Now the first heat of a new season is always special and it was a good opportunity for me to show the Owlerton faithful what I could do.

Thankfully, I made a great gate and led at the first turn and although John Louis briefly threatened on the second lap, I cruised home, at least a quarter-of-a-lap ahead. My dream start continued with three more heat wins (only Kenny Carter beat me, by a wheel, in a rerun Heat 12 after we'd all come to grief) and a match-winning victory in the last which nearly brought the house down.

After the meeting I did an interview for *Speedway Star* in which I stated my aims for 1981: to finally make a World Final (at Wembley), stay injury-free for the season and regain a heat leader berth.

It didn't take me long to achieve the latter, after top-scoring in the opening three meetings at Owlerton and collecting enough points on away tracks to secure me a top three spot.

My early season form hadn't gone unnoticed by the England selectors either, although it was still a surprise when I learnt that I'd been selected to ride against the USA at Belle Vue, after Kenny Carter withdrew through injury. Shawn Moran had been selected for the tourists, so I was looking forward

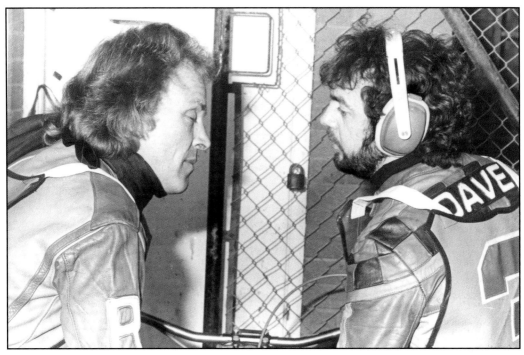

Am I listening to a bit of Rory Gallagher, or just protecting my ears from the unusually loud noise always generated by the bikes in the semi-enclosed pits area at Wimbledon? I had some great laughs with Reg Wilson but, on a more serious note (below), we're putting our 'race faces' on before going to the start at Sheffield in April 1981.

to taking him on. But just as I was about to confirm my availability, I realised that the meeting clashed with a European grass-track competition. To many in the sport, it was a no-brainer, and to represent my country again would surely be my decision.

However, as the grass-track event was an FIM meeting and the Test match was under the BSPA's domestic jurisdiction, the decision was out of my hands, anything sanctioned by the international tracksport controlling body took preference. Even if I'd chosen to miss the grass-track meeting, I wouldn't have been allowed to ride at Belle Vue anyway, so the choice was made for me (Ian Cartwright took my place).

The league season opened with an away fixture at fellow Thursday night track Wimbledon and as an extra incentive, Ray promised us all double points money if we won – and win we did, although the evening was marred slightly when Eric Broadbelt clashed with a number of home supporters, after he took out Dons skipper Roger Johns, who retired from the meeting with a badly bruised leg.

A few days later, we faced a tricky trip to Edinburgh in the first round of the KO Cup, who were languishing in the lower half of the National League. Ray had been true to his word and paid us the extra money for winning at Wimbledon – but promised to take it back if we lost this one.

I knew nearly all the Edinburgh team – Neil Collins, Dave Trownson and Chris Turner, to name just a few, but after an opening maximum from Shawn and Phil White, none of us expected such a spirited, dogged and determined effort from the home team, in what was turning into a most uncomfortable night.

Powderhall was a bit of a trick track – the straights were long and the corners tight – and the tie went to the final heat with us just two points ahead, with myself and Shawn facing Chris Turner and Neil Collins (who had ridden for Sheffield the previous season). I was far too eager at the start, snapped the tapes and was excluded.

Back in the Hackney pits ... in Sheffield's colours.

Reg stepped in and he led from the tapes but by the end of the first bend, Neil Collins somehow squeezed past him, and when Chris Turner followed his partner through the narrowest of gaps, the crowd sensed a famous victory as they roared their heroes home.

But that wasn't the end of the drama. Shawn then not only passed Reg, but both home riders on the back straight of the third lap, only to be re-passed by Collins. As the pair came into the final turn a drawn match looked a certainty, until Shawn's bike reared and he was sent crashing, with Chris Turner performing miracles to lay-down his bike without running into him. Reg passed the pair but deliberately came to a halt just short of the line, allowing Chris to re-mount and take the second place he richly deserved.

It was a great sporting moment but Ray Glover ordered Reg to cross the line to ensure victory for the Tigers. Reg's initial gesture was much appreciated by the crowd but following our promoter's wishes made no difference to the result. Quite rightly, the ref awarded second place to Chris, thus handing the tie to the Monarchs, which sparked incredible scenes on the terraces.

Would I have stopped short of the line to allow an opponent victory? Not a chance!

It had been a great night for the underdog but we took consolation from the fact that Ray didn't take back our bonus money earned at Wimbledon, so despite the disappointment of being knocked out of the KO Cup at the first hurdle, the bonus money stayed in the bank.

Sheffield's inconsistency continued when in the next meeting we won at Belle Vue in the League Cup, but sandwiched between the two cup matches, I for once, failed to make the British Final of the World Championships when I had a poor night at Poole in the semis.

As previously stated, there were very few riders I didn't get on with during my years in speedway but one I really did have issues with was Alan Grahame. We had another set-to during a league match at Cradley, where we resumed our hate/hate relationship from my time at Wolves.

Although the match points had already been settled when we lined up in Heat 12, I was determined to finish ahead of him and end a frustrating night on a high. We broke together and remained within a bike's length of each other for the first two laps. But as we went into the first bend of the third, and with neither of us giving an inch, we collided, and both were catapulted into the fence.

From the terraces and the pits it must have looked a really serious crash but, incredibly, we both dusted ourselves down and walked back to the pits – myself suffering from a sprained wrist and Alan an exclusion.

Our Chris also had a few problems with Mr Grahame throughout his career and had a number of ugly clashes with him. I believe one incident ended with Alan breaking his leg.

At the start of July I was again called up for England, this time for the third Test against Denmark at Coventry, but scored only a solitary point, although I rode with a certain amount of pain in my arm. On the injury front, up until the international, everything had been fine. But as the month progressed, I noticed the nagging pain in my left arm, the one I broke while grass-tracking in France the previous summer, was getting worse after every meeting.

At the gate, as the bike jerked forward, on a number of occasions my arm had locked. So with my gating definitely suffering, I went back to see Carlo Biagi and he confirmed that the screws had come loose and one of the plates had snapped in half.

Carlo advised an operation to put things right but this meant up to six weeks on the sidelines, so I delayed it until the season was over. I could still ride, although it felt a bit uncomfortable.

After a reasonable start to the campaign, Sheffield suffered what can only be described as a mid-season slump, losing 13 out of 16 matches, which included four defeats in front of our own fans. Reg was summoned by the management to explain what had gone wrong and, as the skipper of the team, was reminded that he was responsible for motivating the younger riders.

To be honest, this was a little unfair, because we'd all been responsible for the poor run. But Alan Molyneux had struggled the most, failing to maintain his normal high standards or adapt to the Owlerton track, and as a result he was put on the transfer list.

Thankfully, the hard work we'd put in during the first third of the season was not all thrown away, and we ended the campaign with a more-than-respectable 10th position in the league table, while on a personal level I just failed to top the Tigers' averages, finishing a shade behind Shawn, who completed another impressive season for one so young.

But more importantly for myself, I rode in all my team's league and cup matches in a season for the first time in my career.

A few weeks after the final meeting, I kept my date with Carlo and he put in a new plate . . . and gave me the snapped one as a souvenir.

Here we go again . . . Best Man Chris stands by while I make last-minute adjustments before my wedding to Sharen.
Below: The bride and groom with my parents.

AS an added bonus to my first season at Sheffield, I met a young lady who would eventually become Mrs Morton No.2. In May, Dave Beresford, who wrote for the Sheffield programme and the weekly *Speedway Mail* paper, had organised a fund-raising quiz night at the Hillsborough Working Men's Club as part of Reg Wilson's testimonial year. It was there I spotted this pretty young girl called Sharen Westwell, who was smartly dressed and came along for a night out with her girlfriends, Tina and Karen.

I did my best to catch her eye but she totally ignored me. When the night was all but over, I was about to leave when Reg took Sharen by the arm and told her that I fancied her. To my complete surprise, she came over and kissed me, before walking out without saying a word.

I thought that was that but at the next meeting at Owlerton I spotted her friends and asked them where she was. I was informed that she wasn't a speedway fan, so I arranged for them to bring her along to a nightclub, for another do we had organised for Reg, but not to tell her it was anything to do with speedway or about my involvement.

Sure enough, Sharen came to the club and I tapped her on the shoulder while she was getting drinks at the bar. She soon realised she'd be set-up but we chatted and danced for the rest of the evening and got on really well. It turned out to be our first date and we would marry at St. Bartholomews Church, Sheffield on October 24.

Chapter 16

Safety issues

THE 1982 season was not a good one for British speedway. In April, 18-year-old Aussie rider Brett Alderton sustained fatal head injuries during the second-half at King's Lynn, where he was catapulted into the solid wooden board safety fence after clipping the wheel of a fallen rider. He would die in hospital four days later.

Then in July, Reading's American rider Denny Pyeatt suffered a similar fate after colliding with a lamp standard on the pits bend at Hackney.

My old home track had been the scene of another tragedy three years earlier, when Hawks' favourite Vic Harding died after hitting a metal pylon just before the starting gate, in the horrific crash that left Eastbourne's Steve Weatherley permanently paralysed.

The deaths had many in the sport asking for measures to be introduced to make the sport safer. But amid falling attendances and many clubs struggling to make ends meet, the money needed to improve safety fences, remove protrusions and add padding around floodlight pylons just wasn't available.

PC was one of the high profile riders who aired his concerns in *Speedway Star,* stating that bikes were now so much faster and the tracks, many of them 40-years old, could not accommodate the greater speeds. "It's become more dangerous because we are following the dirt and racing in the danger area near the fences," stated PC.

His recommendations included the doubling of the width of some tracks, to provide more room for passing, which would end the 'follow-my-leader' processions down the straights. Eric Boocock was another leading campaigner for improved safety standards – and with very good reason after having his career cut short by a badly broken arm at Newport.

PC, of course, was right. By creating more room to pass and the ability to manoeuvre around potential incidents, it would not only make the sport safer, but provide more exciting racing that would help bring back the crowds. To be honest, given the number of unforgiving concrete and wooden safety fences (years before the introduction of the cushioned air fences) surrounded by lethal metal lamp standards positioned a matter of only a six feet or so apart, it was a miracle that more riders were not killed or maimed for life.

Throughout my career I didn't really have a track that filled me with dread but Hackney was always fast and had its fair share of accidents and tragedies. Newport, as I have mentioned before, was another that many tried to avoid and Exeter was also a bit dodgy, with its solid steel fence around a narrow but big track, although I always enjoyed racing there.

Bristol was another track that attracted a lot of criticism from riders but, despite its unique sand-based surface, I never had a problem with Eastville when I rode there for Wolves in 1978.

Hopes were high for the start of the '82 season but the League Cup campaign pointed towards another difficult season for Sheffield. Twelve matches in the competition resulted in only two wins and a crushing 54-24 home defeat to Cradley Heath – one of the worst ever at Owlerton.

Ray Glover, however, pulled a master stroke when approaching Ivan Mauger to ride for the Tigers following a long spell on the sidelines following injury. Ivan turned down the offer but agreed to join us in a coaching capacity. Having attended one of his training schools at Stoke in the early 70s,

I knew all about looking after my equipment and the art of gating, so to be honest the majority of the established riders at the club didn't really benefit much from his appointment, although the younger riders certainly picked up some valuable tips, tricks and advice.

I started my 10th season with good equipment and kit but decided to advertise in the club programme for a sponsor, to help with the cost of buying new parts and improving what I already had. Within days I had two good sponsors. Tony and Pat Ackland, a couple who moved to Sheffield from London with their company, were speedway nuts and bought me a new engine as well as other equipment. We became good friends away from speedway and I stayed in contact with them until they eventually moved to France.

The other backer was a chap called Keith Sykes who owned a tool hire company called Aytee's, who provided me with workshop accessories, such as a compressor and spray gun.

From the ad' I also acquired a new set of leathers from a car sales firm in Sheffield called Portland Autos, run by the friend of my mechanic Pete Murphy, so it proved to be quite a fruitful advert.

My fitness, however, was not near the same standard as my equipment as we lined up for our first meeting against Coventry. A win in my first outing and a further five points didn't hide the fact that the operation on my arm had still not fully healed and was not yet strong enough for the rigors of British League speedway. But somehow you adapt your way of riding and I managed stay fit enough to ride in all the league and cup meetings, even though my average was down a little on previous seasons.

The pain in my arm did subside as the season progressed but even today it still gives me problems. I don't have a great deal of strength in it these days. Sometimes, when the weather is cold and wet, I can hardly use it to even stir my cup of tea.

Promoting one of the sponsors I gained after advertising in the Sheffield programme.

The Tigers remained unbeaten throughout the '82 campaign at Owlerton, with only Coventry escaping with a point, but just like the early days at Crewe, the home form was not repeated away. We managed just a solitary win at bottom club Poole and draws at Eastbourne and Halifax, yet still finished fifth in the league table behind winners Belle Vue (who we hammered at home and should have won at Hyde Road), Cradley Heath, Ipswich and Coventry.

For the second season in a row, I was an ever-present, although my eventual average of 6.50 had dropped nearly one-and a half points. Even though I didn't realise it at the time, the injuries and the stresses and strains of top-flight speedway were starting to take their toll.

Shawn Moran was again the star of the season. He was fearless and a good team rider. Being No.1 and going out first, he would always pass on tips and inform us all of the condition of the track. He really was a top, top rider and the 1982 season saw him end it as Golden Helmet holder and runners-up (to Kenny Carter) in the British League Riders'

GREATER LONDON & ESSEX NEWSPAPERS LTD., FRIDAY, JUNE 15, 1979

Hackney cancel meeting following death crash

SPEEDWAY

There will be no speedway meeting at Hackney Stadium tonight following the fatal accident to Hawks rider Vic Harding at the Waterden Road track last Friday.

Following Friday's horrendous crash, the Hackney team did not feel sufficiently composed to contest last Saturday's scheduled Speedway Star Cup match at Halifax.

In deference to his riders' wishes, Hawks promoter Len Silver has offered the Yorkshire team — who were due to contest the second leg at Waterden Road tonight — a walk over in the competition.

East Ham-born Harding, 27, died as a result of a crash with Eastbourne rider Steve Weatherley, who suffered a broken back, during an Inter League Four Team Tournament.

The accident happened as both riders crossed the starting area to enter the second lap of heat 16 from which Hackney needed only one point to ensure qualifying for the finals of the tournament.

The meeting was immediately abandoned with the night's scores standing at: Hackney 39, Eastbourne 22, Wimbledon 18 and Canterbury 11.

Aggregate scores after four rounds of the tournament were: Hackney 115, Eastbourne 112, Wimbledon 110 and Canterbury 40.

"Vic's death and the terrible injuries to Steve were a tragic ending to what had been an exciting tournament" said promoter Silver.

Hackney are expected to contest the finals of the competition at Sheffield on June 24.

As a prelude to last Friday's ill-fated Waterden Road meeting and after having his Golden Helmet, series squared, former World Champion Peter Collins retained his match race championship with a 2-0 win over Scott Autrey.

● Vic Harding

My old track Hackney saw two fatalities in the space of just three years after I left. Home favourite Vic Harding was killed there in 1979, with Denny Pyeatt (below) paying the ultimate price in 1982.

Championship. He also starred for the USA team that won the World Team Cup for the first time in its history.

Dave Bargh was another rider to do well after joining from Newcastle, and his no-nonsense style made him a crowd favourite. Reg and Wayne Brown also finished with averages of more than six and for a few meetings an old associate, Zenon Plech, arrived on the scene, before a car crash in Poland just after he signed curtailed his scoring power.

On August 8 I had the honour of riding in Chris' testimonial. It was hard to believe that he'd spent 10 years with the Aces but his efforts were certainly appreciated by the Hyde Road faithful, who turned out in force on the night.

Testimonials in general were light-hearted affairs and gave the opportunity for riders to try out new equipment and techniques. I was in the True Brits team along with Chris (who top-scored), PC, John Davis, Reg Wilson, Steve Bastable and Les Collins, against a Rest of the World outfit which included Shawn Moran, Larry Ross and Phil Crump. I used the

meeting to experiment with a new type of carburettor, with different settings, but my bike went round Hyde Road like a brick and the carb was never to see the light of day again.

During the meeting a local lad, John 'Golly' Goddard, stunned the crowd with some amazing, death-defying motorcycle stunts and jumps. I had a word with him after one particular leap and asked him if he was ever worried about hurting himself. But to my amazement, he thought what he did was perfectly safe and that speedway riders hurtling around a shale track at 50mph with no brakes were the mad ones. A year later he jumped 16 double-decker buses at Chester races to beat the record held by Eddie Kidd – and he called us mad!

The main stand at the Ballymena Showground in Northern Ireland as it looks today.

There was also another meeting I remember well from the '82 season, when I was privileged to be asked to ride for an Ivan Mauger Select against Cradley Heath in a challenge match organised by Heathens' manager Peter Adams.

What made it so memorable was that it took part at the Ballymena Showground, some 28 miles north-west of Belfast in Northern Ireland and just south of Giant's Causeway on the Antrim Coast.

It's the home of NIFL Premiership football team Ballymena United and has also staged regular stock car racing since 1977 on the 440-yard oval that rings the pitch. Stock car promoter Robert Mathers put up a wooden safety fence around the car circuit and covered the tarmac base with a shale and sand surface.

On July 13, 1982, The Troubles in Northern Ireland were forgotten for one day by the 5,000 enthusiastic and friendly crowd who turned up to enjoy a close run affair in which the Heathens snatched a 40-38 win.

For the record, the scorers were: CRADLEY: Alan Grahame 12, Bruce Penhall 9, Erik Gundersen 7, Phil Collins 6, Lance King 3, Andy Reid 3, Bill Barrett 0. IVAN MAUGER SELECT: Kenny Carter 10, Ivan Mauger 8, Shawn Moran 6, David Bargh 5, Reg Wilson 4, Dave Morton 3, Steve Bastable 2.

Chapter 17

Strange behaviour

AFTER such an encouraging season, hopes were high at Owlerton during the winter months that with investment, the squad could be improved and a shot at the 1983 British League title was possible. But in all club sports, the team with the most money usually comes out on top, and that was the problem at Sheffield – there was a serious cash shortfall as the new season approached.

Ray Glover did his best to bring in a lucrative sponsorship deal but when nobody of note came forward, he had to make do with what he'd got. On the positive side, Shawn Moran signed on for another season and No.2 Dave Bargh was allowed to stay on loan from Belle Vue. However, Wayne Brown was an absentee as we started practice sessions, while Zenon Plech was refused permission to ride in Britain by the Polish authorities.

We started the new season minus Shawn, who broke an arm while grass-tracking, but I felt as fit as I could be, so did my best to fill the void with a string of double figure scores and some fast times around my home track, which earned me yet another England recall for the second Test match against the USA at Sheffield on April 29. At last it was all starting to come together for me again. My gating was sharp and I felt, certainly at Owlerton, that I could match and beat anyone.

But just before the Test, fate dealt me yet another cruel blow in a league match at Ipswich. It was my first outing in Heat 3 and I was off gate four. I made a reasonable start and headed into the first,

The friendly smiles disappeared when Chris and me went at it on track in those old Sheffield-Belle Vue northern derbies.

Being Sheffield's big individual star didn't stop likeable Shawn Moran from being a good team man too.

level with home rider Jeremy Doncaster. Unfortunately, he didn't turn and knocked me off, although the referee didn't see anything wrong and all four riders lined up for the restart. What happened next is all a bit of a blur (it was explained to me later) but, basically, what happened was an exact re-run of the original start.

Jeremy and I both arrived at the corner together and, again, he didn't turn, only this time I was put through the collapsible wire-and-wood fence and landed heavily on the concrete stock car circuit which surrounded the speedway track at Foxhall.

I was out cold. My helmet was split virtually in half and I awoke a couple of days later in Ipswich hospital, lucky I suppose to still be alive. The only thing I could remember about the meeting was getting changed before the off.

Our Chris and his mechanic Ged Blake picked me up the following week and I spent a few days at home recovering. I persuaded Sharen to take me to the Test match at Sheffield but she took some persuading because I'd been acting rather strangely. I was still not fully recovered and on the morning of the Test, she caught me trying to climb out of the house via a window!

Anyhow, along with a number of friends, we set out for Owlerton but, apparently, I talked non-stop throughout the journey, most of it mixed up nonsense. On arrival (according to Sharen), I decided to pull my baseball cap down so my ears stuck out. And with glazed eyes and a stupid soppy grin, it was a wonder the men in white coats weren't called for. If fact, Sheffield team-mate Phil White, who was in our party, was so concerned, he never left my side. He was positive that, given the chance, I would have jumped on a bike and lined up for the first race!

I was passed fit to ride in the home meet with Belle Vue just 17 days after the accident but my brain wasn't up to racing speed and it was quite scary – I was all over the place when it came to trying to slide into the bends.

After riding in Germany in a World Long-track Championship qualifying round, where I reached the semi-final, I again failed to score in the Owlerton clash with Coventry. And when I again struggled in my first outing at Leicester five days later, I realised that I had returned far too early because my vision was still impaired. My confidence was shot, so I decided to visit a specialist. The only cure he diagnosed was a complete rest, which I did before returning with a Heat 3 victory in the home romp against Eastbourne three weeks later.

The team, however, suffered a mid-season collapse and some really heavy away defeats, including a 62-16 thrashing at Wimbledon. The speedway journals and local press had a field day, describing our performance at Plough Lane as 'embarrassing' and the Tigers as 'an excuse for a speedway team'. The criticism obviously hurt but, in our defence, the squad had been badly hampered by a string of injuries, most notably Shawn, who broke a leg at Hackney while guesting for Eastbourne.

I was away riding on the continent when I heard of Shawn's injury. On the return journey (in Ivan Mauger's van), along with Reg Wilson, Bobby Schwartz and Ivan's mechanic, Norrie Allen, we decided to visit Shawn in Hackney Hospital. Not surprisingly, as soon as we arrived he pleaded with us to take him to see Carlo Biagi in Galashiels. It took us over three hours to persuade the London doctors to discharge him, after we confirmed that there was a bed available for him in Scotland.

Poor Reg had already driven in excess of 800 miles across Europe to Zeebrugge, then on to London, before facing a 400-mile trek to the Scottish Borders. He dropped myself and Bobby off, returned the van to Ivan, then picked up his car to complete the journey. Oh, and he carried Shawn into a Chinese restaurant after the Californian complained that he was hungry!

After ensuring Shawn was in the safe hands of Dr Biagi, Reg then decided to drive the 250 miles back to his Sheffield home, arriving there at 4.00am on Tuesday morning, which meant that he hadn't slept a wink since the Sunday morning. But that was Reg all over. He would do anything for a team-mate and we shared many funny moments.

On one occasion we were in Reg's van, along with Phil White, Dave Bargh (who was driving) and Wayne Brown, on our way to Swindon. We were making good time when suddenly we hit road works on the motorway and were down to two lanes. The car in front of us was going far too slow

New-look Tigers for 1984. Left to right: Maurice Ducker (promoter), Les Collins, Martin Hagon, Shawn Moran, Nigel Crabtree, Reg Wilson and Eric Boocock (team manager). Kneeling: Neil Collins and myself.

Eric Boocock was good with the riders because he'd done it all himself, although Neil Collins doesn't seem to share my amusement.

but wouldn't let Dave pass, so Reg jokingly told Dave to move him out of the way, which he did when he drove right up to this guy's bumper and gave him a solid nudge.

The other driver must have shit himself as he promptly moved to one side as we shot past him. Thinking back, I couldn't believe what Dave had done – he was a very quiet guy albeit with a funny sense of humour. After all, he was just following orders from Reg!

Another funny episode with Reg happened on one of Ivan's trips on the way to Germany. We were travelling with Dave Bargh, Shawn Moran, Wayne Brown and Ivan's mechanic Norrie in Ivan's van, along with all our gear. Someone had brought a few cannabis joints to smoke on the journey and before long we all had a fit of the giggles.

Eventually, we stopped at a service station for a bite to eat but as we were in the queue looking at the menu up on the board, Reg and I spotted something listed which, for some reason, sounded amusing, so we kept saying the name of this food (can't remember what it was now) to each other, over and over again. Each time we mentioned this word we would collapse in a fit of the giggles. And having the same silly sense of humour, this went on for some time. Other diners were staring at us in disgust, thinking we were either drunk or just plain stupid.

We went outside to try and calm down and about 30 minutes later, returned to order our food . . . but didn't dare look at the menu board or we would have started giggling like silly schoolboys all over again.

Three home defeats and a solitary away win saw the Tigers back down to 10th in the final 1983 league standings. Ray Glover had done his best to improve the squad and John Davis improved matters at the back end of the season when he fell out with the hierarchy at Poole and was loaned out to us.

But despite a raft of high profile guests, which included PC, Phil Crump and Dave Jessup, the team had gone backwards. New blood was required. But top riders, as stated before, cost serious cash and the coffers at Owlerton were empty.

What followed in the close season was another downturn in the fortunes of Sheffield Tigers.

ONE word can sum up seven days in the 1983-84 close season – and that's chaotic. News broke that Sheffield had resigned from the British League and been accepted into the National League, owing to their money troubles. There was a transfer request from No.1 Shawn Moran, who wanted to ride for a more successful club, and Wayne Brown refused to accept Ray Glover's terms for the new season.

With suitable replacements thin on the ground, and with the new season only a few weeks away, Ray reluctantly offered to sell the club to Shawn's personal manager Maurice Ducker, who owned the A&E Transport business in Sheffield. But his offer, believed to be around £80,000, did not meet Ray's valuation. Subsequently, Shawn was put on the transfer list with a world record price tag on his head, with Poole and Belle Vue at the head of the queue for his services. Wayne was another rider that could command a fair fee and he was the subject of a big bid from Exeter and Halifax, while I discovered that Coventry were interested in signing me and had apparently accepted Ray's valuation of around £12,000. Dave Bargh returned to Belle Vue and Reg Wilson received offers from a number of teams.

However, before the ink had dried on the NL application form, Tigers were back in the senior division following an improved offer by Ducker, who acted quickly by naming Eric Boocock as our new team manager. For me, it was a great appointment, as I'd always got on with Eric, who had been there and done it as rider, promoter and team manager.

The only problem for Eric was that he didn't have much of a team to manage. Given Ducker's close association with Shawn, the No.1 jacket was filled but apart from myself and new signing Martin Hagon (from Hackney), experienced riders were desperately needed if we were going to compete at a reasonable level.

Another plus for Sheffield was the switch back to their traditional Thursday race night, which suited me fine when I had grass-track meetings scheduled for the weekend. Friday's had been trialled

Leading home pair Preben Eriksen and Dave Cheshire on my return to Wolverhampton with Sheffield in 1984.

at the back end of the 1983 season but attendances at Owlerton dipped alarmingly. The club also signed a lucrative sponsorship deal with a local brewery and were re-named the Sheffield Stones Tigers.

Although the management had very little time to assemble a squad, countless phone calls and complex negotiations reaped rewards with the eleventh hour signing of Les and Neil Collins, who were available following Leicester's shock closure. They both seemed destined for Exeter at one stage but ended up staying in the north.

Neil's return to Owlerton in April resulted in Reg joining BL newcomers Newcastle on loan. I was sad to see Reg depart. We'd shared some good times together, both on and off the track, but he was soon recalled by Sheffield after we suffered early season injuries and it was good to welcome him back.

During the close season, I improved the strength in my arms and shoulders. I also invested nearly a grand in a new Godden engine, in an effort to challenge for a heat leader berth. I would be lying if I said it didn't bother me not being one of the top three riders at the club but I wasn't content in just being a second-stringer.

Things didn't begin well for me in the League Cup. A fall in my first outing in the opener at Coventry (where Gerald Short broke his leg in four places) ended my night, while two spills at home to Newcastle resulted in a shoulder injury that was aggravated by another fall against Cradley, which kept me on the sidelines for a few days.

A paid maximum in the KO Cup at Halifax halted a depressing run of scores and my form improved markedly when the league campaign commenced. Tigers won their first three matches, including a narrow victory at Exeter, and the unbeaten run only came to an end at Swindon on June 9, in a last heat decider, after we'd fought back from a 12 point deficit. I mention the date merely because we would not win another BL match until July 19 – a run of eight successive defeats, during which Janno sustained a broken arm in the defeat at Eastbourne, following a three man pile-up which included home rider Colin Richardson and myself, after I ploughed into the back of the two strewn riders.

Incredibly, the hastily assembled Stones Tigers finished a lofty fifth in the table (including wins at Exeter, Newcastle, Oxford and Halifax), a remarkable feat after all that had happened just a few weeks before opening night.

Sheffield's traditional end-of-season fancy dress 'do' was always a laugh. I'm looking a bit embarrassed as Reg Wilson inspects Shawn Moran's underwear.

Of course, a lot of the credit was down to Eric's skills as a team manager and Maurice Ducker's cash injection. To be honest, I didn't really warm to Ducker, who knew very little about the sport and even less about running an ambitious speedway team. He would try to interfere too much, instead of leaving Eric to do what he was paid for, but it was his money and he had a right to say what he really thought.

The undoubted highlight of the '84 season for me was the home victory over an impressive Ipswich outfit, who up to the end of August had been beaten just once all season. I joint top-scored with Les and Shawn and although I finished the season fairly strongly, my average had remained around the six mark. At one stage I'd dropped to reserve owing to a series of exclusions for tape-touching.

This rule had been brought in at the start of the season to prevent riders from moving at the tapes. As hard as I tried, I found it very difficult to adapt to the new rule and sit still on the start-line, after years of nudging the tapes to gain any advantage on my rivals.

So without making excuses, the rule curtailed my average and cost me an awful lot of money. In one twitchy spell I was excluded for tape-touching six times in 18 scheduled rides. And in the final match of the season versus Cradley, I was excluded in my first and final rides of the night – just for touching the tapes. It was a most frustrating way to finish the season and something I would have to cure, and quickly, if I was to remain in the British League.

On a happier note, 1984 saw PC and our Chris win the World Pairs at Lonigo in Italy. It was a tremendous achievement and I was immensely proud of both of them for winning the title for England, Manchester . . . and Partington!

Gunning for glory . . . the Ellesmere Port team at pre-season practice. Left to right: Louis Carr, Miles Evans, Joe Owen, Phil Alderman, Paul Heyes, myself and David Walsh.

Short but sweet . . . my reign as Silver Helmet holder lasted one night.

Chapter 18

Port in storms

TRYING to explain the goings-on surrounding the 1985 season would test a far greater man than me, but the crazy world of British speedway was just about to get even more bonkers. Results being changed at the death, a series of very poor refereeing decisions deciding league points, and a tragic injury to a big name ride that would overshadow our league championship celebrations.

Sheffield were determined to make a real push for the title and signed a number of up-and-coming riders, including Peter Carr and Steve Baker. Maurice Ducker made it clear that he was going to lower the average age of the team when he called me into his office before the season commenced. Although I stepped in for Martin Hagon (who was recovering from an operation) for the first four official meetings and averaged eight points, I was made available for a season loan, although retained as their No.8.

I really wanted to stay in the British League, where I thought I still had something to offer, but the complications of the 48-point rule, and the fact that all BL teams had sorted their line-ups for the season, made it virtually impossible to find a spot. The National League became my only option if I was to continue in the sport.

Long-serving Tiger Reg Wilson, who had been part of the Sheffield scene since way back in 1969, was another of the 'old guard' to be moved on, with Birmingham eventually winning the battle to sign him.

I was on a bit of a downer for a few days after coming to terms with the fact that after 10 consecutive full seasons in the British League, my top flight appearances would be limited. However, the top division had only 11 clubs competing in 1985 after five – Eastbourne, Exeter, Newcastle, Poole and Wimbledon – took what they believed was the more viable option of dropping into the second tier.

So while there wasn't the same level of signing-on fees, bonuses and points money available to riders in the National League, there was nearly double the number of teams and the extra rides would help make ends meet.

To earn a little more, I started up a car repair business, working from my dad's garage, and also dabbled in selling second-hand vehicles.

Barrow, Middlesbrough and Stoke were the first to show interest in my signature, and it was the Potters who made the first concrete offer. But then a phone call from promoter Mervyn Porter, who was reviving speedway at Ellesmere Port after a two-year absence, whet my appetite for a new challenge. Apparently, Eric Boocock had telephoned Mervyn about loaning Sheffield youngster Dave Walsh to the Gunners. Mervyn agreed – but only if he could take me on loan as well.

Although Ellesmere Port had been in the wilderness for a couple of years, Mervyn spent considerable money in assembling a decent squad, which included Joe Owen (from Newcastle) and Louis Carr (from Belle Vue) and he wanted me to complete what he considered to be "a formidable heat leader trio" and also challenge Joe for the No.1 jacket, to keep him on his toes. Mervyn was quietly optimistic that with me onboard he had a team that could bring silverware to The Wirral. A passionate fan, it was his enthusiasm and determination for his Gunners outfit to succeed which convinced me that the move was right, so I agreed to sign for the season.

I believe Mervyn paid Sheffield £2,000 for my services and he was clearly not afraid to splash the cash. Despite the National League's attempts to curb clubs' spending by introducing what they claimed was a strict pay scale, I can reveal that Ellesmere Port did bend the rules, as I'm sure a number of other clubs did in their search for success.

I believe I received a signing-on fee of £1,500, plus a bit over and above the standard points rate. Joe had been a British League No.1 for Newcastle the previous season, while Louis spent the '84 season in the top flight on loan from Belle Vue Exeter, so I assume they were on good deals too. Mervyn invested heavily on a strong heat leader trio.

So for the first time in more than a decade, I was riding in the league that had introduced me to the thrills and spills of British speedway. Not that it would be easy money. For this campaign, the addition of five former British League outfits meant a number of ex-BL riders, including some seasoned internationals, were now plying their trade in a division already packed full of young and hungry riders determined to make it to the top.

Reg Wilson and I were by no means the only ones who dropped into the NL in '85. Former Sheffield No.1 Doug Wyer left Halifax to team-up with Reg again at Birmingham, Gordon Kennett (World No.2 in 1978) rejoined Eastbourne from Wimbledon, while Poole's demise as a long-established top flight team under Reg Fearman saw Neil Middleditch become the new No.1 at Arena-Essex.

By the start of the season there was a clear and growing divide between the two leagues. While the shrinking British League now lacked variety, the National League broadened its appeal and presented a better public image. There seemed a greater unity among NL promoters that wasn't mirrored in the upper section. The lower division even set up its own independent office in Weymouth, where Alan Hodder had been appointed to administer the day-to-day running of the league.

To be honest, I was quite looking forward to riding for a team competing for honours and riding on tracks I hadn't been to for years, plus some that were totally new to me.

The opening meeting of every season is important to the home promoter who wants to put on a good show and see his team perform well in front of what is traditionally a larger than usual crowd, all dead-keen having been deprived of their speedway 'fix' for four-and-a-half months. At Ellesmere Port, the anticipation had been heightened by the fact that the locals hadn't seen a meeting staged there for two years.

So the last thing Mervyn Porter needed was for our eagerly-awaited curtain-raiser, a challenge match at Thornton Road against 1984 league champions Long Eaton, to be cancelled due to the state of the track.

A new delivery of shale had caused the problem and a number of the visiting riders complained about certain parts of the track, and the size of some of the stones strewn all over the circuit. Some home riders also had concerns but, personally, I thought it was okay to ride. Despite attempts to make the circuit raceable, around 30 minutes after the tapes should have gone up for the first heat, referee Colin Thomas called the match off, much to the annoyance of many in the 2,000-plus crowd.

I made my debut for the Gunners in a home challenge versus Stoke, although the meeting was again delayed due to heavy rain, which continued to fall throughout the meeting. Despite the difficult conditions, I enjoyed the perfect start with a four-ride maximum in a comfortable home victory. A few days later in the return clash with the Potters, I joint-top-scored with Joe Owen in another win which saw all three heat leaders score heavily.

We finally began the league campaign with another home fixture, this time against Berwick, but the supporters who again turned up in large numbers had to wait around in the drizzling rain, while riders, officials and the referee tried to sort out a problem concerning British League tyres being used by yours truly and Joe Owen, which were generally wider with a different tread than the NL tyres allowed.

My young pits helper Carl Stonehewer would go on to enjoy a fine career.

But Joe had been given clearance to use his tyres the day before after phoning a member of the Speedway Control Board, so the meeting finally started around half-an-hour late, with Berwick riding under protest. We easily won the contest – only Jim McMillan, in Heat 12, denied me another home maximum – but Bandits promoter Davie Fairbairn was confident that Joe and I would have our points deducted following their appeal and that Berwick would be awarded the league points.

I liked the big Thornton Road track, constructed around a football pitch. Although the straights were narrow and the track flat with hardly any banking, you could pass on the corners, as they widened in the middle, but it was essential to gate well if you wanted to rack up the points.

Mervyn was delighted with the victory but could not apologise enough to the Gunners' supporters in the local press for yet another disrupted meeting. The success of the new venture depended on the number of fans coming through the turnstiles and, sadly, these disruptions at the start of the season put off a number of the newer supporters. Attendances from then on were largely disappointing.

At Exeter, I was given another opportunity of putting to bed one of the most disappointing nights of my career, when I was nominated to ride against Nigel Sparshott for the Silver Helmet. While at Crewe, being an over-confident so and so had cost me my chance of winning the match-race title and it had rankled with me ever since. I wasn't going to fail again. I enjoyed riding the big-banked track at Exeter and I beat Sparshott at a canter.

As we were at Poole the next night, the riders and management stayed overnight at Ken Middleditch's Baillie House guest house, where we celebrated my victory with a few beers – and a few more. Halfway through the evening I put on the coveted Silver Helmet and kept it on until I went to bed in the early hours. It proved to be possibly the shortest reign in the history of the famous trophy, when I lost the title to Wildcats' Stan Bear at Wimborne Road the following night.

After our minor slump we then ran-up seven successive league wins, which included victories at Milton Keynes, Mildenhall and Canterbury, but the meeting that pleased me most in the winning sequence was our home success over Exeter where I hardly figured, after going over my handlebars in the opening heat and landing on my elbow. With Louis Carr also struggling with motor problems,

The home straight and first bend at Thornton Road, a track I enjoyed racing at.

Calm before the storm. Myself, Gary O'Hare, Phil Alderman, David Walsh and Joe Owen walk the Glasgow track before a controversial match that ultimately decided the league title.

the unbeaten home record looked in jeopardy. But it was the impressive performance of the second-strings, who helped grind out the victory, which convinced me that we had a real chance of the title.

It was not just all about having good heat leaders if you were to challenge for the silverware, and this match was a prime example of their importance. Those riding at No.2 and No.4 had to contribute and the Gunners had a number who had already proved they were going to score consistently, which included Dave Walsh, Gary O'Hare, Miles Evans, Phil Alderman and Joe's younger brother, Richie.

I returned briefly to Sheffield to ride in a League Cup match against Wolves, where I scored paid 11, and in a three team tournament at Halifax. But even though I'd only been away a short time, I didn't quite feel part of the set-up. I didn't really get on with Maurice Ducker but at the end of the day, it was an opportunity to show a few folk that I could still compete in the top division.

Part way through the campaign, junior grass-tracker Carl Stonehewer joined my pits team at Ellesmere Port. Even though he was only 13-years-old, he was keen to develop his mechanical skills. After meetings, it was the norm for most of the team, staff and management to head across the road to 'The Gunners' pub for some liquid refreshment, before heading home. It was a good way of discussing the night's racing and talking to the fans – but it was a common sight to see young Carl fast asleep in a corner somewhere in the pub after one too many. Carl, though, took his speedway seriously and would later carve out a really successful career, which included appearing in three successive Grand Prix series.

One night in The Gunners I was at the bar buying a round of drinks when Chris Pusey – my British Lions skipper from 10 years earlier – came in. I bought him a pint but before I had even collected my change, old 'Bert' slapped his empty pint pot on the bar and ordered another!

As the season progressed Middlesbrough and Poole emerged as our biggest rivals. At the start of July we made the journey up to Teesside, where we were narrowly beaten after making a poor start. The next night however, we had the chance to exact revenge in a match we simply couldn't lose if we were to remain genuine title contenders. Mervyn and co-team managers Stan Ward and Chris Bond demanded a big victory and we didn't disappoint, with home riders winning 10 of the 13 heats in a comfortable 48-29 victory, which kept us right on their shirt-tails. After my poor showing the previous night, where I was excluded twice for touching the tapes at Cleveland Park, I top-scored, although the star of the night was reserve Gary O'Hare, who weighed in with nine.

It was a really important win, a clear statement of intent, but following another big home success over Wimbledon, we faced another trio of tricky southern meetings in successive days against teams with impressive home records, which would again tax both men and machinery.

For this trip we stayed in an east London hotel (in Forest Gate, I think) and unlike today's professional athletes who would prepare properly with decent food and drink, we gorged ourselves on fish and chips, burgers, curries and kebabs, laced with a volcanic chilli sauce, courtesy of Joe Owen, all washed down with a few beers. Joe, however, was the true pro among us. He wouldn't go to bed until his bike was spotless and properly prepared for the following meeting.

Wimbledon was the first port of call but they were just too strong for us and gained their own revenge with a 10-point win. The next stop was Arena-Essex and for anybody who has never been there, the track was quite unique in British speedway because it had no safety fence for the first few years the Hammers rode at the Thurrock raceway. To be honest, it wasn't one of my favourite tracks. It was hard to gauge your racing line – you could actually go off the outside of the track, on to the stock car circuit, and rejoin the shale, which to me wasn't proper racing. Anyway, excuses aside, we went down by two points, which meant that the final match, at Hackney of all places, was now of paramount importance.

Hackney had dropped out of British speedway at the end of the 1983 season but Crayford had moved into Waterden Road to become Hackney Kestrels, although my old mate Barry Thomas was

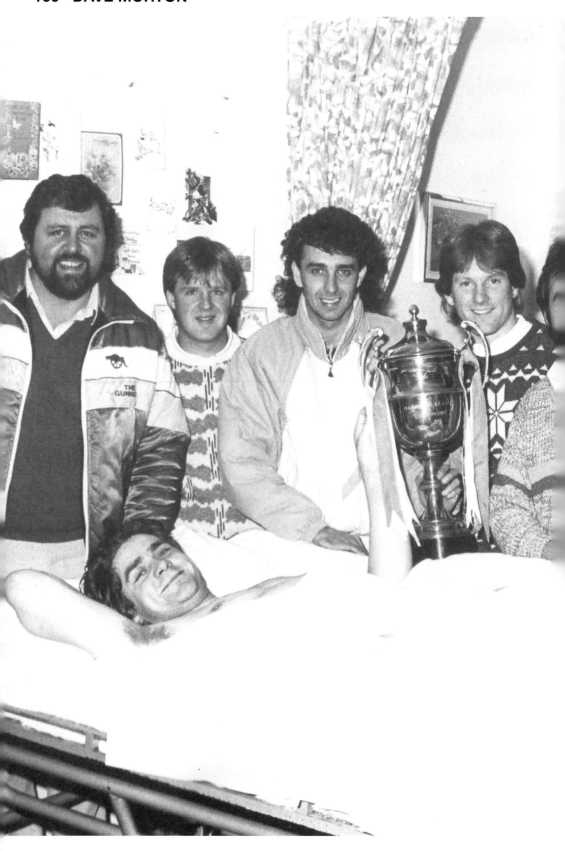

An emotional hospital visit to see Joe Owen, who had done so much to lead us to the championship before tragedy struck. Surrounding our injured No.1 are (left to right): Chris Bond, Gary O'Hare, Louis Carr, Miles Evans, myself, Phil Alderman, Richie Owen, David Walsh, Stan Ward, Mervyn Porter and Paul Heyes.

still part of the furniture. I remember entering the stadium and noticing how run-down it was. The track was also in poor condition compared to the days when I was there.

Hackney led by eight after the first seven heats but, again, Joe took the match by the scruff of the neck and his 14 points gave us a real chance going into the final heat, 35-37 down.

I lined up in Heat 13 with Louis Carr, who for once had had a poor night, facing Paul Bosley and Andy Galvin. It turned out to be a fantastic finale, with the lead changing several times, until the final lap, when we both stormed to the front. As we hit the final bend with victory in sight (with Louis just ahead), we both drifted towards the fence, allowing just enough room for Paul Bosley to challenge on the inside, which resulted in all three of us hitting the deck. Andy Galvin, a good 50 yards behind, calmly negotiated his way past to take the chequered flag, as Bosley remounted.

Surely the referee would award the race to us, wouldn't he?

Incredibly, Galvin was allowed to keep his three points, with Louis awarded second place. Gunners riders and management went potty following the decision but after a re-think, the first two places were reversed, which still meant we had lost.

A protest was immediately lodged and as you can imagine, Mervyn was furious. He told *Speedway Star:* "It was a ridiculous decision. Just what can you say when something like that happens? We had the 5-1 and there was no doubt that the accident was caused by Paul Bosley. So the race should have been awarded as it stood – a 5-1 to us.

"I don't agree that Dave Morton was going down anyway. He could see out of the corner of his eye what was happening and had no chance. And I noticed the track staff were very quick to pick up Dave and Louis' bikes, so they couldn't have pushed home even if they'd wanted to."

Five home wins in a row put us back on track, while an easy passage into the KO Cup semi-final, following an aggregate win over Berwick, kept the double dream alive. But another shocking refereeing decision at lowly Glasgow saw us record our sixth successive away defeat, after a farcical final race again involving Louis Carr and yours truly which took more than 35 minutes to complete.

After 12 heats at Craighead Park we trailed by two points after a series of tape-touching exclusions and falls. I made a good start in Heat 13 and hit the first bend in front. But behind me Louis and Andy

We enjoyed an entertaining night with comedian Ken Dodd. His 'Diddymen' here are (left to right): Mervyn Porter, Louis Carr, David Walsh, Gary O'Hare, myself, Paul Heyes, Richie Owen, Phil Alderman, Miles Evans, Chris Bond and Stan Ward.

Reid had a coming together and the race was stopped. All four riders were recalled for the re-run and, again, I hit the first bend ahead, only this time I had Louis tucked behind me.

It was, I believe, at the start of the third lap, with the positions unaltered, when Martin McKinna took a tumble. Louis and Andy Reid both stopped, despite no red light from the referee, after somebody waved a red flag from the centre green. The track staff were on to the circuit like a flash to help McKinna up and wheel off his bike, so the referee had no other alternative but to order a second re-run. We were absolutely fuming, because the fall and interference from the track staff had, without doubt, cost us a 5-1 and the league points.

I stormed into the pits and threw off my gloves and helmet in disgust. Team manager Chris Bond arrived on the scene and tried to calm me down but I wasn't having it.

"Hurry up, Dave, you'll get timed out if you don't get a move on," Chris shouted above the din, but I was adamant.

"Bollocks to this, Chris, I'm not riding – this is a f****** joke."

"Get your arse out there now," Chris insisted, so I reluctantly got my things together and went to take my place in the second re-run but failed to make it back on track within the two-minute allowance.

There was only way I could vent my frustrations and that was to ride around the track and straight through the tapes. Phil Alderman, my replacement, also felt that the referee had go it badly wrong, and he too fell foul of the two-minute warning after initially refusing to ride. Louis, as a token gesture, rode alone, eventually winning the heat, but it was little consolation. We had been robbed of the points and were all furious with the referee for not awarding the 5-1 following the first re-run. Mervyn immediately lodged an appeal and was positive that the result would be overturned.

After the meeting, while we were loading up in the car park, we were approached by a number of irate-looking home supporters and I thought for a moment that things were about to get ugly. The meeting had been played out in front of a volatile, partisan crowd and our situation was not helped by their centre green man, Dick Barrie, whose silly, sarcastic comments only added fuel to the fire.

But these Tigers fans simply wanted to tell us that they felt the result was incorrect and we had, indeed, been robbed of two precious points.

The defeat left us in third place behind Poole and league leaders Middlesbrough, who were a whopping eight points ahead of the Gunners, albeit we did have two matches in hand. We now had to rely on favours from other teams if we were to pull off Mervyn's dream.

We then had a run of four league matches at Thornton Road and apart from a rather nervy victory over Mildenhall, we hammered Canterbury, Rye House and Arena-Essex and also won the National League Pairs at Hackney, where Joe and Louis for once got the decision over Poole's Stan Bear and Martin Yeates after Louis was put through the fence by Bear on the last lap.

But before we could concentrate on the league, we had Hackney to overcome in the semi-final of the KO Cup. There was no love lost between the two teams following the incident at Waterden Road and our orders were simple – to make the second leg irrelevant by recording a big first leg lead, which we achieved with a 50-28 victory.

But once again Hackney tried to derail the double dream when their promoter Terry Russell complained that Louis Carr's engine was oversized and demanded it be impounded. He then paid to have it checked after the meeting, but his claims proved unfounded as the engine was well within the 500cc limit.

This incident only added extra spice to what would turn out to be a very difficult return leg. Nobody in the crowd could have anticipated what was about to unfold, after I led home Miles Evans for an easy 5-1 win in the first. But with Louis Carr unavailable for the meeting, things turned completely on its head when Joe injured his arm in a Heat 4 fall and withdrew from the action. Hackney smelt blood and despite my 11 points, we went to the tapes for the 13th with Kestrels needing a maximum to take the tie to a replay.

Dave Walsh and I faced Paul Whittaker and Thommo, who had both scored well on the night. We made quite a level break from the tapes but I was bullied to the back of the pack coming out of the first bend, with Thommo chasing Dave in second. Despite numerous attempts to pass him, Barry knew me too well, anticipating my every move, while his own attempts to pass Walshie became more and more desperate.

However, Dave Walsh was a much improved rider and he somehow held on to win the tie for us. We had survived – by the skin of our teeth.

With five league matches remaining, all away from home, we faced a monumental task of winning the title. But we travelled to Berwick on September 29 knowing five wins would give us the championship after Middlesbrough had been beaten at Peterborough.

Bruce Cribb just beat me in the first and although the rest of the meeting turned into a personal nightmare for me as I failed to register another point, Lady Luck smiled down on us for a change. In yet another last-heat decider, we scrambled home to register our first away win in the league since the end of June (Canterbury). Three days later, we repeated our success on the road, with another narrow victory at Long Eaton.

Then, on October 8, we had our most important 'meeting' of the season – a Speedway Control Board tribunal at Belgrave Square in London to decide the results of the controversial Hackney and Glasgow matches. Our title aspirations rested with the tribunal board.

I travelled down to the capital with Louis Carr, Stan Ward, Chris Bond and Mervyn hopeful that at least one match would be ruled in our favour. In the morning, the Hackney meeting was discussed but the board upheld the ref's original decision, so the result remained unchanged (Mervyn had to pay £150 towards court costs).

We broke for dinner but were more hopeful of winning the afternoon appeal, which we did when they ruled that Martin McKinna should not have taken part in the second re-run of Heat 13, as he was not under power when the first re-run race was stopped. They therefore deducted his two points and the original 39-38 home victory was amended to a 38-37 victory in our favour. Glasgow promoter Jim Beaton was also reprimanded and warned as to the future conduct of his track staff.

After the tribunal we completed a quick-fire hat-trick of away wins, this time at bottom-of-the-table Edinburgh. Peterborough was next on the agenda but even though they were a team occupying the middle reaches of the table, they possessed a fearsome 100 per cent home record – and guess what? Yes, it went down to the last heat, with us needing a 5-1 to take home a point. And we did just that, when Louis and I romped home after the fallen Mick Poole had been excluded.

It was very rare that I was involved in any unsavoury incidents with away supporters but on this occasion a number of Panthers fans clearly blamed me for Poole's fall, when trying to go around the outside on the first turn. There were several nasty comments from incensed fans, including one who screamed into my face: "Morton, you're a f****** animal!"

Sometimes in speedway, however, there is a decision made by those at the top that is not only ridiculous, but almost unbelievable. And this time Ellesmere Port were the victims.

Nearly six months after Berwick protested about the tyres Joe and I had used, the SCB ruled in favour of their appeal and awarded the league points to them. Board manager Dick Brache confirmed that the points scored by myself and Joe were void and so the 50-28 victory was amended to a 34-41 defeat – our first at Thornton Road. Can you imagine such a farce in any other sport?

When Mervyn received the news, he thought somebody was winding him up and refused to accept it until he received confirmation from the Board in writing (an appeal at the end of the season proved fruitless).

So it all boiled down to the fact that with one league match to go, at Birmingham, we were one point ahead of Middlesbrough, who had two matches left. The destiny of the championship was again out of our hands.

But first we had a KO Cup to win. Our opponents were Eastbourne who we'd previously thrashed 50-28 at home and drawn with away, so on league form we were big favourites to win the first leg of an historic double.

However, like in all major sports finals, form tends to go out of the window. In the first leg at Arlington, where the track was again really slick, we met an Eagles team at the very top of their game. We were 22 points down after just eight heats, before we rallied to end up 14 behind going into the home leg two nights later.

The Ellesmere Port public turned out in force for the return and it was great to see Thornton Road packed to near capacity. We needed to start well to claw back the deficit but when Gordon Kennett equalled John Jackson's four-year -old track record in the first, we knew we had a massive task ahead and the Eagles deservedly claimed the spoils. It was a bitter blow but the league was the main goal. After a few consolation beers, we turned our thoughts to our final league match of the season, at Birmingham on October 20.

Brummies had nothing to ride for other than pride and although they possessed a couple of seasoned veterans in Reg Wilson and Doug Wyer, our recent away form was good, so we arrived at Bordesley Green with hopes high that a victory would win us the title (Middlesbrough faced a daunting away tie at Eastbourne later that day). Unfortunately, I had been advised by my doctor not to ride, due to a bout of conjunctivitis. Normally I would have defied doctor's orders but my vision was severely impaired, so for once I took his advice.

After arriving early for the meeting, to hand the referee my 'sick note' to confirm our right to operate the rider replacement facility, it started well for the Gunners. After Phil Alderman and Dave Walsh won Heat 8, we led by six. Joe was out next and chasing his fourth successive win but events unfolded in a fateful Heat 9 that would make the result irrelevant.

In an attempt to pass Reg Wilson going into the bend, Joe clipped his back wheel on the home straight and was catapulted over his handlebars (known as a 'high-sider'), landing on his head.

First on the scene was team manager Chris Bond, who had a habit of watching from the centre green where he'd pick up tips and observe the riding habits of opposing riders, but this time we didn't need him to tell us what we all knew – it was a really serious injury. The ambulance arrived and somehow Joe was put on a special stretcher and taken to hospital, eventually being moved to the spinal unit at Oswestry Hospital.

The severity of the crash seemed to knock the stuffing out of the team and, not surprisingly, Birmingham came back to beat us 41-36.

As we awaited an update on Joe's condition, the news filtering through that Middlesbrough had lost by four points at Eastbourne barely registered.

We finished our season with a home challenge match against Stoke, a meeting none of us really wanted to ride in. And it showed as we lost our only genuine home match of the season. But the fans turned up in numbers and a collection for Joe saw a sizeable figure raised, with the Stoke riders admirably donating their prize money to Joe's cause.

D-Day for the destination of the league title was November 1. I was watching television at home when the phone finally rang. It was Mervyn ringing to give me the news: "Dave, they lost – we've done it!"

Glasgow had turned the form book upside down and beaten Boro 41-37. The league championship trophy was duly handed over after the meeting to Gareth Parry, Ellesmere Port's programme compiler, who had made the long journey to Scotland, and it was Gareth who had rung Mervyn with the good news. I was chuffed for Mervyn, a true gentleman, and I celebrated with a few beers and a bar of Galaxy chocolate!

In a way, it was a shame that we couldn't have all been together when news of our title triumph was confirmed – the team spirit at the club was as good as any of the teams I had ridden for – but we met up a few days later to show-off the trophy to our fans at a foggy Thornton Road, after it was presented to us by the Mayor of the town. We then enjoyed a few celebratory beers and a slap-up meal . . . at McDonald's!

A few days later we took the trophy to show Joe, who by this time was in the spinal unit at Southport hospital, nearer his home. Tragically, he had been diagnosed with a crushed vertebrae and was paralysed from the neck down.

It was a difficult visit – most of us hadn't seen him since the accident – but when we gathered around his bed, he seemed really cheerful and glad to see us. I think Joe had long realised that he wouldn't walk again but was surprisingly upbeat regarding his future and what had happened.

Mervyn also took us out a few weeks later, girlfriends and wives included, to The Woodhey Hotel, where along with a number of supporters, we were entertained by Mervyn's good mate, Ken Dodd, who had joined the Gunners supporters' club.

And what a night that was. You certainly got value for money at a Ken Dodd show – he kept us entertained for a solid four hours. If the club boss hadn't called time on the evening, I'm sure he would have continued cracking gags until sunrise.

The Ellesmere Port management were wonderful when it came to raising funds for Joe. They received special dispensation from the Speedway Control Board and Ellesmere Port council to stage a benefit match for our injured No.1 on Boxing Day. On what was one of the coldest days in living memory, an Ellesmere Port Past and Present team (including our Chris) took on an Inter-league Select side. What I remember most from the meeting was racing Chris on vintage Excelsior speedway bikes after the main match. They were slow and hard to handle, they vibrated like hell, and were virtually impossible to slide around the corners, but it was great fun. Despite the freezing weather, a big crowd turned out and a large sum of money was collected.

None of us knew at the time, but it was to be the last ever speedway meeting at Thornton Road.

Artist and Gunners fan Jeff Baker was the man behind this drawing

Chapter 19

Downhill slide

AS well as winning the title, the Ellesmere Port riders received an extra bonus for securing the most away points in the National League (eight wins and two draws from 18 matches) – a skiing holiday in the French Alps, courtesy of Silver-Ski, a company run by my old boss Len Silver.

Before the off a few of us got in some much needed practice on a dry ski slope at Rossendale, and even though I had a really bad cold by the time of departure in early January, 1986, I wasn't going to miss this 'free jolly'.

The party consisted of the majority of the squad (Richie Owen didn't travel due to injury), accompanied by girlfriends and wives, and Mervyn Porter's wife Shirley and daughter Dawn. We stayed in the resort of Meribel, in a lovely warm and friendly chalet-type hotel where we spent our nights in front of a huge log fire, drinking and chatting the night away.

Although I hadn't been skiing since I was a lad, I soon got the hang of it again and as my confidence grew, I accompanied the more experienced among us on the steeper and more dangerous slopes. On one occasion I decided to have some fun with the lads at the bottom awaiting the ski lift. I got within about 10 yards of them and decided to stop with a sideways slide in the hope of covering them in freezing snow.

But it was just like taking the wrong line on my Weslake when going into the first bend – I completely overcooked it, knocked poor Dave Walsh off his feet and he, in turn, took the rest of the lads out like skittles.

On another day we all decided to try out the hotel's outdoor ice skating rink. Everybody was keen to have a go and Louis Carr was soon speeding around the rink like a true pro. But I was the total opposite. If you can remember the film *Bambi,* the bit when the little deer first steps onto the frozen pond, then that was me. I tip-toed onto the ice and within seconds went arse over tit, causing all the change in my pocket to spill out all over the rink. The coins immediately froze to the surface, so I had to take off one of my skates and chip them off, which took me about 20 minutes, much to the amusement of the others.

That was enough for me and I gave it up as a bad job – I didn't want to injure more than my pride. It was one of many funny episodes during the trip.

Unfortunately, there would be nothing to laugh about a few weeks after returning from France, when we learnt that Ellesmere Port faced an uncertain future, or even closure.

As the days passed rumours intensified, and I heard that a large sponsorship deal was paramount if we were to run in 1986. Despite winning the league championship, the current level of support could not sustain the club alone and despite Mervyn's efforts to get prospective sponsors on-board, his pleas fell on deaf ears as the new season approached.

As a possible alternative option, I was hoping that I still had some sort of future at Sheffield, and would have been quite content to remain the club's No.8 and be loaned out again to the Gunners, as I didn't really want to go back to the British League full-time. But the Tigers' management wanted to raise funds to invest in new riders (Peter Carr from Belle Vue being one), so I was placed on the transfer list. Mervyn enquired almost straight away but Maurice Ducker wanted around £8,000 for

What we didn't know for sure as we headed off to France on a skiing trip was that Ellesmere Port were already on the slippery slope to oblivion. Left to right: Miles Evans, David Walsh, Paul Heyes, myself, Phil Alderman, Gary O'Hare and Louis Carr. Below: Walshie (left) and Gary' O'Hare looking the worse for wear after a liquid night in Meribel.

me and there was no way Mervyn could afford that sort of fee.

It got worse for Ellesmere Port's team-building plans when Gary O'Hare, who had been loaned to us by Stoke the previous season, failed to get in touch. And with Dave Walsh recalled by Sheffield and Richie Owen likely to be out for the majority of the season due to a pending knee operation, the situation seemed desperate.

I was now in limbo and wholly reliant on somebody agreeing a financial package with Sheffield. A number of NL clubs got in contact, including Boston, Glasgow and Edinburgh, but I was hoping a team nearer home would come in for me.

Then, completely out of the blue, Eric Stead, who owned a car dealership in Sheffield, got in touch, about me riding for Newcastle. Eric's consortium, which also included John Dews, John Turner and Ray Sant, had resurrected the Byker club after a season's break. Although the Brough Park track – built inside the greyhound circuit – was fairly small and slick, I was assured that it would be in top condition and have plenty of dirt on it.

Newcastle had an impressive record as one of the powerhouse teams of the National League since their revival in 1975, winning silverware galore with Tom and Joe Owen as their brilliant spearheads, but had made the mistake of trying to emulate their success in the British League, where they bombed spectacularly, finishing bottom and going out of business after the conclusion of the 1984 season.

But the new promotion were ambitious and keen to bring the good times back to the North-East venue, so I was delighted when they agreed terms with Sheffield (believed to be around £6,000) and offered me the No.3 jacket. They also snapped up my Ellesmere Port team-mate Gary O'Hare.

I looked forward to the new challenge but just after signing, I was somewhat saddened to hear that Ellesmere Port had withdrawn from the NL and Mervyn had, regrettably, moved the club, lock-stock and barrel, to Long Eaton. He had been badly let down by local businesses and council, who wouldn't support his venture at Thornton Road.

The defunct champions, however, had one final obligation – I agreed to ride for them under the banner of 'Ellesmere Port 1985' in a farewell challenge match at Stoke, which had been arranged prior to the decision to pull the plug at Thornton Road. It was a good way of saying our 'goodbyes' to the Gunners fans who were understandably shocked and upset at the sudden demise of their team. Sadly, history proves that there just weren't enough of them coming through the turnstiles.

You have to ask what more Mervyn Porter could have done to have made a bigger success of the club. He pushed the boat out by assembling a title-winning team, one that went close to winning the coveted league and cup double. If that couldn't pull the crowds in, then what chance of 1986 turning out any better?

As for Gunners' final meeting at Stoke, it was no happy ending. We were duly hammered at Loomer Road, where I spent more time picking myself off the soggy track than actually racing, scoring a solitary point from my five rides.

It was a miserable conclusion, made worse when a number of Gunners fans turned on poor Mervyn. It was out of order, although I understood their frustrations. We met the supporters afterwards to sign autographs and bid a final farewell but by now I was a Newcastle rider, so had to put my emotions and feelings to one side and left for home without comment.

There was an awful amount of work to do to get the Newcastle track, facilities and stadium ready for the season but somehow it was achieved, albeit causing a late start. There was also a name change for the Geordie fans to get used to, as the team were re-named the 'Newcastle Federation Specials', which did not go down too well with the traditionalists, who preferred the original Diamonds nickname that has been synonymous with Newcastle since pre-war days.

But the Federation Breweries were the club's main sponsors – 'Special' being one of their most popular beers – and it was their money that had made the resurrection possible.

As I hadn't previously ridden the Newcastle track much, I was hoping to work out my lines and tactics in a number of pre-season challenge matches. But the rain gods had other ideas and in the first six weeks of the '86 season four home meetings were called off. It was not a good start for the new promotion in terms of turnstile revenue, or the riders, who received little in terms of points money.

We lost our opening NL matches at Wimbledon and Arena-Essex, without being disgraced, and then won at Boston in the KO Cup before making a winning start in our first home league match against Long Eaton. None of the heat leaders, Dave Perks, Paul Stead and myself, were exactly tearing up trees, but it was a fairly solid start.

Then the wheels fell off with a humiliating home thrashing by Eastbourne – Newcastle's biggest defeat at Brough Park to date – in which Paul Stead was the only home rider to taste victory.

We continued to scrape home wins but didn't pick up anything on the road. After further home reversals to Stoke and Exeter, we found ourselves bottom of the table by mid-August. What made it worse was the fact that our 'noisy neighbours' Middlesbrough were top of the pile and were our next opponents at home. As derby matches went, this was one of the biggest and a large away following made for a cracking atmosphere.

Local pride and bragging rights were at stake and we made a dream start, winning the opening heats 5-1 and 5-0 (after both away riders fell). The next two were shared but when Dave Blackburn and Dave Perks put us further ahead in Heat 5, the home support sensed a big victory. And that's just what they got as we trounced our biggest rivals 54-23, with every home rider winning at least one heat. The result was, as *Speedway Star* put it, 'UNBELIEVABLE!'

Confidence is everything in sport and following our big derby win, we remained unbeaten at home

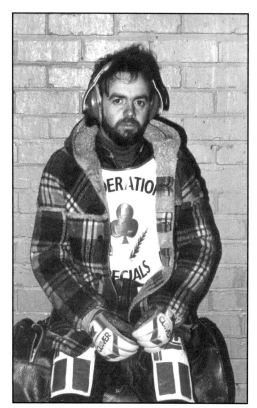

Getting down about the condition of the Newcastle track.   I always put a lot of thought and effort into making fast starts.

Challenging Paul Woods in the dust at Rye House.

It was pleasing to finish 1986 as Newcastle's No.1 even though I realised my top flight days were over.

The Diamonds are back. Lining up at the 1987 press/practice day are (standing, left to right): Paul Bentley, David Blackburn, Tom Owen, Steve Wicks and Gary O'Hare. Mark Courtney and me are either side of team manager Joe Owen.

in the league for the rest of the season, although failing to pick up a single point on our travels. The facts didn't quite tell the story, though, as on 14 occasions we scored 30 or more points. But most importantly, we managed to ease away from bottom place to avoid the dreaded wooden spoon. Ironically, Mervyn Porter's Long Eaton were the only side to finish below us, in 20th place.

I was an ever-present and finished top of the Newcastle averages, with figures a shade under 8.25. It was a real bonus to be No.1 and re-pay the faith the promotion had in me. I'd developed a method of riding the Brough Park track that proved quite successful. I found you could bomb down the straight and into the corner fairly wide and then cut the next corner off to make the next straight much longer. By doing this, you could pass on the inside while the opposition riders were still sliding out of the corner.

During the season I received an offer to guest for Stoke in an Inter-League challenge and I just couldn't turn it down – it was against Sheffield, an opportunity for me to show Maurice Ducker and co. what they were missing. I'd ridden at Owlerton for a National League Select earlier in the season, scoring in all three of my rides, but this would be far more competitive. When you've dropped down a grade and performed at that level for a while, it's very difficult to move back up again.

Despite being desperate to put on a show and leave with my head held high, I finished at the back in all four of my rides. If I didn't know it before, I knew now . . . my days as a top flight rider were officially over.

One off-track memory I have of the 1986 season was when I nearly wiped out half of the Newcastle team following a meeting at Peterborough. To save on fuel costs, I would often travel to away fixtures in my transit van with Gary O'Hare and Bernie Collier. On our way home from the East of England Showground, travelling back up the A1 towards Sheffield, the weather took a turn for the worst, only adding to existing poor driving conditions due to a lack of road lights and a worsening mist.

We had been travelling for about an hour and I was bombing along at about 75-80mph on the inside lane. To be honest, I was quite tired and not really concentrating on what I was doing. Thankfully, Bernie was wide awake and, just in time, spotted a tractor and trailer – poorly lit and travelling about 20mph – just in front of us. Anyway, I moved to the outside lane, pretending that I'd seen the tractor, but if Bernie hadn't seen it I would have ploughed into the trailer and killed all three of us and Gary's mechanic, 'Turbo Tim'.

This really shook me up and for the rest of the journey, I kept to the legal speed limit and was wide awake until I reached home. Gary and Bernie never suspected a thing, believing that, as usual, I was driving normally and leaving things to the last minute. Well, sorry lads . . . and thank you, Bernie!

The car business I was building up continued to flourish and I suppose I was preparing for my future after speedway. But it was bloody hard work, especially in the winter months when it was freezing in Dad's garage. One day, while underneath a second-hand motor I was doing up, I was welding away when I smelt smoke – a lot of smoke. I had set fire to the carpets, mats and the back seat above the welding job I was doing, which were ruined by the time I had put out the 'Partington Inferno'. I spent the next few days trying to purchase a new seat and carpets to match the others that weren't burnt, and also had to put the car through an expensive valet to rid the interior of the smoke smell.

Anyway, I managed to sell the car on – I think I just about broke even on the job – but was lucky the car's petrol tank hadn't exploded, otherwise it probably would have been the end of the business, the garage and me!

But the car repair business was still a side-line operation and I wasn't about to hang up my leathers just yet. I was quietly content at Newcastle, we'd made progress during the latter half of the season, but the club was put up for sale in December. Despite the brewery sponsorship deal, Newcastle was haemorrhaging money amid plummeting attendances – a far cry from the glory days when the stadium was packed to the seams.

JANUARY passed without a decision on the future of Newcastle, although I was positive that new owners would soon be announced and I would be offered terms for the new campaign. However, when February also sailed by and there was still no definite news, I was a little anxious to get something sorted.

First, with more and more tracks closing down (membership of the NL dropped from 20 to 16 teams in 1987), competition for places had intensified, with some good riders out of work. Secondly, speedway was an expensive sport and individual sponsorship was important, but how could you approach potential sponsors in Newcastle if you didn't know you would actually be riding there?

This state of limbo seemed to drag on and on until, just a few weeks before the commencement of the new season, the original promotion announced that they were to run for a second term, after failing to agree any sort of deal in time with prospective buyers.

Furthermore, a new deal was agreed with the Federation Brewery. To keep all parties happy, a new name change meant the return of the famous 'Diamonds' nickname, as we were re-christened the Newcastle Federation Special Diamonds for the '87 season.

Of the original '86 team, the majority were retained, with former Belle Vue rider Mark Courtney signed from rivals Middlesbrough, but it was the return of the Owen brothers that caused most excitement in the city. Former Diamond Tom rejoined us from Stoke, while wheelchair-bound Joe took on the role of team manager following his horrific crash.

Although they are both Newcastle legends, Joe made it clear from the off that he had not been brought in as a publicity gimmick to bring a few more through the turnstiles and wasn't prepared to manage a run-of-the-mill outfit. It was good to see him back in speedway and although he obviously

Out in front at Brough Park and searching for the dirt against Peterborough.

lacked experience as a TM, he was keen to learn all the rules and regulations. He was certainly a great motivator and wanted to be as successful off the track as he was on it.

In March, before the main season kicked off, PC rode in what would be his farewell meeting at Hyde Road, after a year-long battle with a knee injury sustained at the start of the 1986 season. I had shared some great times with him during our days in speedway and while we were grass-tracking, and in terms of my all-time list of the greatest speedway riders, PC without doubt figures in my top 10.

With one Belle Vue legend retired, the news that the world famous Hyde Road stadium was to be demolished at the end of the '87 season was another bitter blow for the sport and the speedway-loving public of Manchester. It was a sad day when they started to demolish the place where I'd enjoyed many years as a boy and later as a rider, but the stadium, with its wooden stands, was falling down and would have cost too much to put right to meet new safety regulations that affected many sporting stadia in the wake of the Bradford City FC fire tragedy of 1985. During my British League career, the visit to the old Belle Vue was the one meeting I looked forward to most when the new fixtures were published.

The '87 season finally started for us in early April with a Tyne-Tees Trophy dust-up with Middlesbrough. Newcastle had the proud record of winning the previous 10 competitions and it was really important that we started well to keep hold of the extra fans who had turned up for Joe's first meeting in charge. For a change, the track had plenty of dirt on it and I found a number of strips that were particularly deep when coming off the bends. I ended up winning all my four rides and to be honest, even though Brough Park was not one of my favourites, there would be no complaints from me if track conditions were as good as this for the rest of the season. Alas, they weren't.

While walking the circuit before our opening home NL meeting versus Stoke, I noticed how slick it was. It was hard enough to pass on such a small and narrow track, especially if you missed the gate, as it basically had only two racing lines. And without that extra drive created by the deep patches of dirt, it was difficult to make up any ground at all.

After the Potters fought back from eight points down to win by the same margin, I made my feelings known to Joe and Eric Stead about the slickness of the track. At home you are supposed to have a big advantage but a slick track made it a more even affair, often dictated by the position of the riders coming out of the first bend. With passing limited, it did not make for exciting racing.

Being the senior rider at the club, Joe and Eric listened to my concerns and agreed to purchase a large amount of fresh shale, which was laid for the next home meeting.

Joe made it abundantly clear that he wouldn't tolerate sub-standard performances and when we travelled to Edinburgh four days later, he demanded an improvement. We again started well, leading by eight after the first six heats, but in the next, with a 5-1 almost in the bag and with just one lap to complete, Mark Courtney nearly took out his race partner Dave Blackburn, fell and was excluded. In the re-run we lost it 5-1 and imploded from then on. Joe was furious with us for throwing away the points for the second match running.

Victory at Boston and a home win versus Berwick in the KO Cup eased tensions in the camp but a number of home riders had complained about the deepness of the shale in the match against the Bandits. It suited me down to the ground, I top scored on the night, but was fighting a losing battle on the slickness issue.

Dave Blackburn preferred it slick and being the team's up-and-coming star, his preferences carried a lot of weight. As the season progressed, the majority had got their way, so the track became slicker and slicker.

A narrow loss at Middlesbrough in the second leg of the Tyne-Tees Trophy meant we won the silverware, before a home win versus Mildenhall in which I secured another maximum, including two wins from the back. This was a prime example of what you could achieve on a track with a bit of dirt on it. In the first, I completely missed the gate but found tremendous drive on the back straight and had just Mildenhall's Mel Taylor ahead of me by the end of the first lap. I shadowed him for another two laps, then completely caught him on the hop when I performed some fence-scraping and took him on the outside.

Taylor was again my victim in the second from-the-back three-pointer. As we left the gate, I had to shut off the power to avoid colliding with the rider on my right shoulder but then slipped through on the inside of the bend before pulling away to lead by turn two. The fans loved it and so did I.

But in the home league match with Middlesbrough, in front of a bumper Bank Holiday crowd, it resulted in another mid-match collapse, again on a track lacking any deep patches of dirt.

With a healthy 10-point lead frittered away by Heat 10, everything went wrong in Heat 11, when our promising Aussie youngster Shane Bowes was controversially excluded for dangerous riding, after allegedly barging past visiting rider Mark Burrows. I was on gate four in the original heat but asked to be switched to gate two – Shane's original starting position. The referee was adamant that I couldn't changed grids, but I insisted that I should be allowed. As a result, I was excluded for delaying the start. And just to make matters worse, we lost the re-run by 5-1.

Thankfully, we grabbed a share of the league points when Dave Blackburn won the last but I could have stolen it for us on the final bend if I'd been able to squeeze under Steve Wilcock, who kept his nerve and racing line to secure the draw.

Joe didn't really blame me for the result but did single me out after we lost the return at Cleveland Park a few weeks later. We went into the derby match with confidence sky high following six successive victories which had catapulted us up the league ladder. But in the all-important Heat 12, with us trailing by five points, I blasted from the tapes and didn't even make the first turn after my bike packed up.

For some reason Joe had a right go about my performance in the local press, although I took the criticism on the chin. Being one of the heat leaders, I was expected to perform at a certain standard and I'll admit I fell short of it that night. Cleveland Park was a track where, if things didn't go to

Looking for a way past leader Steve Lawson and Martin McKinna during Newcastle's 1987 visit to Workington, which became Glasgow's temporary home.

plan, it was difficult to put right. Then again, when you think that Dave Blackburn scored only one more point than me on the night, I thought being singled out for the defeat was a little unfair.

Joe's mood following the derby defeat did not get any better when he received news that Boston had resigned from the league at the start of August, thus robbing us of a precious away win achieved earlier in the season. And when Workington (who started the season as Glasgow riding at Workington) were thrown out of the league by the BSPA following numerous problems, we lost another four points, having won there in June and hammered them at home in July.

Five matches without a win at the end of the campaign saw us finish in the bottom half of the table, which wasn't a true reflection of the team's overall performance in 1987. Dave Blackburn deservedly finished top of Diamonds' averages and dominated the Silver Helmet competition by defending his title on 11 occasions, as well as finishing a creditable third in the National League Riders' Championship.

Tom Owen finished second in the Newcastle averages and myself third, but my CMA had slipped a full point. It was with deep regret that just after the final meeting, I put in a written transfer request, citing the track as the main reason why I wanted away.

I had no problem in travelling up to the North-East, or with those marvellous Geordie supporters. The truth is, I was a big track rider plying his trade on a relatively small circuit that I just couldn't warm too. My Jawa was also not ideal for Brough Park but I couldn't justify the expense of buying a GM engine, which would have been better suited to that circuit.

The lack of sponsorship in the area was another issue. I was only making ends meet due to sponsorship retained from my Sheffield days, courtesy of Tony and Pat Ackland and Aytee Portable Equipment.

Skipper Tom Owen was disappointed with my decision, he still thought I had a big part to play in the revival of the club, but my mind was made up and, reluctantly, he and Eric agreed to let me go.

Much as I still enjoyed racing, my aching body was crying out for a rest. Deep down I was hoping for one last campaign on a track not too far from home, where I enjoyed racing. If the right offer was not forthcoming, I would concentrate on my car repair/selling business and hang up my leathers for good.

Chapter 20

Final regrets

ISPENT yet another Christmas with my future up in the air. Mervyn Porter at Long Eaton made an approach just after New Year but could not reach an agreement with Eric Stead.

Before finalising their plans for the 1988 season, Newcastle made one last bid to change my mind. After assurances that the track would be more to my liking (and better prepared), I withdrew my transfer request and decided to spend my third season at Brough Park. It was nice to be wanted and Eric and Joe were doing their best to assemble a decent team.

But things started to turn sour again when Joe's main target for the season, Stoke's Daz Sumner, signed for rivals Middlesbrough instead of the Diamonds. With the Rapierace promotion team running the show at both Newcastle and sister track Stoke, it was widely expected that the Sumner signing was a done deal, and a fee approaching £10,000 had been agreed. Joe was furious and launched a stinging attack on his Newcastle peers. If Sumner had signed for any other club Joe would have understood. But our bitter rivals?

Whether the promoters were looking for a new face to take over anyway or Joe was asking for too much money, I'm not sure, but they certainly didn't let sentiment get in the way and they sacked him – just two weeks before the commencement of the new season.

With captain Tom Owen also announcing his retirement due to business commitments, and with no major signings on the horizon, things took another turn for the worse when Newcastle supremo Eric Stead split from the Rapierace promotion and decided to go it alone. Personally, I didn't think this was a wise move. With the team being at least three riders short and the season only days away, a united promotion had a better chance of attracting the riders we desperately needed.

Just five days to go before our first meeting, I was informed (by George English, I believe) that Newcastle had dramatically withdrawn from the National League. Eric had done his best to put some sort of squad together but rather than start with a team which included reserves and juniors, he decided to pull the plug.

Crowds had not been brilliant at Brough Park since speedway returned there in 1986 and just like Ellesmere Port in 1986, a struggling team would simply not generate the support needed to pay the bills.

As most NL sides had their heat leaders in place, I was about to announce my retirement when Mervyn offered me an unexpected lifeline. Long Eaton were virtually the only outfit who had not finalised their plans, and a loan deal was somehow arranged. I was delighted to still be a professional rider, albeit at a club who had finished either bottom or second-bottom of the league for four of the past five seasons.

The track at Station Road was one I generally enjoyed riding and Mervyn had a number of experienced riders on the books, including my old Hackney team-mate Keith 'Chalkie' White, Gerald Short and Richie Owen, who I all knew well. Just before our first meeting, a Trent Trophy challenge match at Stoke, I ensured my main bike was in tip-top condition thanks to a Bruce Cribb tune-up.

For the 1988 season the old format of 13 heats was extended to 16, which basically ended the second-half programme.

Loomer Road was one of my happier hunting grounds and a dozen points on my debut was a good start to my Invaders career. But that's about as good as it got.

On my home debut I really struggled to impress on a poorly prepared track (rutted and full of pot holes, due mainly to stock car racing also held at Station Road). One win from five outings was a disappointing return but without making excuses, the track really was that bad – without doubt one of the worst I had ever raced on.

Our National League campaign kicked off at Rye House on April 17, a significant date in my career, as it was on this day I won my final competitive heat in British speedway. After a last place in the opener, a third in Heat 5, I won Heat 8, but took no further part in the meeting after being taken out by team-mate Wayne Elliott, who was still racing when crossing the finishing line. Maybe I should have taken the hint.

I was fit enough to take part in a challenge meeting versus Middlesbrough at Station Road but the track again caused me umpteen problems. In Heat 15, when trying to pass on the outside, my bike lifted and I just managed to miss the fence. However, on landing, I badly jarred my arm, which caused a great deal of pain.

In the next three away meetings I scored just four measly points while the team continued its winless start. We did manage a narrow first leg victory in the KO Cup, first leg versus Middlesbrough but it was never enough to see us through.

I'd been signed as a heat leader but was now heading for a reserve berth. For the first time in my career, I wasn't enjoying racing anymore. Everything now seemed a chore and if you didn't put in 100 per cent, then your risk of injury increased. Looking back, I should have retired when Newcastle

Tyred out: Press and practice day at Station Road in 1988.
Left to right: Stan Ward, Wayne Elliott, Keith White, Gerald Short, Mike Spink, Chris Bond, Richie Owen and myself, looking none too enthusiastic. I should have quit at the end of the previous season.

The smile didn't last long at Long Eaton in 1988.

Team Managers: Chris Bond & Stan Ward
Captain: Keith White

LIFELINE INVADE

No	Invaders	Av.	1	2	3	4	5	6	TOTAL	BONUS
1	Keith White	7.89	1	3	2	3	2	2	13	
2	Dave Morton	7.16	R	NS	NS	NS	/		0	
3	Glenn Doyle	8.28	2	3	2	3	1	1	12	
4	Gary O'Hare	4.26	2	/	/	/	1	F	3	
5	Mike Spink	7.30	/	2	NS	1	/	F	3	1
6	Wayne Elliott	2.42	2	1	/	/	1	NS	4	2
7	Richie Owen	4.78	3	1	FX	NS			4	
8										

COLOURS: BLUE, WHITE AND RED

Total 37

HEAT		RIDER	SUBSTITUTE	GATE NUM	Hel. Col.	Pts. Scd	HEAT RESULT H	A	MATCH SCORE H	A
1 Time **66.8**	1	Keith White			R	1	1	1		
	2	Dave Morton			B	Ret				
	1	Nigel Sparshott			W	2	5		5	
	2	Trevor Banks			Y/B	3				
2 Time /	6	Wayne Elliott			R	2	5	6		
	7	Richie Owen			B	3				
	6	Ian Clark			W	1	1	6		
	7	Paul Atkins			Y/B	Fell				
3 Time **68.9**	5	Mike Spink			R		2	8		
	4	Gary O'Hare			B	2				
	5	Mark Carlson			W	1	4	10		
	4	Troy Butler			Y/B	3				
4 Time **68.3**	3	Glenn Doyle			R	2	3	11		
	6	Wayne Elliott			B	1				
	3	Carl Baldwin			W	3	3	13		
	7	Paul Atkins			Y/B					
5 Time **68.6**	5	Mike Spink			R	2	2	13		
	4	Gary O'Hare			B					
	1	Nigel Sparshott			W	1	4	17		
	2	Trevor Banks			Y/B	3				
6 Time **69.2**	1	Keith White			R	3	4	17		
	2	Dave Morton	RICHIE OWEN		B	1				
	3	Carl Baldwin			W	2	2	19		
	6	Ian Clark			Y/B					
7 Time **68.5**	3	Glenn Doyle			R	3	3	20		
	6	Wayne Elliott			B					
	5	Mark Carlson			W	1	3	22		
	4	Troy Butler			Y/B	2				
8 Time **71.2**	2	Dave Morton	WAYNE ELLIOTT		R	1	1	21		
	7	Richie Owen			B	F/X				
	2	Trevor Banks			W	2	5	27		
	7	Paul Atkins	IAN CLARK		Y/B	3				

Race Points: Win 3 points. Second 2 points. Third 1 point. Clutch Start 4 Laps. Helmet Colours
HOME Red (R), Blue (B). AWAY: White (W), Yellow/Black (Y/B). Track Signals: Flags displaye
during the course of a race means, YELLOW/BLACK: Riders entering last lap. BLACK ANI
WHITE CHEQUERED: Race finished. BLACK: individual rider excluded. RED LIGHTS around th
track indicates race stopped.

MILTON KEYNES KNIGHTS

Team Manager: Roger Jones
Captain: Trevor Banks

No	Knights	Av.	1	2	3	4	5	6	TOTAL	BONUS
1	Nigel Sparshott	8.27	2	1	1	2	1		7	3
2	Trevor Banks	8.49	3	3	2	2	3		13	1
3	Carl Baldwin	7.46	3	2	3	2	3		13	
4	Troy Butler	6.90	3	2	3	3	3		14	
5	Mark Carlson	7.00	1	1			EX		2	1
6	Ian Clark	5.27	1		3	1	1	2	8	1
7	Paul Atkins	2.00	F	NS					0	
8										

COLOURS: RED,
WHITE AND BLUE

Total 57

HEAT		RIDER	SUBSTITUTE	GATE NUM.	Hel. Col.	Pts. Scd	HEAT RESULT H / A	MATCH SCORE H / A
9 Time 70.2	5 4 3 6	Mike Spink Gary O'Hare Carl Baldwin Ian Clark	GLENN DOYLE		R B W Y/B	2 3 1	2 / 4	23 / 31
10 Time 69.8	1 2 5 4	Keith White David Morton Mark Carlson Troy Butler	MIKE SPINK		R B W Y/B	2 1 3	3 / 3	26 / 34
11 Time 68.6	3 7 1 2	Glenn Doyle Richie Owen Nigel Sparshott Trevor Banks	GARY O'HARE		R B W Y/B	3 1 2	3 / 3	29 / 37
12 Time 70.8	1 4 3 5	Keith White Gary O'Hare Carl Baldwin Mark Carlson			R B W Y/B	3 1 2	4 / 2	33 / 39
13 Time 71.7	3 5 1 4	Glenn Doyle Mike Spink Nigel Sparshott Troy Butler			R B W Y/B	1 2 3	1 / 5	34 / 44
14 Time 72.6	2 6 2 6	Dave Morton Wayne Elliott Trevor Banks Ian Clark	(2nd ride - NS) KEITH WHITE		R B W Y/B	2 3 1	2 / 4	36 / 48
15 Time 74.0	3 5 3 5	Glenn Doyle Mike Spink Carl Baldwin Mark Carlson EX2	IAN CLARK		R B W Y/B	1 Fell 3 2	1 / 5	37 / 53
16 Time 72.8	1 4 1 4	Keith White Gary O'Hare Nigel Sparshott Troy Butler			R B W Y/B	2 Fell 1 3	2 / 4	39 / 57

INTERVAL: — TIME AND WEATHER PERMITTING THERE WILL BE A TEN MINUTE INTERVAL PRIOR TO THE SECOND HALF EVENTS

Thanks to Long Eaton historian Ian Gill for his immaculate filled-in programme which records the sorry details of my unhappy last night as a speedway rider.

closed down at the end of '87 and bowed out with a bit of dignity.

Things finally came to a head in the home meeting with Milton Keynes on May 25 – my eighth official match in Long Eaton colours. It had been raining heavily all day and on inspection, the sodden track was again strewn with pot holes and bumps but, to my surprise, referee John Eglese passed if fit just before the off.

I reluctantly went out in Heat 1 with Chalkie White, with rain still falling.

From the gate, I found myself at the rear of the pack, behind Knights' pairing of Trevor Banks and Nigel Sparshott, but after just a couple of laps, and covered in cold, wet shale, I pulled up. I returned to the pits, where co-team manager Chris Bond was first on the scene, wanting to know what had happened.

"Sorry Chris, I can't do this anymore," I sighed, as I started to pack up my gear and load the van.

I then went into the bar to find Sharen, who was having a drink with friends. "Are you ready – we're going home," I told her.

Chris and Stan Ward informed Mervyn, who duly indicated to the referee that I was refusing to ride. I was then told that unless I carried on I would be fined and reported to the Speedway Control Board for my actions.

Now that really pissed me off – they were trying to force me to race in dangerous conditions. Had they forgotten what had happened to Joe Owen, their No.1 rider, only a few seasons ago?

"Fine me as much as you want, I'm retiring anyway," were my final words, as I left the stadium still fuming at what had gone on.

As the Invaders slumped to another heavy defeat, we travelled home in complete silence and I went to bed without mentioning what had gone on. The following morning, Sharen asked if it was just a heat of the moment thing but my feelings hadn't changed overnight, so I told her that my racing days were finally over.

There were three main reasons for packing up. Firstly, I was fed up riding on poorly prepared tracks and feared that a bad accident was just around the corner.

Secondly, I didn't want to continue racing and be labelled a 'has-been'. By retiring now, I would hopefully be remembered as a successful and respected rider with a decent average.

Finally, I had started my garage business, but couldn't fully commit to it while still riding full-time. Retiring from speedway gave me the time to take on more jobs and run the business properly. We had some savings and with Sharen working, we weren't going to starve if the business flopped.

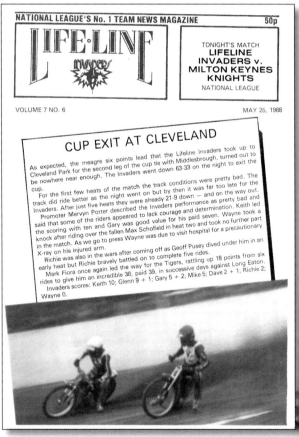

NATIONAL LEAGUE'S No. 1 TEAM NEWS MAGAZINE   50p

LIFE·LINE
Invaders

TONIGHT'S MATCH
**LIFELINE
INVADERS** v.
**MILTON KEYNES
KNIGHTS**
NATIONAL LEAGUE

VOLUME 7 NO. 6   MAY 25, 1988

CUP EXIT AT CLEVELAND

As expected, the meagre six points lead that the Lifeline Invaders took up to Cleveland Park for the second leg of the cup tie with Middlesbrough, turned out to be nowhere near enough. The Invaders went down 63-33 on the night to exit the cup.

For the first few heats of the match the track conditions were pretty bad. The track did ride better as the night went on but by then it was far too late for the Invaders. After just five heats they were already 21-9 down – and on the way out.

Promoter Mervyn Porter described the Invaders performance as pretty bad and said that some of the riders appeared to lack courage and determination. Keith led the scoring with ten and Gary was good value for his paid seven. Wayne took a knock after riding over the fallen Max Schofield in heat two and took no further part in the match. As we go to press Wayne was due to visit hospital for a precautionary X-ray on his injured arm.

Richie was also in the wars after coming off as Geoff Pusey dived under him in an early heat but Richie bravely battled on to complete five rides.

Mark Fiora once again led the way for the Tigers, rattling up 18 points from six rides to give him an incredible 38, paid 39, in successive days against Long Eaton.

Invaders scores: Keith 10; Glenn 9 + 1; Gary 5 + 2; Mike 5; Dave 2 + 1; Richie 2; Wayne 0.

The cover of the programme for my last-ever meeting at Long Eaton on May 25, 1988.

It was not the way I had imagined bowing out – no farewell meeting, no last goodbyes – but, then again, very few riders get to choose the perfect end to their career. Our Chris spent 18 years with his beloved Belle Vue (1973-90) but when he decided, in 1993, that he hadn't quite got speedway out of his system, he came back for one last blast at Sheffield.

I suppose the one who came up with the perfect exit strategy was Bruce Penhall, who quit on the rostrum after winning his second consecutive World Championship in 1982. That was some Hollywood script.

I later regretted dropping Mervyn, Stan and Chris in the shit but I'd contemplated calling it a day a few weeks earlier and only carried on because the team was short of riders due to an injury to

How the local press reported on my sudden exit.

Gerald Short.

I was fined £100 by referee Eglese and also by Mervyn, who quite correctly suspended me as well, but I didn't pay them or serve my suspension because I never climbed aboard a speedway bike again.

Thankfully, after the dust had settled, I became friends again with Mervyn, Chris and Stan. I didn't like leaving the way I did and don't look back on my unhappy exit with any pride. The fact that the Invaders ended up rock bottom again, in 16th place, made it another miserable year for the East Midlands club.

Just to ensure I had no second thoughts, over the next few weeks and months I sold all my equipment, including my main bike (Jawa fitted with a Weslake engine) for £650 and a similar back-up machine for £540. In hindsight, I wish I'd kept them – today they would be worth thousands!

I do enjoy meeting up with old friends at speedway reunions. Above: This one of me with Zenon Plech and Barry Thomas was taken at the Hackney reunion, organised by supporters Paul Tadman and Chris Fenn, at Paradise Wildlife Park (home to the National Speedway Museum), Broxbourne, Hertfordshire in 2005. Below: With another ex-Hawk, Laurie Etheridge, at the WSRA dinner-dance, held at the Leicester Marriott Hotel in March 2015.

Epilogue

LOOKING back, I was a professional speedway rider for 16 years and eight months, travelling the world and earning a good living for the majority of that time for doing something I loved.

So what do I consider to be my greatest achievement in my racing career? Being a No.1 for my club was a great honour and also being picked for England was another momentous moment. Listed in *The Guinness Book of Records* as the world's fastest speedway rider was, I suppose, really special too.

But the one event that stands out for me above everything else was winning the New Zealand Championship in 1975. It was the first meeting where I felt under pressure to win it – thanks to Colin Tucker, who convinced me on the day that I was the best rider in the world and there was only John Davis to beat to be crowned champion.

Probably my biggest – and this will surprise some people – was signing for Hackney from Crewe. I was desperate to ride full-time in the British League but, as I've stated several times, I wanted to join one of the northern clubs, Halifax, Sheffield or Belle Vue, where a bigger track would have suited me much better. I should have been more patient and held out for the right opportunity, rather than immediately jump at the chance Len Silver gave me to progress from Crewe to his senior interest at Hackney.

That's not to say that I didn't enjoy my time at The Wick and performing in front of those magnificent supporters at Waterden Road, or appreciate the efforts of Len, who did everything in his power to help me climb the speedway ladder and was, without doubt, the biggest influence in my career.

But at Hackney I struggled with the track and the travelling and also suffered my worst injury, just at a time when I was at the very top of my game and capable of beating the very best in the sport.

What could I have achieved but for the painful events of that fateful Friday night in May 1977? Would I have qualified for a World Final and even made the rostrum?

Of course, the injury could have happened at any stage of my career, on any track, riding for any club. Fact is, though, after the leg break, I was never quite the rider I was, although it wasn't for the want of trying.

Following my decision to retire in 1988, I did get the urge to race again but somehow I never found the time to have a few practice laps 'to keep my eye in'. And the longer I left it, the harder it became to make the effort – even though I wish now that I'd have had one last go. I was also approached several times to race in testimonials and, I must admit, I was again tempted a few times. These fun meetings with old-timers racing at some stage during the night were great for the supporters but unless you had practiced beforehand, you were a prime target for a fall or even serious injury.

What kept me from accepting any of these offers was knowing I couldn't just 'take part'. If I climbed back onboard a bike again, I knew the adrenalin would kick in and even though the brain would be telling me that I was still good enough to compete, the body told a completely different story. My one big fear was making a complete idiot of myself, getting injured and being unable to earn any money to make a living.

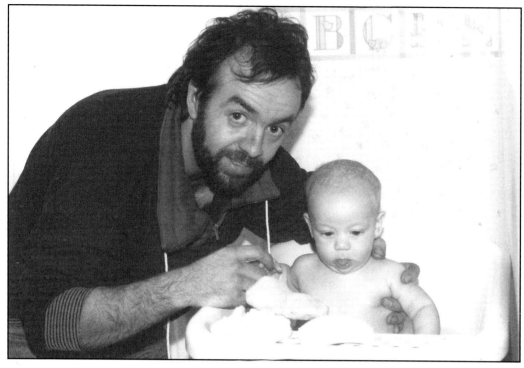

Bath-time for son Rory.

So I never did get on a speedway bike again and for a while, I basically walked away from the sport. It was around five months after retiring before I finally went to another speedway meeting, when I persuaded myself to go to Belle Vue. I was glad I went along and enjoyed the evening . . . the sounds, the smells and the general 'buzz' of a race night, and it was good to see some familiar faces and chat about old times.

I didn't completely wash my hands of the sport and be content to watch from the terraces or on television. When Chris became involved as a promoter at Belle Vue I could have taken on any number of jobs there but decided against it. However, a few years later, when Chris was involved at Buxton, he asked me if I'd be interested in being starting marshal for a few meetings, so I thought this might be a bit of fun, to be in 'their shoes' for a change.

It was not as easy as it looks, though, trying to get the riders to do as they are told when approaching the tapes and starting line. As a rider, I used to take little notice of the starting marshal – instead, I'd be concentrating on finding the best starting position on my gate, while attempting to make the opposition riders as nervy as possible.

So despite my best efforts in my temporary role, I knew the riders weren't taking the slightest bit of notice of me, even at that level of racing, so I would like to apologise here to all the start marshals I ignored over my 16 years in the saddle!

I try and attend as many reunions as possible and usually go to the annual World Speedway Riders' Association dinner-dance, where I always look forward to seeing old friends (and enemies!). At one dinner a few years ago, I was standing at the bar waiting to be served when Jeremy Doncaster tapped me on the shoulder, said 'hello' and then apologised for putting me through the fence at Ipswich and in hospital while I was riding for Sheffield. He looked full of remorse as he explained what had happened on the night, blaming the crash on his reckless riding, but I found it quite funny to be honest. Poor, old Jeremy must have had this incident on his mind all those years!

One of the most memorable reunions was in 2010, when the Ellesmere Port Gunners management, riders and partners celebrated the 25th anniversary of the league championship victory. Mervyn organised the event at a hotel in Worsley and even managed to bring along the old National League trophy, which he loaned for the weekend from Mervyn Stewkesbury (ex-Poole), who had bought the trophy when the top two leagues combined. It was testimony to the tremendous team spirit we had in 1985 that all barring Paul Heyes (who was in Australia) turned up for what turned out to be a really special night.

More than a quarter-of-a-century after hanging up my leathers, I'm still rather humbled whenever I'm recognised in the street or at work, and sometimes I even get asked to sign autographs.

I still have my final set of leathers and all my trophies and pennants, as well as a few body colours. I've also kept a number of scrapbooks to remind me of those halcyon days. I'm very grateful to have ridden in the 70s and 80s, speedway's last golden era.

As for working for a living, I ran the garage business for six years, the first three with my old Newcastle team-mate Bernie Collier, but it was hard work making enough money for both of us, so I decided to end the garage lease and worked for myself at home.

One day I was signing on to pay my stamp when I saw an advert for a job at Manchester Airport, working for Servisair as a mechanic maintenance fitter, repairing ground support equipment. The initial job was for three months but after my trial period, I was offered full-time employment and I've been there ever since (Servisair were bought out by Swissport in 2014).

On the family front, we were blessed with the birth of a son on June 16, 1989 but, unfortunately, my marriage to Sharen didn't last and we parted in 1995. It was all my fault – I'd been seeing someone else behind her back, as I found it really hard to cope with the life changes after young Rory (named after my favourite singer, of course) was born.

Poor Sharen did nothing wrong and didn't deserve what I did to her. She was a good wife and mother and, thankfully, was an emotionally strong person but we weren't good at the marriage game together. Gradually we managed to sort out our differences and became friends again. She would eventually marry Eric Broadbelt's former mechanic, Dave Beresford, who also did some spannering for me at Sheffield, Ellesmere Port and Newcastle. Dave and I were (and still are) good mates and

On holiday in Criccieth, Wales with daughter Kara and son Rory.

Playing the banjo is a favourite pastime.

we'd often get the bus from Partington into Manchester, where the real ale pubs would get some hammer.

In April 1993, my partner at the time, Wendy, gave birth to a daughter, Kara, who in October 2013 made me a grandfather when darling Isla was born. Almost two years later, she presented me with a second granddaughter when Kendall came into the world. It's amazing really that since Kara returned to Partington, she and Sharen became good friends and spend a lot of time doing things together.

It's also great that my new partner, Bernadette (who I met in 2009 through the Internet while learning to play the banjo) and I often go out as a foursome with Dave and Sharen.

As for being a grandad, words can hardly describe the joy I get from seeing Isla (and now baby Kendall) growing up. It's lovely to have her over and spoil her rotten but it's also good to hand her back to Kara and husband Liam when things get difficult!

I still enjoy watching speedway on Sky Sports and Eurosport, as well as the Superbikes, but my main hobby is playing the banjo. My love for the instrument began when I was a youngster, after I watched the American sitcom, *The Beverly Hillbillies,* on television. The signature tune was played by Earl Scruggs and Lester Flatts and heavily featured the banjo. I remember we had an 8-track player in the garage and when Chris and I were preparing our bikes, we'd always play *Foggy Mountain Breakdown* by Earl Scruggs, from the film *Bonnie and Clyde.* I now have four 5-string banjos and a banjola (a cross between a banjo and a mandolin), plus a mandolin. Recently I managed to purchase an Ashbury American banjo off the Internet which has a beautiful pearl inlay on the fretboard, at a bargain price of just £350 (they're worth at least £500 with no inlay).

I also enjoy narrowboat holidays on the canals. Ironic that for the majority of my speedway career I could safely navigate around the track at over 50mph but during my early days on the water I had some difficulty in steering a safe path at 4mph! On one excursion on the Macclesfield canal, I was enjoying the sunshine and peace and quiet as I plotted a course around a sweeping blind bend lined with tall bullrushes. I could hear another barge coming in the opposite direction, so I slowed down

I like this photo of Bernadette taken at the Bryn Guest House in Conwy, North Wales with our banjos in 2010. We were there for the three-day Conwy Bluegrass Music Festival.

as I steered towards the outside 'racing line'.

Unfortunately, the elderly gentleman in charge of the tiller coming ever closer was not looking where he was going, and with us only yards away he still hadn't spotted me. There was no time to reverse the engines and although I screamed out to him to steer away, it was too late . . . BANG, CRASH! Even at that speed the impact was terrific and I just managed to stay on my feet, while below deck the television and a whole host of items crashed to the floor. Only then did he look up to see what he had collided with. As we eventually passed he offered his apologies, and I offered mine – something to do with getting his eyes tested, or words to that effect.

In the last few years I've started collecting pocket watches (both working and non-working) and I have quite a few very rare American watches which are beautifully engraved and are more than 100-years-old.

I also enjoy live music and am a regular visitor to Ireland to enjoy a weekend of Rory Gallagher tribute acts.

Television? Other than speedway, I enjoy watching re-runs of *Monty Python's Flying Circus* and *Steptoe and Son* but through the wonders of satellite television, my favourite programmes are found on the History, National Geographic and Discovery channels. However, my secret vice is *Emmerdale,* of which I've been a fan for as long as I can remember.

Finally, I conclude with my thoughts on speedway today, a sport which would struggle to survive if the financial backing received from Sky was ever pulled. The costs of running an Elite League club and to race are now astronomical and apart from a few reasonably supported tracks, the fans aren't coming through the turnstiles in any significant numbers. The majority of GP riders come and go as they please and generally cost a small fortune to keep happy. Personally, I think the racing in the lower leagues is better and I prefer to watch these meetings. But I fear that the glory years, the 60s 70s and 80s, will never be repeated.

By writing this book, it gives me an opportunity to thank everybody who was involved in my speedway journey, from my parents and the riders I competed with and against, to the promoters, management, track staff, tea-ladies, car park attendants and programme sellers of the clubs I had the honour to ride for.

"And Morton – what do you want to do when you leave school?" asked my teacher at high school.

"I want to be a professional speedway rider, sir," I replied.

So I'm among a very small percentage of school kids who actually lived out their adolescent dream. And apart from my injuries, I enjoyed every second. Thanks for reading.

With Briggo at Herxheim, Germany for the 2014 World Long-track Championship qualifying round.

May 2015 and I'm alongside the statue of my musical hero Rory Gallagher at Ballyshannon, County Donegal, Ireland, where I attended the Rory Gallagher Festival.

And finally . . .

MY old mate Barry Thomas wanted to say a few words to help conclude the book. I thank him for his kind words:

WHEN Mort joined Hackney for the 1974 season it was obvious from the word go that here was a likeable bloke with plenty of talent. He was one of those riders that looked neat and part of the bike, as most small riders do.

I rate Mort as one of, if not the fastest outside riders at Hackney that I have ever seen. He would pick up so much speed on the apex of the bend that I sometimes thought he couldn't possible make it, but he did. But he was also very adaptable and could ride anywhere on the track.

He went exceptionally well on large tracks, which could have been a legacy of his Crewe days.

As a team man, Mort fitted in well and would often have a couple of beers with the boys and supporters after a meeting, even though he had a long drive home.

I spoke to his brother Chris at Malcolm Simmons' funeral in 2014 and he reckons that Dave and I changed the way the Hackney track was ridden. And when I think back to Colin Pratt riding the white line at Waterden Road with great success, he might have something there.

Anyway Mort, it's been a pleasure to have known you. Good luck with the book and all the best for the future.

Thommo

Thommo enjoying a fag as we watch the four team tournament action at Hackney in 1977.
White City's Marek Cieslak is behind.

Thommo and me at Hackney in 1975. Happy days!

Action from Hackney's home match against Swindon in 1976, when I was at my peak and averaging more than 10 points a r

Career Statistics

CLUB-BY-CLUB RECORD

SEASON	TEAM (DIVISION)	M	R	PTS	BP	TP	AVE
1971	Crewe (BL2)	2	6	3	2	5	3.33
1972	Crewe (BL2)	27	94	125	30	155	6.60
1973	Crewe (BL2)	24	101	202	11	213	8.44
	Hackney (BL1)	4	15	17	3	20	5.33
1974	Crewe (BL2)	37	167	348.5	22	370.5	8.87
	Hackney (BL1)	26	99	147	10	157	6.34
1975	Hackney (BL1)	32	141	297	4	301	8.54*
1976	Hackney (BL1)	36	154	386	6	392	10.18*
1977	Hackney (BL1)	5	24	49	3	52	8.67
1978	Wolverhampton (BL1)	35	151	313	11	324	8.58
1979	Wolverhampton (BL1)	23	101	162	10	172	6.81
1980	Wolverhampton (BL1)	17	50	60	7	67	5.36
1981	Sheffield (BL1)	45	210	405	16	421	8.02
1982	Sheffield (BL1)	42	168	249	24	273	6.50
1983	Sheffield (BL1)	37	139	187	16	203	5.84
1984	Sheffield (BL1)	42	154	203	28	231	6.00
1985	Ellesmere Port (NL)	44	171	328.5	15	343.5	8.04
	Sheffield (BL1)	4	12	20	4	24	8.00
1986	Newcastle (NL)	42	174	340.5	18	358.5	8.24*
1987	Newcastle (NL)	32	139	236	15	251	7.22
1988	Long Eaton (NL)	8	28	18	5	23	3.29
Totals		**564**	**2298**	**4096.5**	**260**	**4356.5**	**5.76**

Figures relate to official League and Cup matches only.

* Dave finished the season as his team's number one rider.

Key: BL2 = British League Division Two (second tier); BL1 = British League Division One (top tier); NL = National League (second tier); M = Matches; R = Rides; PTS = Points; BP = Bonus Points; TP = Total Points; Ave = Final average.

From the book, *The Complete History of the British League* edited by Peter Oakes.

198 DAVE MORTON

Looking tense before the England v Sweden Division Two Test match at Eastbourne in September 1973.

Club Honours

1972 British League Division Two championship winner (Crewe)
1972 British League Division Two Knockout Cup winner (Crewe)
1985 National League championship winner (Ellesmere Port)

Individual Honours

September 21, 1973 K.R.C. Trophy at Peterborough
January 14, 1975 New Zealand Championship at Palmerston North
February 22, 1975 Auckland Senior Championship at Auckland
August 9, 1975 Supporters' Club Trophy at King's Lynn
August 26, 1978 Artdeans Trophy at Swindon
June 18, 1981 Bluey Wilkinson Memorial Trophy at Sheffield
June 14, 1984 Stones Open Championship at Sheffield

International Appearances

England v Australasia 1973
September 12 - Third Test at Hull - 4pts

England v Sweden 1973

September 30 - First Test at Eastbourne - 1pt
October 1 - Second Test at Crewe - 15pts
October 4 - Fourth Test at Middlesbrough - Reserve (did not ride)

England v Czechoslovakia 1974

April 24 - Sixth Test at Workington - 5 pts

England v Poland 1974

July 8 - Third Test at Crewe - 13 pts

England v Sweden 1975

July 11 - Third Test at Hackney - 5 pts

Sweden v England 1975

August 26 - First Test at Kumla - 5 pts
August 27 - Second Test at Eskilstuna - 10 pts
August 29 - Fourth Test at Vetlanda - 12 pts
August 31 - Fifth Test at Mariestad - 10 pts

Australia v England 1975-76

November 14 - First Test at Perth - 9 pts
November 28 - Second Test at Perth - 7 pts
December 5 - Third Test at Newcastle - 3 pts
December 6 - Fourth Test at Sydney - 8 pts
December 26 - Fifth Test at Liverpool - 3 pts
December 27 - Sixth Test at Sydney - 9 pts
January 10 - Seventh Test at Brisbane - 7 pts

New Zealand v England 1976
January 24 - First Test at Auckland - 12 pts
January 30 - Second Test at Christchurch - 10 pts
February 9 - Third Test at Auckland - 13 pts

Rest of the World v England 1976
July 25 at Vojens - 3 pts

England v Australasia 1978
July 24 - Second Test at Birmingham - 8 pts

England v Denmark 1981
July 1 - Third Test at Coventry - 1 pt

*I am indebted to Kevin Tew for compiling my career statistics.